Praise for *SAY IT FORWARD*

"Oral history changes lives. It changes the lives of the narrators, the listeners, the editors, and the readers. And for students of any age, there is no more impactful and even life-changing project they can undertake. Claire Kiefer and Cliff Mayotte have made a profoundly clear, fluid, and accessible guide to doing your own oral histories, and teachers, students, and parents: I beg you to try it."

> —Dave Eggers, Voice of Witness cofounder and author,
> *The Monk of Mokha* and *What Is the What*

"Stories are humankind's connective tissue, and *Say It Forward* reminds us the process through which we document a story is as important and powerful as the story itself. This book—a collection of oral historians' own stories and perspectives—is at once a how-to guide, a call to action, and a thoughtful, loving usher through oral history's framework, ethics, methodology, and highest ideals. *Say It Forward* is a vital guide from a vital organization, and it couldn't come at a more critical time. More stories, please, and more justice—and more stories justly told."

> —Lauren Markham, author, *The Far Away Brothers:*
> *Two Young Migrants and the Making of an American Life*

"*Say It Forward* provides not only a practical blueprint for storytelling methodology and approach; it does something more meaningful—it contextualizes and validates the purpose and multilayered nuances of capturing and honoring deeply personal accounts. The storyteller becomes the teacher in their own unfiltered testimony. *Say It Forward* is equally useful as an introductory tool for new oral history practitioners and a refresher for the more experienced. No small feat, done thoughtfully in this essential resource."

—Linda Sotelo, New Americans Museum

"*Say It Forward* is a useful guide for anyone new to recording the oral histories of vulnerable populations. Voice of Witness makes plain how to work with sensitivity, respect, and care."

—Danielle Jackson, cofounder, Bronx Documentary Center

SAY IT FORWARD

A Guide to Social Justice Storytelling

WRITTEN AND EDITED BY
CLIFF MAYOTTE AND CLAIRE KIEFER

WITH ASSISTANT EDITORS
NATALIE CATASÚS AND ERIN VONG

Haymarket Books
Chicago, Illinois

Cover design by Michel Vrana.
Cover photograph © Yaissy Solis. Nautica Jenkins (right), community orga-
nizer at Project South, and Patricia Cipollitti (left), national coordinator at the
Alliance for Fair Food, share words of solidarity at a rollicking rally with more
than one hundred farmworkers and consumers in Atlanta during the Coalition
of Immokalee Workers' (CIW) Return to Human Rights Tour in March 2017.
To learn more about the CIW's historic movement for dignity and respect in the
fields, visit www.ciw-online.org.

Published in 2018 by
Haymarket Books
P.O. Box 180165
Chicago, IL 60618
773-583-7884
www.haymarketbooks.org
info@haymarketbooks.org

ISBN: 978-1-60846-958-1

Trade distribution:
In the US, Consortium Book Sales and Distribution, www.cbsd.com
In Canada, Publishers Group Canada, www.pgcbooks.ca
In the UK, Turnaround Publisher Services, www.turnaround-uk.com
All other countries, Ingram Publisher Services International,
IPS_Intlsales@ingramcontent.com

This book was published with the generous support of Lannan Foundation
and Wallace Action Fund.

Printed in Canada by union labor.

Library of Congress Cataloging-in-Publication data is available.

10 9 8 7 6 5 4 3 2 1

CONTENTS

PART THREE: STORYTELLING AND ORAL HISTORY RESOURCES

INTRODUCTION:
MAKING THE INVISIBLE VISIBLE

*Sometimes I walk down the street and I look at all the people I'm passing
and I think, damn, all these stories walking right by me. So, so many
stories that I will never know. All the heartbreak, all the joy. There's a
quote from William James's work where he says something like (I've been
trying to re-find this quote for years and so who knows, maybe I made it
up?): "If you took all the thoughts of all the people in a single city on a
single night, your head would explode." I think this sort of work makes a
little bit of a dent in this idea. You know what I mean? You get a little
closer to people you never knew and never were going to know.*

—Peter Orner, novelist, and editor of *Underground America*,
Hope Deferred, and *Lavil*

Say It Forward was created to address the varying needs of both beginning
and experienced oral history practitioners. All of us in this field have the
desire to listen to—and share—stories in order to learn firsthand about
the experiences of other people. Under the right circumstances, story
sharing can be empowering, transformational, and life-changing for
both audience and storyteller. There are countless relevant and engaging
unheard stories to listen to and learn from, as well as many individuals
and communities that long to share them.

Part of the transformative power of oral history stems from the intimacy and vulnerability that comes with listening to and sharing personal stories. And with that power comes the responsibility to be mindful

about the planning and execution of oral history projects. There are many practical and ethical questions to explore that are profoundly important to the oral history process—questions that usually emerge like bolts of lightning, when you least expect them. Or sometimes when you do expect them, but don't necessarily have the experience or a particular plan to acknowledge or address them. Sometimes these questions are straightforward: How am I going to find people to interview? Other times they are more complex: How do power and privilege affect my project?

The first part of this book introduces some of the most crucial questions and concerns that have emerged in our work as oral historians at Voice of Witness. We don't necessarily have answers to all of these questions, but it's our intention to help facilitate a dialogue. We see *Say It Forward* as a conversation about the experiences of practicing oral historians. In that sense, much of the content of this book is an oral history of ways to approach oral history.

The second section contains eleven chapters, or "field reports," in which new and experienced oral historians document the development of their own oral history projects. All field report authors were drawn from the larger Voice of Witness learning community, including teachers, students, and independent practitioners who are familiar with our oral history methodology. We chose field reports that reflected a wide geographic range and a variety of content. There is overlap in the essential questions and thematic issues these eleven reports raise, and this is indicative of the overarching, recurring concerns that come up when doing oral history with purpose and intentionality. However, each of the field reports also brings to light its own set of specific lessons. We want the guide to be as far-reaching and comprehensive as possible.[1]

Field reports are based on real projects—a few complete, many still in progress. With each project, we asked the authors to consider lessons learned as they went along, and each field report is an intimate record

---

1. For more on how these field reports were selected and developed, see pages 55–56.

of some of the challenges, successes, direction changes, and surprising moments of oral history work. Our hope is that readers will use these hard-won lessons as guideposts for their own oral history approaches. We have also included an extensive oral history resource section with materials ranging from a mini oral history project-planning template to a list of recommendations for recording equipment to resources for trauma and self-care.

We believe even experienced oral historians need to approach their projects with open minds and a beginner's curiosity. That is because behind the simple act of asking others to share their stories, there are nuanced and always-changing uncertainties related to story ownership, trust, retraumatization, and sometimes the very safety of individuals sharing their stories. In essence, *Say It Forward* seeks to make visible much of what is invisible in the oral history process.

Say It Forward will give newcomers the confidence to begin their oral history projects. It will guide them through the initial planning phases— *How should I frame my project? Where will I find narrators? How do I make sure I've gotten permission to print these stories?*—and into the deeper, more essential questions that examine the ethics of the practice.[2] In this book, we address a lot of the ideas that many people aren't sure how to talk about, those related to questions such as, *How do I interview people who belong to a very different community than the one I'm from? How can power dynamics affect a narrator's comfort? How do I deal with secondary trauma when listening to difficult stories?*

Oral history is merely a formal term that describes the process of listening to and sharing stories. It's an accessible way for human beings to exchange social, cultural, and historical knowledge with each other. It's

---

2. At Voice of Witness, we use the term *narrators* instead of *interviewees* or *interview subjects*. While these last two are commonly used elsewhere, Voice of Witness prefers the term *narrator* (and *narrator communities*) because the people we sit down with are storytellers narrating their own experiences rather than simply providing answers to our questions. Also, in some contexts, *interview subject* can feel clinical and impersonal, running counter to the Voice of Witness mission of putting a human face on contemporary human rights and social justice issues.

a traditional art form that retained its appeal and power to connect us across continents and cultures, even in an age when digital communication seems to transform how we talk to each other. By its very nature, oral history can be thoroughly subversive because it makes space for stories that otherwise might not be heard. It creates a platform for individuals and communities that don't feel connected to more dominant, established narratives to speak up and share their own personal experiences. The oral history process can liberate people to count themselves as a part of history, and not separate from it, especially individuals and communities that have been marginalized or silenced.

Because oral history is a universal form of storytelling, the main ingredients for participation are a story, a storyteller, and an audience to experience it. At Voice of Witness, we share the stories of people impacted by injustice with a broad audience of readers, educators, activists, and storytellers. We also strive to create more community-based spaces for stories that might otherwise go unheard. *Say It Forward* is an extension of this work: making space to listen to, and learn from, a larger circle of stories, storytellers, and the people who help bring those stories to light.

PART ONE

ORAL HISTORY PRIMER

HISTORY ON A HUMAN SCALE

Though often overlooked, oral history is a vital form of historical narrative and has been for much of human existence. In fact, for centuries oral history didn't even need a name. It was simply the primary vehicle for communities and cultures to share common history and create strong intergenerational links. Although the term *oral history* can feel overly stuffy, given storytelling's revered position in world culture, it serves the useful purpose of signifying a history that exists in between and underneath "official" history. The very substance of oral history clearly demonstrates that all of us are participants in history. Why? Because we share, interpret, interrogate, and draw conclusions about our individual and collective experience every day. What is that if not history? Our stories don't need to appear in a textbook or newspaper for us to think of them of as historical. Of course, this idea calls into question the nature of history itself. Who decides what is historical? Oral history can be a powerful reminder that the number of stories that need to be heard is infinite—contrary to the messages we receive from the stingy gatekeepers of history.

There are those who feel that oral history is not real history or not true because it's not factual. A familiar argument goes, "How can you be sure people are telling the truth or remembering things as they actually happened? We all know how tricky and fallible human memory can be." This is a faulty argument given that many of the indisputable "facts" of history were originally based on oral reports or testimony that were later written and recorded as fact.

So how has oral history become the poor stepchild of "legitimate" history? The primary reason is oral history has the audacity to be surprising, inconclusive, complex, and a little bit messy—which is, of course, consistent with human experience.

Recently, oral history seems to have gained (or regained) traction as the desire for deeper and more personal versions of history and events has reflected a larger societal need. Some of this has to do with the reductive, superficial sound-bite reporting that has become so prevalent in journalism and media. Much of this style of reporting and storytelling does little more than reinforce existing stereotypes about individuals, communities, and cultures. As writer Chimamanda Ngozi Adichie rightly points out, "It's not that stereotypes are untrue, it is that they are incomplete." Through our intuition and curiosity, we know that there's more to someone's story, and we want to know what it is. Oral history has a way of honoring our curiosity.

The resurgence of oral history is also a reaction to the constant shouts and pitches from advertising and mass media, which makes it impossible for accounts of our own personal experiences to be heard above all the noise. As humans, we instinctively seem to know that storytelling is an opportunity for connection and learning, but we've been pummeled so relentlessly by language so disconnected from human experience that we're desperately seeking more reflective and participatory forms of communication.

Oral history helps us bring our history down to a more human scale. It's easy to forget in the grand gestures of historical reporting that history happens to actual people—people with names, families, and stories. Using the Voice of Witness book series as an example (just one of many), a book like *Underground America*, which focuses on undocumented immigrants, allows us to look at the issue of immigration from another angle—one that goes beyond familiar arguments such as "They take our jobs" or "They're bankrupting our public health system." Through oral history, we have the opportunity to hear the personal story of Lorena, who struggles with maintaining her job while pursuing a college education. She shares her hopes, her fears, and her dreams for the future. We get a more complete snapshot of who she is, which makes it easier for us to relate to Lorena as a human being, thus having our thinking complicated in useful ways. After hearing her story, we realize that Lorena is far more than her ascribed identity as an undocumented American.

To participate in oral history is to palpably experience the human scale of history firsthand. The process puts the storyteller in the driver's seat, empowering them as teachers, with interviewers (or those who listen) as their willing students. This is history constructed and exchanged between two people, history that invites you into an ongoing conversation, history that you can participate in. Oral history embodies a desire to understand the world and human experience in a personal, emotional way. It includes individual experience and emotional response as part of a critical dialogue about history. Oral history helps us to take history personally, allowing us to place ourselves inside of it, which is the ultimate vantage point for acknowledging our differences and celebrating what connects us.

What Is Oral History and How Does It Relate to Social Justice?

Research is formalized curiosity. It is poking and prying with a purpose.

—Zora Neale Hurston, *Dust Tracks on a Road*

According to the Oral History Association (OHA), "Oral History is a field of study and a method of gathering, preserving, and interpreting the voices and memories of people, communities, and participants in past events. Oral history is both the oldest type of historical inquiry, predating the written word, and one of the most modern, initiated with tape recorders in the 1940s and now using 21st-century digital technologies." While the OHA definition is admirably concise, it only scratches the surface of the many aspects of doing oral history: seeking out storytellers, establishing and adhering to ethical guidelines, conducting and recording interviews, transcribing the interviews verbatim, editing, fact checking, sharing stories through various kinds of media, and storing or archiving the stories for future generations to access. Oral history attracts a diverse group that includes academics, artists, social workers, advocates, teachers, librarians, historians, activists, journalists, and more. Some oral historians pursue formal training, and some do not. What most of them have in common is a desire to explore history in a way that is relatable and engaging. They are also interested in narrowing the wide gaps that exist in our interpretations of history. Beginning and experienced oral historians alike feel an urgency to preserve first-person accounts in order to gain clarity and insight into events that feel incomplete without them. An essential question for many oral historians is, who decides what constitutes "history" and who does not?

The OHA definition clearly articulates a focus on the everyday experiences and memories of individuals, as opposed to larger, more monolithic readings of history and events. It encourages the collection and sharing of first-person accounts that rarely (if ever) have a platform to be heard, let alone be considered historical. Oral history presses for an examination of history without seeking approval from authority to be considered legitimate.

Historian and activist Howard Zinn popularized the practice of "people's history." His description creates a useful distinction between top-down history, or "winner's history," and underrepresented accounts from individuals whose stories complicate or contradict dominant narratives. Zinn's term also serves to illustrate that history should include the voices of our friends, families, neighbors, and community members. Oral history seeks to grab the mic from the constantly amplified voices of the powerful and privileged and direct it toward ordinary people with stories that deserve hearing. This impulse is an oral historian's response to the inequity that results from ignoring or silencing the mosaic of stories that make up any historical event, time period, or social issue. As playwright and poet Bertolt Brecht states in his poem "Questions from a Worker Who Reads": "Philip of Spain wept when his armada went down.

Was he the only one to weep?" Brecht's lines eloquently capture the intersection of oral history and social justice, asking, how would those who are not in power write history differently?

Applications for Oral History

Most oral history projects are variations on a theme—*How can we share stories in a way that reveals the past, illuminates the present, and informs the future?* With such an open-ended theme, the applications are limitless. New approaches for oral history are cropping up all the time, and as the world will never run out of unheard stories to listen to, it stands to reason that the variety of ways to utilize oral history also feels infinite. The following applications are only meant to serve as a primer, but they do articulate some of the ways in which Voice of Witness has taught strategies for activating oral history. While the descriptions below share a lot in common, we chose to differentiate them here to illustrate some of the needs and intentions that drive oral history projects.

Family and Cultural History
This oral history application is probably the most time-honored. Long before the written or printed word, this type of storytelling was how communities taught future generations about shared history, tradition, culture, family, and the significant events that shaped them. It remains essential even in the age of digital communication.

Oral history connects generations through the sharing of personal narrative between elders and youth. Teenagers who interview their parents, grandparents, and other community elders are surprised to hear stories of struggle and triumph they'd never heard before. Recording and preserving these intergenerational stories is one of the most basic functions of oral history. The nonprofit organization StoryCorps features many examples of this approach through their website and books such as *Listening Is an Act of Love* and *Ties That Bind*.

Whether storyteller and audience identify as family or not, there is usually a sense of urgency behind these oral histories, as elders are often imparting their lived experience before these vital connections to the past are lost.

Historical Memory

This application expands the theme of family history to include personal accounts of broader historical issues and events, such as American labor issues of the 1930s, the women's rights movement of the late nineteenth century, Negro League baseball, Japanese American internment, and more. Compelling examples of this approach are J. Todd Moye's *Freedom Flyers: The Tuskegee Airmen of World War II* and *Survivors: An Oral History of the Armenian Genocide* by Donald E. Miller and Lorna Touryan Miller. A more recent example is the publication of Zora Neale Hurston's long-delayed *Barracoon,* which features her 1927 interview with Cudjo Lewis, one of the last known survivors of the Atlantic slave trade. In this collection of field reports, the application of preserving historical or cultural memory is represented by Lauren Taylor's Resilience project, which chronicles the decades-old experiences of New York City elders, and OG Told Me, in which Pendarvis Harshaw collects the advice and stories of elder Black men in Oakland, California.

Community History

This oral history approach is popular with universities, historical societies, libraries, schools, and other community-based institutions. Some of the essential questions that guide this type of project include, *What are the stories and events that have shaped our community's history and identity? What has impacted how we see ourselves? What is our dominant narrative and how does that complement or contradict personal experience?* This application has the potential for uncovering dormant stories just below the surface of established narratives, revealing a history many did not think existed or had forgotten. Oral history is particularly adept at connecting a community's past and present. Studs Terkel's groundbreaking *Division Street* is an absorbing survey of Chicago in the sixties and thoughtfully captures the city's nuances and contradictions. The oral history–based play *The Laramie Project*, by the Tectonic Theater Project, explores the lives of the residents of Laramie, Wyoming, in the aftermath of the brutal murder of Matthew Shepard, a gay University of Wyoming student. Other examples are found in the work of Vermont Folklife Center, which applies oral history to "strengthen communities by building connections among the diverse peoples of Vermont." Projects related to this theme in the present collection include Project LRN, Genevra Gallo-Bayiates's look at the racial past and present of Evanston, Illinois, OG Told Me, Resilience, and the school/community–focused project Our Town, Our Stories.

The Process of "Forcing Space"

Voice of Witness is committed to advancing human rights by amplifying the voices of people impacted by injustice. While there is great value in preserving stories of any people or community, at Voice of Witness we focus solely on the stories of people who have endured deep injustice. Oral history is a medium that gives primary agency to the person whose story is being told, which makes it an ideal form for amplifying the stories of those who have been marginalized, disenfranchised, or harmed. Voice of Witness has described this process as "forcing space" for these marginalized voices to be heard. Titles in our series include *Inside This Place, Not of It: Narratives from Women's Prisons* and *Palestine Speaks: Narratives of Life under Occupation*. Another powerful example of this approach is *Voices from Chernobyl: The Oral History of a Nuclear Disaster* by Nobel Prize winner Svetlana Alexievich. Field reports in this book that apply oral history to address injustice are "Behind the Wire: Mandatory Detention in Australia," "Reentry Stories: Life after Prison and Jail," and "After the Disaster: Rebuilding Lives and Communities in Fukushima."

Whether or not oral histories are explicitly focused on injustice, they can still serve as meaningful tools in seeking social or political change, as they can offer testimony to problems that require urgent attention. For example, Groundswell: Oral History for Social Change is a national network of oral historians, activists, and others that apply oral history to "support movement building and transformative social change."

The Student Experience

Empathy is the highest form of critical thinking.

—Katherine Geers, Mission San Jose High School,
Fremont, California

The skills of the oral historian, particularly communication and critical thinking, are vital tools for teaching and learning, and have broad application in educational settings. By their very nature, oral history projects reconstruct history and allow students to grapple with perspectives that are subtle and complex. Oral history has the capacity to nurture empathy and promote critical thought in classrooms and community learning spaces. Oral history inspires students and educators to establish personal relationships and connections to the events and issues. For example, students begin to place themselves inside a narrator's story and ask themselves, how would I have felt about that? Or, what choices would I have made in that situation? Educators have described oral history as "taking history personally." These types of experiences, in and out of the classroom, transcend the passive routine of remembering facts, figures, and dates and give teachers and learners a tangible, meaningful point of entry into a history they might otherwise not feel connected to.

Many schools and organizations that engage in service, project-based, or immersion learning harness the power of oral history as a means to develop mutually beneficial community relationships that can deepen the quality of learning. To make active listening a crucial part of the learning process is to acknowledge power and privilege, and amplify the need for cultural awareness, humility, and action. Oral history projects create space for students and teachers to grapple with issues of representation, ethnicity, culture, class, gender, and socioeconomics in a direct and meaningful way. The oral history process can therefore help to create more equitable models for teaching and learning. A persuasive example of how oral history influences learning, and classroom and school culture, is *111th and Roberts: Where Our Stories Intersect*, a book by the students of Amos Alonzo Stagg High School in Palos Hills, Illinois. What began in 2014 as a schoolwide exploration of empathy, led by English teachers Lisa Thyer and Chris Wendelin, culminated in a self-published oral history collection that explores the lives and identities of students, teachers, staff, and alumni. The course from which the project emerged has since become a popular yearly offering, successfully weaving oral history into the fabric of the school. Along with building much-needed communication, literacy, and critical-thinking skills, the application of oral history in educational settings promotes the creation of culturally relevant material by placing student experience at the center of the curriculum. The field reports collected here that speak to the ongoing collaboration between oral history and education include "After the Disaster"; "Our Town, Our Stories"; "DREAMers Testimoniando"; and "Unsettled: Relocating after Katrina."

ESSENTIAL QUESTIONS AND ETHICS

Oral History: An "Experiment in Equality"

In Alessandro Portelli's groundbreaking collection *They Say in Harlan County*, he addresses a seminal question for oral historians: How do you communicate your intentions in an open, respectful way that acknowledges power dynamics, privilege, and difference?[1] In the case of Portelli, a politically left-leaning Italian researcher who knew very little about coal mining and the daily struggles of the residents of Harlan County, Kentucky, being an obvious outsider helped to open doors to him that may have otherwise been shut. His decision to lead with his curiosity, interest, and relative ignorance was part of an honest, straightforward approach that ultimately led to some very rewarding interviews. Reflecting on the experience, he writes, "When I first started doing this work I was afraid that people would resent me because I am such an outsider. I didn't find much negative reaction. I think basically it's been because I didn't know much and wasn't in a position to teach anybody anything." Portelli continues: "It was a lesson in the methodology of fieldwork: the most important things I had to offer were my ignorance and desire to learn. . . . I was not there to study them, but to learn from them. It was what I didn't know that encouraged people to talk to me, knowing that they were helping instead of being 'helped.'"

Later in the collection, he writes:

---

1. Alessandro Portelli, *They Say in Harlan County: An Oral History* (New York: Oxford University Press, 2010).

There were lines of age, class, gender, education, religion, language, color, and nationality between myself and most of the women and men who spoke to me in Harlan County. The mutual effort to speak across those lines taught me to speak of the interview as an experiment in equality, where the trust is not achieved by pretending that we are all the same but by laying the difference and the inequality on the table . . . and making it the implicit subject of the conversation.

Portelli articulates two key concepts in the practice of oral history. One is the importance of framing the interview process as an opportunity for learning and growth, creating an opening for the narrator to be teacher and for interviewer to be student (not the other way around). The other is openly acknowledging power, privilege, and difference as (an often unspoken) part of the oral history process. These dynamics influence our daily interactions anyway, and given the potential intimacy of an oral history interview, they need to be considered a crucial part of the oral history experience. As Portelli demonstrates, this kind of acknowledgement can lead to an increased connection between narrator and interviewer. You could describe this phenomenon as "connection through acknowledging difference." Several of the field reports that appear in part two mention this dynamic. In Lauren Taylor's report on Resilience, she shares the following reflection:

I have led a sheltered life in comparison with most of the people I interviewed for this project. My training has made me sensitive to the potential impact of racial, ethnic, age, and class differences between interviewer and narrator. I feel it appropriate to let people know I am doing the interviews as a volunteer, as I do not want the narrators, many of whom are economically disadvantaged, to think I might be making money from their stories. Cultural sensitivity is critical in the interviewing process, but the need to tell stories is universal.

In "Reentry Stories," *Say It Forward* cowriter and editor Claire Kiefer describes how her passion and curiosity, along with acknowledging the limitations of her project, helped strengthen her connection to narrators:

I haven't been in jail or prison myself, and my life hasn't been deeply impacted by familial incarceration. What I had going for me, as an interviewer, was persistent curiosity coupled with a passionate concern about prisons, probation/parole, and reentry in American society. I couldn't promise any sort of tangible change; I couldn't assure any of my narrators that their lives would specifically benefit from talking to me. In a way, though, I think that acknowledging that uncertainty deepened the trust between my narrators and me, because it meant that we were embarking on this journey together, both taking a risk and hoping for the best possible outcome.

Why Should I Share My Story with You? Ownership, Identity, and Storytelling

Many oral historians are motivated by general curiosity and a deep desire to understand, but what is it that moves someone to share their story, to sit down—often with a virtual stranger—and openly talk about some of the most difficult things that have happened to them?

Regarding her motivation for sharing her story for the Voice of Witness book *Inside This Place, Not of It: Narratives from Women's Prisons*, Ashley Jacobs says: "Knowing that someone had listened and shared my pain was amazing. I was free to cry, and I no longer feared speaking about my life. After the interview, I felt relief. It was healing for me." Of course, not everyone feels so unequivocally positive after being interviewed. It's important that we as oral historians are acutely aware of the potential trauma that asking deep questions can unearth. Recounting one's life can be a triggering experience, which begs the question: Why do people do it?

There's a range of reasons why people choose to share their stories. Some people hope that awareness will inspire change, and others simply want to be heard. It's interesting how often, after an interview, a narrator will say, "No one's ever asked me that before." This sentiment speaks to a cultural proclivity toward limiting communication to small talk. Interestingly, narrators often report that even the people with whom they interact daily don't know some of the stories of the deeper, more difficult parts of their lives. It's far more common to ask a neighbor about her favorite restaurant than about her journey to the United States from her home country. For many people, being interviewed results in a type of catharsis.

One of the important tenets of oral history is to let narrators guide the telling of their own stories. It can be hard to go into an interview with no agenda; often we want the narrator to confirm our feelings about a particular issue through their personal testimony. This is natural. At the same time, having the narrator—rather than the oral historian—guide the arc of the story is essential. If the interviewer is too pushy or tries to direct the interview in a certain way, 'the narrator might not feel comfortable fully opening up. Letting narrators meander as they tell their stories allows for a more authentic experience. This may lead to a long interview, and it's all too easy to edit and tailor that raw material to create the story that we, as editors, want to tell. At Voice of Witness, while we make substantial edits for length, coherence, and clarity, we strive to ensure that narrators maintain ownership over their stories throughout the entire process, from the first interview to the final, printed story. At various stages during a project, we seek narrator input (narrators sometimes want to clarify parts of their story or remove sections altogether), including final approval before publication. For us, this kind of narrator participation is crucial to preserving the integrity of our work.

There are countless unanswerable questions in oral history. So much of the work we do is just puzzling things out, using a combination of best practices and our intuition to make thoughtful choices throughout the process. One of the more challenging unanswerable questions that the narrator may ask is, *How will sharing my story with you change my situation?* For people in the midst of a crisis, taking the time and energy to recount their life and its trials can be particularly difficult. Notably, when we were in the process of doing interviews for *Out of Exile: Narratives from the Abducted and Displaced People of Sudan*, a Sudanese woman named Mary posed this very question to the book's editor, Craig Walzer. When he asked her to describe the story of her life, she said:

Even if I tell you my life, what will you do about it? I have been asked these questions before and nobody has come to our help. We have never been helped. They say money will go to building schools and hospitals. We have been told this all the time, and nothing ever happens. I have been living this bad life, and many people come and say they will do everything, and nobody has been doing it.

So often, there aren't satisfying answers to the questions that Mary poses. Oral history is so often an experiment in risk and faith; we risk sharing our stories with people, despite the pain in our retelling of them and the uncertain outcomes that will follow, with the faith that somehow, in some way, our story will have an impact on other people. Tracking the impact of our work at Voice of Witness has taught us that stories inspire change at the cultural, social, and policy levels by challenging preconceived notions and generating empathy.

The Chain of Trust and Collaboration in Oral History

The fun for me in collaboration is . . . working with other people just makes you smarter; that's proven.

—Lin-Manuel Miranda, interview, *Smithsonian Magazine*, November 12, 2015

Collaboration is an essential element of oral history. In the midst of your project, it can be useful to revisit the essential questions that inspired you to create it in the first place. For example, you might ask yourself: *Who else in my community, family, or network of contacts might have experience exploring this topic or may know individuals or organizations that I can reach out to? How can my project support an ecosystem that works on behalf of communities I'd like to collaborate with?* These questions help illustrate an approach that Voice of Witness and many of the following field reports utilize—a concept called the "chain of trust."

Our organization learned of this concept from Annie Holmes, coeditor of our book *Hope Deferred*, and Just Associates, a social justice organization with offices in South Africa and London. The driving idea behind the chain of trust is to develop relationships with individuals and organizations that are directly involved with, or have access to, the collaborators, community partners, and potential narrators your project will be centered on. Social service organizations, nonprofits, libraries, schools, universities, local historical societies, cultural organizations, senior centers, and advocacy organizations all have the potential to become vital and trusted project partners. If your project is a collaboration between two organizational partners, the chain of trust approach can help determine if your values are aligned in ways that are mutually beneficial.

Initial engagement with potential collaborators can take a variety of forms and opens up possibilities for partnership that can go deeper than mere networking. Volunteering, attending organizational meetings or community events, conducting research, sharing resources, and generally being an ally can help support the chain of trust that forms the basis of successful oral history collaborations. If you are already aligned with your narrator community, the chain of trust approach is still valuable, as it reflects an ongoing commitment to deepening relationships and engaging in continual learning. If you are a relative outsider, this approach may not totally diminish the challenging dynamics that exist in the partnership, but it demonstrates a sincerity that nurtures trust and goodwill between project partners. By employing the chain of trust model, oral historians can address community concerns about whether their projects entail more than just "parachuting in" to collect stories and then abruptly leaving. This is especially important when seeking out potential narrators to interview. It communicates that the interviewer and narrator are working in collaboration and for mutual benefit, and that it is not a transactional experience in which all that happens is a narrator gives and an interviewer receives.

The chain of trust approach promotes the belief that the oral history process should not be extractive and that it is based on relationships that require personal and professional integrity. No matter how long these relationships last, whether for weeks or a lifetime, the care you take in developing them will resonate throughout every aspect of your oral history project. Your openness and willingness to collaborate will certainly be valuable assets as you begin the process of contacting narrators and scheduling your first interviews.

How Do I Find Narrators for My Oral History Project?

Each person has a literature inside them.

—Anna Deavere Smith, interview, *People*, August 30, 1993

For burgeoning and experienced oral historians alike, this is the most crucial (and sometimes oddly overlooked) question in the oral history process. Most oral historians have great ideas, intentions, and goals, and have already chosen how the stories will be shared—books, podcasts, live performance, and so on. And yet the question remains: *How am I going to find narrators for my oral history project?*

Seeking out potential narrators is an extension of the chain of trust approach. If you are collaborating with an organization, potential narrators may not be familiar with you, but if they have a trusted relationship with a partner organization, they may be more willing to consider participating in your project. In any case, there is a lot of listening and learning involved. In reaching out to potential narrators, you'll need to hear about what interests them about the project, what they'll need in order to participate, how they'd like to be represented, what they're hoping to get out of it, and so on. This process highlights the need for creating the necessary space for narrators to choose interviewers as much as the other way around. The chain of trust places a high value on narrators maintaining agency over their stories and alleviates interviewers from the untenable position of trying to convince people to be interviewed for their project.

Spending time on relationship building will help address insider/outsider and power dynamics, and hopefully inspire project partners and narrators to help out when you inevitably ask, *Do you know anyone else I should be talking to about this project?* This approach will also help you determine the most effective way to reach out to potential narrators, since you'll have more informed ideas of the community you're working with. In some cases, reaching out via phone or email will be fine. In others, it may be more beneficial to post flyers or publicly address group meetings or gatherings. Of course, it is always important to be willing to meet in person with any interested individuals. The chain of trust can also help you identify interpreters for the community in the event that you have narrators who do not speak English or are deaf or hearing impaired. Interpreters who are present during the interviews add another layer to the development of trust, as narrators must have faith in the interpreter's translations of their story. By searching within the network you have already developed, an interpreter can serve as a bridge between interviewer and narrator.

Many of the field reports that follow offer differing glimpses into the chain of trust model and the collaborative process of finding narrators. For example, in the report for After the Disaster, Jon Funabiki details his tireless work in bringing the stories of Fukushima residents to light by working with two university programs and nonprofits committed to Japanese history and culture. Lauren Taylor found her narrators for Resilience by working directly with seniors receiving services through the Carter Burden Center for the Aging in New York City. Genevra Gallo-Bayiates's chain of trust began with her involvement with the local YWCA, which connected her to other organizations and individuals in Evanston, Illinois, for Project LRN. In Tales of Tar Sands Resistance, Stephanie Thomas collaborated with East Texas churches, community groups, and nonprofit advocacy organizations in seeking out potential narrators. Ashley Jacobs was able to connect with narrators by mentioning her Cycles of Domestic Violence project to a friend while attending a poetry reading. You never know where you're going to find links in your chains of trust, so be open to any leads that might come your way.

Creating Safe/Brave Spaces for Sharing Stories

The sharing of joy, whether physical, emotional, psychic, or intellectual, forms a bridge between the sharers, which can be the basis for understanding much of what is not shared between them, and lessens the threat of their difference.

—Audre Lorde, *Sister Outsider*

This essential idea about sharing human experience is particularly resonant for oral historians. They often address it by asking, *How can I create an environment in which my narrators feel safe enough to share their stories?* By raising this question, oral historians demonstrate that they are not consciously courting traumatic stories from their narrators, but are still acknowledging that interviews can inspire many unanticipated moments. This is, of course, one of the outcomes of oral history. It can also present a challenge that requires mindfulness and advance preparation.

It is a reasonable position to argue that creating a safe space is not entirely possible (or even desired), since the world, for many, is inherently unsafe. By that logic, the term *safe space* has its limitations. For example, if you can create a genuinely safe space for sharing stories, how far in time does that space extend? Just for the length of the interview, or for days or weeks afterward? Our colleagues at the University of San Francisco School of Education taught us a useful variant of the term *safe space* that they themselves learned from others. Rather than insisting on an elusive *safe space*, they have instead articulated the need for a *brave space* for sharing stories.

Creating a *brave space* for sharing stories opens up possibilities that *safe space* seems to constrict. While a safe space promises comfort and ease, a brave space invites nuance, complexity, ambiguity, joy, discomfort, humor, and contradiction. In short, a fuller range of human experience. This is not to say that creating a safe space can't contain these possibilities, but that by calling it a brave space, you are probably more accurately describing the interview process.

In our work at Voice of Witness, we often begin our trainings and workshops with the question, *If you had a meaningful story to share with someone, what would you need in order to feel safe, to feel brave?* This prompt elicits many of the realities and considerations that have already been mentioned, namely, those of power dynamics and representation. Here are a few possible responses you may receive:

- Listening without judging your narrator
- Awareness of cultural norms or family practices
- Confidentiality
- Making enough time so as not to feel rushed
- Respect
- Clear intentions
- A comfortable environment during the interview
- Sharing food
- Mutual sharing between interviewer and narrator
- Offering the option of audio instead of video recording
- Having family or trusted friends present
- Establishing topic boundaries
- Narrator agency through ownership of story

And of course, there are many others. These multifaceted responses hint at the power that sharing stories has and articulate some of the universal topics related to conducting oral history. An exploration of this question can also bring to light considerations and needs specific to any given project. Certain cultural norms will inform you how to approach topics of trust, respect, and environment with your narrator, keeping in mind different understandings regarding eye contact, tone of voice, and personal space. In the field report for DREAMers Testimoniando, Shelby Pasell describes how her evolving relationship with narrators helped determine what their version of a safe/brave space needed to be. In the report for Cycles of Domestic Violence, Ashley Jacobs describes how her openness and desire to learn helped to create a safe space for her narrator:

> Mona was my first interview. I was nervous about interviewing her because I knew she was a history professor and a poet, so when I spoke with her on the phone, I told her I wanted to do her interview first so that she could critique me and give me input on how to make it better. She said, "Not a problem." At that moment, I'm sure any doubts she had were erased, because she took this as not just an interview, but as a teaching moment.

The point here is for participants to ask themselves, *How many more needs can we articulate that will be crucial to our narrators and other project participants?* All of the collected responses and strategies for addressing those needs can also serve as a valuable set of group agreements for project participants. It's a useful touchstone and a tangible way of making sure your ethical considerations directly bear on the technical and creative choices that you make throughout your oral history project.

Avoiding Retraumatization

When talking to someone about recollections and experiences that can be deeply painful, using a trauma-informed approach can help to facilitate safety and trust. Trauma-informed care is a framework through which practitioners understand the far-reaching impacts of trauma on people's lives, recognize the signs of trauma, and prioritize emotional well-being and the prevention of retraumatization in their interactions with clients (or, in the case of oral historians, narrators).

Sometimes, avoiding potential triggers is common sense; most of us can imagine a war veteran experiencing post-traumatic stress symptoms when they hear fireworks or a survivor of physical abuse being retraumatized by playing contact sports. Other times, triggers can be unexpected. These triggers can cause the survivor to experience feelings and thoughts associated with their original trauma. Retraumatization not only shuts down the interview process, but can result in psychiatric crisis for the survivor. While oral historians are not expected to have the expertise of clinicians, it is important that we understand the ways in which trauma can manifest throughout people's lives and take steps to be collaborative, supportive, and responsive to our narrators in order to be ethical storytellers.

The following guidelines provide a place to start when planning your interviews:

1. *Allow enough time for the interviews.* When narrators feel rushed, they are likely to feel undervalued, unheard, and uncomfortable in their vulnerable state. Furthermore, it is important to budget extra time for breaks, in case the conversation becomes emotionally challenging and the narrator needs to take a moment. These breaks can be instrumental in preventing retraumatization.

2. *Respect narrators' self-determination.* If a narrator does not want to tell a particular story or expresses hesitance when you ask about an aspect of their journey, it is important to respect their boundaries, regardless of how compelling a story it may be. Shelby Pasell describes one such experience she had interviewing a narrator: "There was a topic one narrator was always very guarded about. In the interviews, I pushed a bit, and got some answers that could have aided the *testimonio* [testimonial narrative]. During that conversation they told me directly that they didn't see the relevance of my questions, at which point I immediately changed the subject, disappointed but mostly uncomfortable with knowing I had pushed too far." Sometimes, experiences are just too raw and painful, and a narrator may not be ready to talk about them yet. Let the narrator guide the conversation, be perceptive to cues that indicate distress, and be prepared to change directions if they want to talk about something different than you intended.

3. *Emphasize narrators' anonymity.* If the narrator you are interviewing is telling a story about a person or system that has harmed them, they may be anxious about their vulnerability to future abuse or retaliation. Take time to explain the specific methods

you will use to preserve anonymity so your narrators feel able to share their stories.

4. *Solicit input from your narrators and give them choices.* If you are doing an oral history project about sexual abuse, for example, be mindful about interview circumstances that may trigger your narrators' trauma. Ask them if they feel more comfortable being interviewed by someone of their own gender, if they would like to have a support person present during the interview, or if they prefer a public space to a private one. People are less likely to experience retraumatization when they are given control.

Yet, even if you do everything right and take every measure to ensure your narrators are given the respect, autonomy, and consideration they deserve, you may end up in a situation in which a narrator experiences retraumatization during an interview. People are so conditioned to masking pain that when they do tell stories of their past traumas, it can elicit discomfort, distress, or panic. As interviewers, it is important to have a plan in case retraumatization occurs. Plans will differ according to the narrator, subject, and location but should include both immediate and longer-term interventions so that if a narrator begins to experience trauma during the interview, the interviewer is prepared not only to terminate it but also to make referrals for the narrator to seek support following the interview.

Prior to the interview, determine who you will first contact in the event of retraumatization. If the interview is taking place at the narrator's home, perhaps there will be a family member or friend available to help support the narrator if they experience signs of trauma. You may also have identified a counselor or social worker to call if the narrator needs additional help. If you are working with an organization or agency, they may have a specific protocol for managing this type of situation.

Talking openly with your narrator—expressing gratitude for their vulnerability and generosity, reminding them that it is okay to become emotional and also okay to stop the interview at any point—is often an important step toward avoiding retraumatization. This transparency will help your narrator understand the parameters and gain a sense of control over the process, which can mitigate harm. Establishing rapport and mutual trust can also help the narrator feel more comfortable sharing and will likely result in a fuller, more authentic story.

Come prepared with a list of referrals for the narrator in case retraumatization occurs. These referrals will vary depending on the circumstances but may include free or sliding-scale counseling services, information for community support groups, or contacts at organizations specific to the subject of your interview (legal clinics for undocumented immigrants, agencies that help ex-offenders to expunge their records, or women's shelters, for example). Remember that along with demonstrating empathy and care, the most responsible way to handle crises is to make referrals to trained and skilled professionals. More resources about trauma and retraumatization can be found in the Trauma and Self-Care portion of the book's Oral History Resources section (pp. 255–57).

Protecting Narrator Safety

One of the most compelling aspects of oral history is its capacity to decentralize a dominant narrative by presenting the firsthand experiences of individuals. The process results in stories that elevate the personal and the particular over "objective" and generalized representations of events, people, and places. By its very nature, oral history grants authority to the underrepresented lived experiences of specific individuals. Oral histories can tell us, *I saw that, I was there.* In this way, the individual becomes the authority on his or her own experience, and our investment as an audience depends on our knowledge that we are witnessing a real person recount events.

In some cases, however, revealing a narrator's identity may conflict with preserving their safety. The concern about the narrator's safety can take various forms. *What risks may this person be taking by sharing their story with me? How may sharing this story affect their job security, legal standing, physical safety, reputation, or family?* One of the questions that may come up during an oral history project is whether in some cases it may be appropriate, or perhaps necessary, to preserve a narrator's anonymity. Because of oral history's emphasis on individual experience and personal narrative, it is common practice to include the real names of narrators. The Oral History Association suggests that some exceptional circumstances could warrant withholding the narrator's true identity. In the case of an undocumented immigrant, for example, sharing a story of immigration using a real name could entail a significant risk. Revealing true identities of certain narrators could lead to deportation if their status were to come under investigation. For incarcerated narrators, speaking about living conditions in jail or prison, or the dynamics between inmates and officers, could put them in a precarious position within a place they cannot leave.

In this collection, the authors of the Behind the Wire field report address some of these very issues. They describe the debate they had over whether or not to interview certain subgroups of the community of asylum seekers they were working with, such as currently detained refugees and released refugees whose visa status was still pending. The facilitators were concerned that even if they changed the names, the unique qualities of the narratives themselves would identify the narrators and could then be used as evidence against the refugees in their open immigration cases. This dilemma is a striking reminder of how intimately the narrator's identity is woven into the fabric of the stories they tell.

Power, Privilege, and Representation in Oral History

Being oppressed means the absence of choices.

—bell hooks, *Feminist Theory: From Margin to Center*

The realities of power and privilege have come up several times already and will be explored in detail in several of the oral history field reports that follow. How could it be otherwise? If the practice of oral history is one that is rooted in collecting and sharing stories, then it would be irresponsible not to address the social, cultural, and historical forces that shape those stories. It is also vital to delve into how the steps in the oral history process intersect with the power dynamics that affect our everyday interactions.

Many factors exert influence over how we see, hear, and experience each other: ethnicity, class, language, gender, religion, sexual orientation, socioeconomics, age, and more. Not surprisingly, these visible and invisible boundaries assert themselves in the creation of many oral history projects, including the ones featured in this collection of field reports: a middle-class white woman interviewing elderly Black and Latino men in a Harlem senior center, young Australian human rights activists interviewing narrators with direct experience of illegal detention, American college students interviewing victims of the Fukushima disaster, and so on. Through the Voice of Witness Education Program, we've seen several versions of oral history projects that detail the process of affluent (usually white) students interviewing community members (usually people of color) about the effects of gentrification. According to oral historian, educator, and Voice of Witness advisor Rick Ayers, it's not that these kinds of projects shouldn't be considered, but that it's useful for project planners to challenge their own assumptions in order to discover more equitable and inclusive ways to collect and share stories. A prompt that Ayers uses to foster dialogue on this topic is, *Who is the looker, and who is being looked at?* These questions simultaneously acknowledge the power in naming the framework of these stories and emphasize the role of the interviewer and their identity relative to the stories they are collecting. Ultimately, it forces oral historians to explore how they are going to "position" or place themselves in the story-gathering process. This dynamic is often referred to as *positionality.*[2]

Examining positionality is useful for oral historians as they address power, privilege, and representation in their projects. Ayers's prompt encourages thoughtful reflection on a variety of questions that spring from one central question: *How will the very fact of who I am affect how stories are*

---

2. The "positions" of the interviewer and narrator with respect to education, class, race, gender, culture, or other factors influence the questions the interviewer asks and the answers the narrator provides.

collected and shared? In other words, am I positioning myself as a trusted, reliable, and relatively unbiased source, or am I positioning myself to share and shape the stories I want to hear, as opposed to the stories I'm actually hearing?

In any case, it's crucial to openly acknowledge power dynamics and differences like the ones mentioned above and strategize with project partners on how best to proceed. In some cases, this may include gathering interviewers who are more closely positioned to the narrators being interviewed. Or, project partners may determine that relative outsiders to the community may be a better choice (remember the advantages Italian historian Alessandro Portelli had in conducting an oral history with Kentucky coal miners, for instance).

Another key strategy is to identify ways in which the oral history project is mutually beneficial to narrators, interviewers, and audience. This strategy inspires the question, *Who is benefiting most from the oral history project and why?* Consider, for example, a student who completes a great oral history project and gets an A+ in her class. The student may have shaped interesting, engaging narratives, but what do the narrators get out of the experience?

Ayers's question about who is the looker and who is being looked at can be very generative, and it invites another round of questions worth addressing: *How are the project's narrators being represented? Are the viewpoints presented in ways that they themselves feel are authentic, or do the stories merely satisfy the needs of the interviewer and the audience they're intended for?* There are no easy answers to this. The point here is that you enter into dialogue and relationship with project stakeholders to work out how best to address issues of power, privilege, and representation. It can take openness and bravery on all sides, but it has the potential to create a deep and meaningful story-sharing experience for everyone involved.

Insider/Outsider Dynamics

A narrator's level of comfort with an interviewer is paramount. In some instances, a narrator will express a preference to be interviewed by someone from within his or her own community; in other cases, narrators may feel more comfortable with an outsider—someone who has little prior knowledge of their life and who they imagine can be more objective. But often the interviewer/narrator pairing is somewhat arbitrary, and it is incumbent upon the interviewer to assess the narrator's sense of safety and comfort and to keep the complications of insider/outsider dynamics in mind during the process. Cowriter and editor Claire Kiefer says this about her experience conducting an interview as an outsider:

> The first interview I did for a Voice of Witness book was in the summer of 2010. That morning, I got up before the crack of dawn and drove from my parents' house in Atlanta, Georgia, to Aid for Inmate Mothers, a nonprofit organization that serves incarcerated women and their families, in Montgomery, Alabama. I was excited and a little bit nervous to meet Lisa, a woman who had only been out of prison for a couple of months and yet had agreed to sit down and share her story with me, a volunteer oral history interviewer from California.
>
> Lisa was shy but incredibly kind. I tried to make her feel as comfortable as possible by explaining in detail why I was there (we were working on *Inside This Place, Not of It*, a book that documented first-person narratives from people serving time in women's prisons, focusing on the specific human rights abuses that occur in correctional facilities for women). I told her that I really believed that stories like hers needed to be told, because there are so many people in the world who have no idea what goes on inside women's prisons and therefore aren't moved to help enact change. I explained to her why I believed in this book project and thanked her for being so incredibly brave.
>
> But it was Lisa who ultimately put me at ease. From the beginning of the interview, it was very clear that I was an outsider. I hadn't realized it, but I'd been harboring all kinds of silent, insidious fears: *What if she doesn't trust me because I've never been incarcerated? Will she doubt my intentions? What if the fact that I am a young, white woman who lives in a West Coast city is alienating to her?* Lisa's openness showed me that, for whatever reason, she trusted me, and the chemistry between us as interviewer and narrator quickly quieted my worries about being an outsider.

The lived reality of being an insider—part of the community of affected people to which your narrator belongs—or an outsider can certainly affect the outcomes of an interview. In some cases, being an insider can work to your advantage, as it can help your narrator feel a sense of safety and solidarity with you. Some oral historians enlist community members to conduct interviews when they recognize that narrators would feel more comfortable talking to someone from their own community; this is the ultimate "insider" approach. Pendarvis Harshaw, who documents his interviews with elder Black men in Oakland in his OG Told Me field report, says this about his insider status:

> I think it's important that I'm a young Black man conducting this experiment . . . I'm familiar with my target audience. I'm digging into my own community and capitalizing on a phenomenon I've noticed, time and time again. If I weren't a young Black man, or if I weren't from Oakland, I wouldn't get the same results. Being able to relate to other Black men can be as deep as the shared experiences of our ancestors or as simple as having similar skin tone. These similarities and differences can affect how comfortable a narrator is with an interviewer.

In other cases, a narrator may feel more comfortable sharing their memories with someone who can't question the validity of their stories by saying, "That's not how I remember it." Sometimes it's easier to explain things to someone who hasn't had similar lived experiences.

In many cases, we are both insiders and outsiders. In Pendarvis's case, he is an insider in that he is a Black man who grew up in Oakland, but he is an outsider in that he is decades younger than the men he is interviewing. Lisa and Claire are both women who were raised in the South, but these two things they had in common didn't change the fact that the experience Lisa had just endured—eleven years of abuse and severe medical neglect in prison—was something entirely foreign to Claire.

As oral historians, we are often compelled to shun the notion of "the other" and capitalize on shared human experience. In a way, this is the express goal of empathic listening: to blur the differences between ourselves and the people we listen to in order to achieve mutual understanding. But at the same time, it's important not to ignore what could easily become an elephant in the room: sometimes we are outsiders, and that can create discomfort or mistrust. Shelby Pasell describes her experience as an outsider interviewing undocumented college students in Minnesota:

> I tried not to bring up their undocumented status until late in the first interview. Some of the participants never said the word at all, replacing it with references to their "situation" or wordy phrases like "I wasn't able to tell them something really important about myself." Though I wanted to feel and show that we were equals, there were moments that made it impossible to ignore the great gap between our experiences.

The world of oral history would be far less interesting if oral historians only interviewed people who shared their specific backgrounds and privileges. One of the beautiful things about this field is the unexpected connection that can occur between two virtual strangers. The best we can do is to offer up our most genuine, authentic selves to the people whose most genuine, authentic stories we seek.

Curiosity and Flexibility in Oral History Projects

"Curiosity never killed this cat"—that's what I'd like as my epitaph. It won't kill me, no sir.

—Studs Terkel, *The Oral History Reader*

The most compelling oral history projects are ones in which storytelling functions as a point of entry or mode of inquiry into a particular topic, time period, or event. As such, beginning with a vital question to be explored not only yields powerful and nuanced stories; it remains true to the essence of oral history, which is a potent blend of memory, culture, and a strong desire to be heard. Projects that are too specific or set out to prove a thesis are inevitably frustrated by the complex and contradictory nature of human experience. If most of an oral historian's project interviews end with the unspoken thought, *Why can't my narrators stay on topic?*, then chances are the interviewer has too narrow a focus and lacks the capacity for one of the great joys of doing oral history—the capacity for being surprised.

Just as with an inspiring interview question, crafting an exploratory question to frame a project has the potential to be both beautifully specific and flexible enough to move in several directions at once. The work of famed oral historian Studs Terkel provides a great example of the innate (and ever-changing) curiosity that guides great oral histories. The subtitle for his influential book *Working* is a case in point: *People Talk about What They Do All Day and How They Feel about What They Do.* Voice of Witness editor Audrey Petty also comes to mind with respect to the open-ended questions that guided *High Rise Stories*, her collection of oral histories from former residents of Chicago public housing: "The eventual destruction of these landmarks stunned me. The absence of the twenty-eight buildings of Robert Taylor Homes compelled me to reckon with their enormity as a community. *What were those communities really like? I wondered. And where on earth did all those people go?*"

While framing oral history projects with a series of open-ended questions can accommodate some of the thematic shifts that occur as narrators share their stories, it's not a guarantee that your project won't move in unanticipated directions. Shelby Pasell, in the DREAMers Testimoniando field report, articulates this phenomenon this way: "There is nothing straightforward, efficient, or predictable about oral history. Before entering a project in this field I had to let go of all expectations, and be prepared to let the process shape both my final publication and my own understanding." This example speaks to the importance of being flexible and adapting to changing circumstances. In many oral history projects, the main topics or themes only emerge after conducting the initial interviews. In Lauren Taylor's project, Resilience, the primary theme took shape only after she listened to some of the stories and realized what the narrators shared in common. At some point, most oral history projects grapple in small or large ways with the realization, *I thought this oral history project was about* _____. *Turns out, it's about* _____.

Oral history uncovers the stories that have been consciously or unconsciously submerged under the stories you thought you were hearing or expected to hear. Archaeologists often have an idea of what they're looking for at an excavation site and are often surprised to make an incredible discovery they weren't originally anticipating. This is a useful reminder for beginning and experienced oral historians that flexibility is a key asset in oral history, and that it is realized through a commitment to staying receptive and letting the actual interviews shape the theme and scope of the project. Doing so opens up the required space for variation, detail, and surprise—for interviewers, narrators, and an oral historian's intended audience.

Editing Oral History Transcripts: Honoring Your Narrator's Voice

At first glance, transcribing an oral history interview can feel really overwhelming. If you've done a two-hour interview, you might have over one hundred pages of transcription and no idea where or how to start shaping it into a polished narrative. Wading through that much text can be daunting, particularly since the nature of conversation is seldom linear, and narrators skip around considerably when recounting their life stories.

There are, of course, countless ways to begin, one of which is to simply start from the beginning. Remove the interviewer's questions, delete extraneous "ums" and "you knows," and splice sentences together to reflect the flow of the conversation. If you start at the beginning of the transcript, you can work your way through, creating paragraphs as you go, and leave the reordering until the end. Once you're done cleaning up the entire transcript, it will be easier to move sections around so that the story reads naturally and coherently.

If you know that you're only going to use certain sections for the finished narrative, isolating those sections is a great way to make the task of editing feel more manageable. Alternatively, you can read through the transcript and find a "hook." Just like any good story, an oral history narrative is most compelling when the first sentence draws the reader in.

Often, oral history interviews begin with general questions, the answers to which may not necessarily be an ideal beginning for a story. You may find something your narrator said halfway through the interview to serve perfectly as a hook, and that's totally fine! Feel free to play with the order of the transcript, and craft a narrative that has a compelling fluidity, flow, and some kind of story arc.

The ultimate goal of editing an oral history transcript is to honor the narrator's voice. Because spoken language is often very different than written language, transforming recorded speech to coherent text often involves more finagling than simply removing the interviewer's questions and stringing together the narrator's answers as they were spoken. Conversation is sometimes winding and disjointed, so a transcript scrubbed of the interviewer's questions would be unlikely to yield a very cohesive story. As editors, it is our job to hone the syntax and grammar in a way that best reflects a narrator's tone, rhythm, personality, and intention.

But here's where the nuance comes in: while it's generally best to "correct" an occasional grammar mistake, it's important to preserve the narrator's linguistic quirks and idiosyncrasies. There aren't many hard-and-fast rules when it comes to carrying out this priority; in many cases, we have to rely on our own instincts. For instance, if your narrator is a person for whom English is a first language, and they accidentally use an incorrect verb ending, it's usually best to change it because the small error might be interruptive to the text's flow or portray the narrator in an unflattering light. However, if your narrator is a native Louisianan who speaks with specks of Cajun dialect, keeping their alternative grammar and syntax intact may be the approach that is most true to their authentic voice.

A good measurement of whether you're on the right track is to ask yourself: *Would my narrator want me to keep this sentence or leave it out? Would they prefer me to standardize the grammar or keep it as it was spoken? How would my narrator want to be portrayed?* At Voice of Witness, we try to maintain contact with our narrators throughout the entire process. That way, if any sort of question comes up, we can ask them directly how they'd prefer us to handle an editing dilemma. In some cases, however, the narrators aren't reachable. Because our books tell stories of human rights crises around the world, some of our narrators are incarcerated, in refugee camps, or otherwise unavailable for follow-up interviews. In these cases, we do our best to shape their narratives in a way that lends the most honor, respect, and authenticity to their voice.

Sometimes, it is necessary to add words to a narrator's sentence in order for it to make sense. For example, if an interviewer asks, "When did you arrive in the United States?" the narrator might simply answer, "In 2002." While this answer makes sense in the context of the question, "in 2002" can't stand alone in an oral history narrative. In these cases, you can find contextual information that the narrator said in neighboring sentences. They may have said, "When we moved to the United States . . ." in another sentence from the same paragraph. In this instance, you could splice together the first half of that sentence with "in 2002" to yield a complete thought. But if the necessary information isn't there, and you have to supplement text for a sentence to make sense, you should put the words you supplied in brackets. Many editors will choose alternative sentence structures, or even to omit information, to avoid using brackets, as they can be distracting in a story. It is Voice of Witness's preference not to use brackets, because it makes for a more seamless, immersive experience for the reader.

Granted, oral historians have varying viewpoints on the ethics of editing interview transcripts. Some prefer to leave the transcripts untouched, even if the result is a less coherent narrative. In her chapter on Project LRN, Genevra Gallo-Bayiates says this about the editing process:

> I do think something is inevitably lost in the editing process, because every time I touch the story, I inevitably change it (either intentionally or unintentionally). The narrative becomes one step removed from the narrator with each manipulation . . . and so providing a way for others to access the material in both written and audio forms (with minimal editing) remains very important to me.

There are limitations to any process, and certainly something is lost in the "translation" of an audio interview to a written story. Two questions that often serve as useful guideposts are the following: (1) *How can*

I make the written story most reflective of the experience I shared with my narrator during the interview? (2) Does editing help the written story mirror the fluidity of the narrator's speaking voice? Asking the latter question, in particular, can help editors know when to put the brakes on, lest they impose too much of their own voice onto narratives.

As an oral historian, you will inevitably be asked, "Do you fact-check your narrators?" While fact-checking is generally considered to be an essential part of responsible journalism, the issue is a bit less cut and dried with oral history. When you sit down to record someone's account of their life, you are not only preserving history; you are preserving your narrator's specific memory of their own history. One of the beautiful things about oral history is that the same story could easily be told fifteen different ways depending on the person who is telling it.

Nonetheless, some details in an account deal with objective reality and can be fact-checked without it impinging on a narrator's rightful claim to their own account. Oral historians should check all proper nouns to ensure that they are accurate. This can usually be done with a quick internet search. It is also important to fact-check historical details that are verifiable. Facts stated by a narrator should fall into one of three categories: established, probable, or not established but possible. For instance, if a narrator tells a story about evacuating New Orleans for Hurricane Katrina in 2003, that is obviously an error and should be changed to 2005, because it is an indisputable fact that can be easily verified.

However, if that narrator gives an account of a subjective experience, it is generally best to take their account for granted, as the point of oral history is to listen to and honor your narrator as an authority on their own life. For example, if they talk about the days before Hurricane Katrina as "chilly," this may stand out as strange and unlikely, and you may be tempted to look up the temperature in New Orleans in August 2005. In this case, though, the narrator's perception of the air as chilly leading up to the hurricane is more relevant than the facts of the weather during those days.

Self-Care, Compassion Fatigue, and Developing a Capacity to Listen to Difficult Stories

> *Practice self-care. Listening to and working with traumatic stories is a transformative experience, with both positive and potentially harmful effects. Secondary stress and "compassion fatigue" are common but avoidable consequences. Create boundaries, talk to other people who can relate to what you're dealing with, get enough rest and exercise, and accept your limitations (don't make yourself feel guilty for not "doing more" than you're capable of for someone).*

—Mimi Lok, Voice of Witness cofounder

Most of us who work with people who have experienced trauma—whether as teachers, physicians, advocates, or oral historians—were drawn to this work by a deep sense of care for others. Often, people who work in these fields have a great capacity for empathy and grow accustomed to prioritizing others' needs. The very nature of our work can rely upon crisis after crisis: emergency room doctors juggle patients with acute trauma; child social workers have to continuously manage the unmet needs of children in the system; firefighters wait for a literal blaze and then rush toward it. But while mitigating trauma and giving people the help and support they need may be exactly why we do this work in the first place, it can also take a significant toll on our minds and bodies.

Also known as vicarious trauma or compassion fatigue, secondary traumatic stress (STS) is a condition common among individuals who work directly with trauma survivors, characterized by a gradual lessening of compassion over time and long-term emotional duress caused by witnessing or hearing about someone else's trauma.

When conducting oral history interviews with people who have faced human rights crises or other trauma, we often focus on how to meet the needs of our narrators: how to make them feel safe, supported, and cared for. This is a crucial practice; facilitating a space that encourages bravery and openness requires that we are particularly attuned to our narrators' needs. It's also important, however, to allow ourselves this same kindness. While the interviews themselves can be connective experiences, what follows is often solitary: processing, transcribing, and editing the interviews. Describing her profession, social worker SaraKay Smullens says, "In the truest sense, we are alone—we are the givers, and our fulfillment comes from seeing the growth, hope, and new direction in those with whom we are privileged to work."[3] Although Smullens is talking about social workers specifically, her sentiment applies to anyone working directly with people who have endured trauma.

The position of being alone and thriving on the fulfillment of stewarding other people's growth is inherent to the work of a social worker, case manager, educator, or human rights–focused oral historian. This sense of aloneness is not likely to go away. Being mindful, however, of our own proclivities (toward isolation, depression, irritability, substance abuse—all potential manifestations of STS) can save us from suffering and enable us to sustain our work for longer periods of time.

In her book *Trauma Stewardship: An Everyday Guide to Caring for Self While Caring for Others,* Laura van Dernoot Lipsky writes, "The most important technique in trauma stewardship is learning to stay fully present in our experience, no matter how difficult."[4] She argues that being intentionally present and allowing yourself the space to feel the emotions that arise when bearing witness to trauma is essential to maintaining well-being. This requires a mindfulness and patience that can run counter to our self-preservation instinct to rush through negative feelings in order to get past them. Often, we attempt to distract ourselves to escape the deeply rooted sadness that can result from listening to very difficult stories.

---

3. SaraKay Smullens, "What I Wish I Had Known: Burnout and Self-Care in Our Social Work Profession," *New Social Worker,* Fall 2012, www.socialworker.com/feature-articles/field-placement/What_I_Wish_I_Had_Known_Burnout_and_Self-Care_in_Our_Social_Work_Profession/.

4. Laura van Dernoot Lipsky, *Trauma Stewardship: An Everyday Guide to Caring for Self While Caring for Others* (San Francisco: Berrett-Koehler Publishers, 2009), 12.

The kinds of social justice–based oral history work that Voice of Witness does, focusing on the stories of people who have experienced human rights crises, can often result in STS. These stories can be triggering, induce survivor's guilt, and inspire deep sadness, particularly for people who have a great capacity for empathy. If you are working on an oral history project centered on emotionally difficult stories, it's important to be aware of the symptoms of STS and to practice self-care.

When dealing with STS, you may experience fatigue, anger and cynicism, hypervigilance, a sense of hopelessness, numbness to other people's pain, and a sense of diminished creativity. These can all be frustrating effects of doing this kind of important work. While there's no easy way to prevent these effects, there are self-management techniques that can help you cope with them:

- *Acknowledge your feelings.* Rather than sweeping feelings such as sadness, despair, anxiety, and guilt under the rug, acknowledging them and giving them space to exist will help you to move through them. Bypassing these negative feelings will often cause them to rear back up unexpectedly and with greater intensity.

- *Practice self-care.* This looks different for every individual. For some people, talking with colleagues or friends who do similar work can be cathartic. For others, running or other forms of cardiovascular exercise can help to release endorphins and lower stress. Some people benefit from meditation, others from playing games with friends or watching lighthearted television to achieve a sense of levity and balance. Listen to your body.

- *Remember that you are separate from the person whose trauma you are witnessing.* When we spend a lot of time and energy with someone who is suffering, it's all too easy to co-opt their pain. Creating healthy boundaries between ourselves and those with whom we're working is essential to doing this work in the long run. This is especially important when interviewing someone who has experienced a type of trauma that is intimately familiar to you. Hearing a narrator recount a trauma story that mirrors an experience of your own can be triggering and result in retraumatization. In situations like these, it is crucial to maintain consistent boundaries and ensure that you are giving proper attention to the feelings that may manifest.

- *Reconnect with the purpose that drew you to do this work.* Remember that helping people to create a living record of their stories is vital and important work.

In an oral history interview, both the narrator and the interviewer are creating space for stories that can be tragic, life-affirming, and ultimately transformative. It's necessary to take good care of yourself as you move through this process.

Preserving and Archiving Oral History

The oral history archiving process is a formal way to save the stories in your oral history project for future audiences. Passing on history and culture through in-person community storytelling has long been a primary function of oral history. In essence, the archiving process is our modern way of staying true to the oral traditions of our elders.

There are many considerations to grapple with when deciding on how best to store or archive your oral histories. Beginning oral historians can become overwhelmed by these considerations, as they usually occur when they are surrounded by a mountain of unorganized audio and video files, transcripts, photos, and partially edited narratives. To reduce this anxiety, it's a good idea to address archiving needs during the initial planning of your project. It is also useful to bear in mind that the storing and archiving process is ongoing and can be time- and labor-intensive. For larger-scale projects, it can also be expensive. Even with small projects, there always seem to be stories that need to be transferred, stored, and archived. During your planning, think of your project several years into the future—after the public readings, launch parties, and community gatherings have subsided—and consider the following questions:

- What is the ongoing value of these stories to narrator communities?

- Who is the wider audience for the stories, and how can they access and learn from them?

- What kinds of media and technology best reflect our archiving goals?

- What kinds of collaborations would be mutually beneficial for archiving our project?

Similar to other aspects of the oral history process, the ethical choices about archiving work in tandem with the technical ones to ensure the stories are preserved for project participants and potential future audiences. Ethical considerations related to narrator agency, representation, and access are essential to this aspect of oral history. For example, how can a given project's archive design choices create the easiest and most reliable access for the communities that shared their stories? And what collaborations or partnerships are worth pursuing that best reflect that commitment? We'll take a brief look at archiving considerations from four different perspectives: audience, access, collaboration, and technology. All of these perspectives overlap and affect each other. The resource section at the end of the book provides information about web and cloud-based storage and archiving platforms, as well as examples of well-curated archives.

Audience
An essential question for any oral history project, and one that should be addressed long before the first interview, is, who is the audience for these stories? We've seen earlier how exploring this question affects the "delivery systems" used to share oral history (books, websites, podcasts, and so on). During early project planning, create a working profile of your audience. Chances are you already have some of this information through your preparatory work with narrator communities and other partners. As part of your audience profile, you should consider how your intended audience prefers to experience stories: Are they tech-savvy, public gathering–minded, bookish, urban, rural, radio listeners, multiple-language speakers? Are they extremely limited in their media access? Are they primarily academics, scholars, or researchers? Are they some or all of the above? Addressing these questions

will inform your choices for preserving and archiving stories. Ideally, your oral history book, film, website, or podcast will mesh with the needs and desires of your intended audience and their ongoing engagement with the stories. For example, for DREAMers Testimoniando, it may make sense for project coordinator Shelby Pasell to consider creating an archive at Jóvenes Sin Nombres, a student-immigrant art collective / activist organization, instead of at the University of Minnesota. For After the Disaster, the stories of Fukushima survivors could be stored at the Dilena Takeyama Center for the Study of Japan and Japanese Culture, since they are already trusted partners on the project. By contrast, Claire Kiefer may consider connecting the Reentry Stories project with existing media platforms that serve the needs of formerly incarcerated individuals with limited media access. It can be challenging to find the perfect match between audience and archiving priorities, but listening to project participants and understanding audience needs can help steer your archiving choices in a more inclusive direction.

Access

Considerations of audience and access go hand in hand. It is crucial to determine the most unencumbered way for narrator communities to access their own stories. These determinations should address the dual needs of narrator agency and audience access. How can you work together with your narrator communities to ensure their agency and access while making the stories available for other audiences?

Oral historians utilize different approaches for creating this access. Some maintain "hard copy" archives at a local library, community center, neighborhood gathering place, or historical society, where narrators and others have easy access with a minimum of required passwords, access codes, or other potential impediments. This approach requires building relationships that need to develop over time, and it will be discussed further in the next section.

Archive access choices will depend on the intended audience for the stories. Is the audience exclusively the narrator community, or does it include members of the general public, researchers, and other historians?

There are a large range of options and choices to explore when it comes to determining what your intended audience prefers and how your archive choices affect their access.

Archivists can also create a digitized or online platform that can be easily accessed. For OG Told Me, Pendarvis Harshaw simply uploads the ongoing stories from the project to his website, creating easy access for all audiences. If your oral histories are intended for a wider audience, oral historians or archivists (often the same person) can create dual tiers for access: one for narrator communities and one for wider audiences. If access to wider audiences needs to be limited for issues of narrator safety, or to protect anonymity, oral historians can use access codes or passwords, or require interested parties to contact them or a narrator community representative directly before gaining access to the archive. Oral historians often use variations of all these approaches to create multiple points of entry for various audiences. The archiving choices for oral history projects should first and foremost strive to uphold the agreements made with narrator communities. Once that has been addressed, the stage is set to create an access and archiving scenario that serves the needs of every type of project participant: narrator, oral historian, archivist, and audience member.

Collaboration

As stated above, seeking out collaborative partners for oral history archiving can be a beneficial way to preserve and share stories. It's actually a continuation of the chain of trust concept mentioned earlier. Community centers, libraries, historical societies, museums, universities, and community colleges are all traditional locations for oral history archives, but which one seems to fit within a holistic approach to archiving your project? How can this aspect of your project build on the existing relationships you've nurtured? It takes time to create viable partnerships—especially if finances are involved—so as you enter into dialogue about an archive collaboration, patience, flexibility, and active listening are indispensable. These are, of course, the practices that have probably served you well throughout your entire oral history process, so you can extend them into your archiving work.

In pursuing partnerships, take some time to get to know one another and learn about each other's values, organizational cultures, and particular challenges. This learning process is vital in any collaboration but can be particularly valuable when it involves organizations of varying sizes and budgets. Individuals and smaller organizations tend to be more facile in moving ahead with projects and partnerships, whereas larger organizations tend to move a bit more slowly and have more moving pieces to attend to, and more voices to consider before making decisions. There are also questions of access, representation, copyright, and ownership. Universities and large nonprofits may ask for or require conditions stating that the content of a particular archive "is the sole property of . . ." This may not be a consideration for your project or it may be a deal breaker. When exploring these realities, it can be useful to take a step back and think about one of the narrators who feels emblematic of your entire project and ask yourself, *What would they most appreciate?*

There are many other details and logistics to work out, and they'll vary from partnership to partnership, but the following topics are usually taken into account when developing relationships with other organizations:

- consensus on the goals of the partnership (both individually and collectively)
- a mutually agreed-on decision-making process
- a co-drafted memo of understanding (MOU)
- parameters and agreements about finances and fundraising
- mutual understanding of project sustainability issues
- the need for additional staff
- a system for addressing grievances

While far from comprehensive, this list can serve as a template for collaborative partnerships. As with the other priorities addressed in this section, the majority of your choices regarding collaboration should be led by your project's commitment to agency and access for your narrator communities and other audiences.

Technology

Rather than giving a detailed analysis of equipment, this section focuses on the general technological choices involved in preserving and archiving oral history. The Oral History Resources section (p. 241) provides information and useful links about the pros and cons of various kinds of equipment, tools for preserving physical media, and the benefits and challenges of digital archives and preserving oral history in the cloud.

Many libraries, universities, and historical societies still maintain oral history archives that consist of hard copies, analog audiotape, photographs, and other forms of older media. They are archived in a way that would resemble a collection at your local library. Since this form of archiving requires a lot of physical space and tends to contain physical media that falls apart or disintegrates, most oral history archives have transitioned to a digital storage approach that ranges from maintaining multiple hard drives to using web-based archiving through organizational websites and relatively easy-to-use platforms such as Wix, Weebly, and WordPress. On a larger (and more expensive) scale, there are online platforms such as the Oral History Metadata Synchronizer, developed by the University of Kentucky, that will help to organize your archive in addition to providing storage. Many oral history projects utilize cloud storage services such as Google Drive, Dropbox, OneDrive, and Box. All of these services have free versions, which is fine for archiving small-scale projects, but most oral history archives purchase more space from these services in order to store larger ongoing projects. This is especially true for video and audio files, which require more storage space.

There are certainly pros and cons involved with "on-site" archives (hard drives and servers) and "off-site" archives (web-based platforms and cloud storage). For example, on-site storage allows archivists to better control the parameters of location and access, which reduces the risk of viruses or cyberattacks. A potential downside of on-site archives is that they are vulnerable to damage or theft. Also, on-site archives cannot be accessed remotely, which may prove to be an inconvenience for archivists and other stakeholders. Some of the benefits of off-site storage are simplicity, efficiency, and easy access. One of the challenges (particularly with cloud storage) is the difficulty of knowing if your archive is fully operational and truly secure.

Whatever approach you decide to employ, the technologies you choose for your oral history archiving project should be practical, sustainable, and reflect the needs of your intended audience.

PART TWO

ORAL HISTORY
FIELD REPORTS

A NOTE ON THE FIELD REPORTS

We chose the following eleven field reports from a pool of concept submissions that came from the larger Voice of Witness community. Our education program reaches thousands of students and teachers every year through our oral history resources, curricula, trainings, consultancies, and site visits. Many of the contributing authors came from that pool of teachers and learners, and all contributors have had varying degrees of exposure to Voice of Witness oral history methodology, including familiarity with many of the guiding questions and concerns outlined in part one. In short, we selected field reports that show what it means to put aspects of Voice of Witness methodology into practice.

Of course, every field report author has their own unique background, training, oral history experience, and set of practical concerns, and each project was developed independently of Voice of Witness. For this reason, we view each field report as both an example of and a complement to the work we do. While there are strong affinities among the different approaches you'll read about here, each project coordinator employed a unique approach that sought to best reflect the needs of their narrator communities.

Our main aim is to share with readers some of the hard-won lessons, successes, and surprises encountered in producing oral histories. For the sake of ensuring all the reports covered a core set of topics, we provided the authors with a series of writing prompts (though many had already started their oral history projects long before). Examples include, *How can an oral history project be beneficial to all participants?*, and, *How can we share stories in such a way that honors both narrator and interviewer?* Every contributor obliged by responding to those prompts, but we also encouraged them to share whatever wisdom they had gained through their own process. As a result, some field reports share similar viewpoints, while others seem to differ, at least a bit, on topics ranging from editing and transcription approaches to ways of ensuring narrators feel their stories are portrayed respectfully.

We open each field report with a brief introduction that addresses some of the major themes of the piece. This is to allow readers to easily search for content that might apply to their own project concerns. Several of the field reports conclude with a short postscript that gives an update about recent developments or ongoing project work, or points toward a project conclusion. In any case, every field report is wide-ranging, and we believe there's great value in reading them all to draw a full comparison between the many creative, inspired approaches and solutions our contributors developed in producing their projects.

BEHIND THE WIRE: MANDATORY DETENTION IN AUSTRALIA

ANDRÉ DAO AND SIENNA MEROPE

Behind the Wire began as an oral history project committed to sharing the unheard stories of asylum seekers in Australia being held in mandatory detention facilities. To limit access to journalists and advocates, these facilities have recently been moved to foreign jurisdictions on remote islands in the Pacific Ocean, and they have been internationally condemned as unjust and inhumane. André Dao and Sienna Merope undertook the project as volunteers. In this field report, André and Sienna explore the interview power dynamics unique to working with an especially vulnerable population.

Excerpt from "Behind the Wire"

They took me to very small room. Very small light inside, video camera on the corner. All the walls and also the floor was covered with very hard sponge, like mattress, but very hard. No bed, no pillow, no blanket, and air conditioning on 24 hours, and the light on 24 hours. There wasn't any switch inside the room to turn the light off or on. A small window in the door, you know, for security guard to see me inside, what I'm doing. They took my clothes away. They gave me one of the white surgical gowns that people wear for x-ray at hospital. They gave me one of those for one month and they didn't give me another one to change into. One month I was wearing that, without T-shirt, without pants, without underpants, without anything.

One month I was in isolation. My hunger strike [hit] day 46, and someone from Immigration or medical center in detention, they came with a piece of paper and they said, "Mr. Ruddock send us email or fax, something like that, and he said if you don't start to eat in next 48 hours doctor can force you.[1] Could you please start eating?" I said, "I'm sorry. No." And in that time I didn't have feeling to move, you know. They use wheelchair to take me to bathroom or sometimes outside.

Day 48 they opened the door, I was lying on the floor. Five or six big security guards. I was feeling sick and shocked as well. What do you want to do to the person who didn't eat anything for a long, long time? What can these big officers do? Two of them hold my legs while I was on the floor. Two of them hold my hands, this is four. Supervisor she put my head between her knee. Another officer with video camera filming it. Nurse and doctor try to use tube from my nose to my stomach. And doctor inject some liquid thing.

That was really, really torture, because it wasn't easy to breathe, with something going from your nose to your stomach, while they didn't put you to sleep using anesthetic injection. I couldn't breathe. I didn't have any energy or power to move, because I was sick and held by big security guards. Nothing I could do that time. And they gone. They shut the door and they gone.

Nighttime, they come, open the door, your food. I said, "No, put it outside, I don't want it. I don't want it." I was there for another few days, then they said, "We're going to take you to Juliet Block. And we are not going to release you until you start eating." I was there also for one week. They brought one of the detainees there for some different reason, and he said, "Look, it's not going to work. People

---

1. Phillip Ruddock was the immigration minister in the government of Prime Minister John Howard from 1996 to 2003.

are waiting for you inside the compound, you have to go and join them in doing something together."

I was really tired. Really tired mentally, because I didn't see anybody, my friend, for a long time, and the treatment of the security company and Immigration also make me more sick. I start to eating. They released me from isolation.

—Ali Bakhtiarvandi

The idea for Behind the Wire came from a combination of our anger at the treatment of asylum seekers in Australia and belief in the power of storytelling to advance social justice. When we started this project at the beginning of 2014, things were going from bad to worse in Australian refugee policy. The government was locking up men, women, and children arriving by boat, refusing to process their applications for refugee status, and detaining them indefinitely. Asylum seekers were being held in overcrowded, hot detention facilities on islands in the Pacific as well as Papua New Guinea. Stories emerged of disease, insufficient water, and rampant self-harm and sexual abuse in detention. Amnesty International and the United Nations condemned Australia's detention facilities as inhumane, and the minister for immigration shut down journalists' access to refugees coming by boat by putting the issue under the jurisdiction of the Australian military.[2]

There was—and continues to be—a lot of outrage in Australia about these policies. Many articles have been written on the subject, and advocates have sought to humanize asylum seekers by telling their stories of persecution before arriving in Australia. We began this project after realizing that there was almost no information about what it was actually like to *be* in immigration detention. Discussions about detention take

---

2. Amnesty International, *This Is Breaking People: Human Rights Violations at Australia's Asylum Seeker Processing Centre on Manus Island, Papua New Guinea* (Sydney, Australia: Amnesty International Australia, 2013), www.amnesty.org.au/wp-content/uploads/2016/09/Amnesty_International_Manus_Island_report-1.pdf; UN Office of the High Commissioner for Human Rights, "Australia's Detention of 46 Refugees 'Cruel and Degrading,' UN Rights Experts Find," August 22, 2013, available at https://newsarchive.ohchr.org.

place at a high level of generality and proceed along well-worn lines: commentators either condemn it as inhumane or argue it is necessary in order to deter other asylum seekers from coming to Australia. The voices of asylum seekers themselves are largely silenced in this discussion. We set out to develop Behind the Wire to tell the story of the lived reality of immigration detention, by the people who have experienced it. Our original goal was to compile around a dozen detailed oral histories from asylum seekers who had been held in Australian detention and to edit them into compelling literary narratives that could be published as a print book and e-book. We wanted to create an anthology of short, nonfiction stories of life in detention.

Revealing Resilient, Suffering Human Beings

We quickly chose to focus Behind the Wire specifically on the experience of being in Australian immigration detention, rather than the experience of being a refugee in Australia more generally. By showing the detailed reality of life in detention, we aimed to shift public discourse away from shallow rhetoric and to create a historical record of a very dark period in Australia's history.

Mandatory detention was introduced by the Australian government in 1992 to deal with a perceived "asylum seeker problem." Under the policy, all asylum seekers arriving by boat and without a valid visa are placed in detention until their applications for refugee status are reviewed. Depending on the refugee and the government in power, that time has ranged from a few weeks to several years. Likewise, under Australia's policy, asylum seekers have been detained in a range of different locations—from facilities in suburbs of Australia's major cities, to remote parts of outback Australia, to other countries like Papua New Guinea that Australia pays to house our detention centers.

We believe that the brutality of Australia's treatment of refugees is only accepted by the public because asylum seekers are systematically dehumanized. Their faces are kept from the media, they are referred to in government communications by case number rather than by name, and they are invariably discussed publicly under broad and collective labels—"boat people," "asylum seekers," or "illegal immigrants"—rather than in a way that ever recognizes their individuality.

We chose an oral history approach because we believe it allows narrators the freedom to provide details and perspectives about their experiences and thoughts that might not emerge in a more structured interview format. The narrative feels like the story of an individual, rather than a case study.

So often, social justice narratives are regarded as "pity narratives" because they focus on the extreme in an attempt to shock and to elicit pity. The risk is that these experiences are so alien to the reader's own life that the audience no longer identifies with the storyteller. Pity narratives also dehumanize narrators, portraying them as two-dimensional victims rather than as complex, multifaceted human beings. As we began collecting interviews, it was the small human details that moved us the most: the young woman with ambitions to become a journalist who started her own newspaper in detention, the couples who met and married while detained, the group of Middle Eastern men who cooked lunch for their center guards.

By sharing personal stories, we hope the public will become less willing to accept some of the actions taken by the government in the name of "stopping the boats." Beyond government policy, we also hope that Behind the Wire will enable ordinary Australians to better understand and relate to refugees now living in the community—who may be their neighbors, coworkers, or classmates—thereby providing an entry point for building new, more positive relationships across communities.

We were confident that an oral history approach to telling the story of the camps would allow narrators to maintain control over their representation and minimize the extent to which we were speaking on their behalf. We also know that when documenting a story of vulnerability, there is an inherent power imbalance between the narrator and the interviewer, creating the risk of developing an extractive relationship. We wanted to support narrators to speak out on their own terms, rather than stripping them of their stories, by adopting an open-ended approach and committing to multiple interviews with each narrator.

From the outset, we talked a lot about whether and to what extent we could ensure narrators retain some control over their story once it's published. Deciding to launch a website as well as a book was important in this respect. Because a website, unlike a printed work, does not need to be restricted to a handful of representative stories, every narrator who participates in Behind the Wire can be sure that their story will be published, if that is what they want. It also allows us to remove a story after it's published if a narrator decides they no longer want their story disseminated. Importantly, a website format also allows narrators to access the content of Behind the Wire easily. While a book—especially an e-book—is not necessarily a content delivery method used by our narrators or their communities, almost every asylum seeker we have met is extremely internet literate, due to their having to keep up with news and family in other countries. One impediment to access, however, is the fact that as of this writing, all of our published stories, whether in book form or on the website, will be in English. This is simply a consequence of lacking the resources for translation. The advantage of a website is that it allows us to publish translated work if and when the resources for translation become available.

I Couldn't Imagine My Life without Them

Although Behind the Wire started as a personal project coordinated by the two of us, we quickly drew upon the support of our networks. This was of critical importance, as the scope of the project was large: former detainees are scattered all over Australia, come from a huge range of countries, and were detained over a period of more than twenty years.

We had originally conceived of Behind the Wire operating in a decentralized manner, with the two of us acting as coordinators one step removed from the interview process, overseeing a team of interviewers in different locations. But we eventually moved to a model in which the coordinators would be much more hands-on in conducting interviews.

This led to the recruitment of three more coordinators: Michael Green, Angelica Neville, and Dana Affleck. We decided to move to this model in large part to ensure our discussions about ethics and honoring narrators' stories were front and center in as many of our interviews as possible. While we've still gone ahead arranging interviews by interviewers who are not involved in the central coordinating team, we've tried to make sure that those interviewers have had as much one-on-one time with a coordinator as possible to go through those issues.

The decision to recruit more coordinators was also logistical and strategic. Given the mounting time commitment associated with Behind the Wire and the fact that we were all working in a volunteer capacity, it made sense to spread the workload. In addition, each of the new coordinators brought new skill sets to the project. Michael Green is a freelance journalist who writes on social and environmental issues, while Angelica Neville, who is based in Sydney (the rest of the team is predominantly Melbourne-based), completed a master's in refugee studies at Oxford University. Dana Affleck has excellent refugee contacts through her long-standing advocacy in that area. Having a larger team also meant we had a broader network through which to reach narrators.

In order to contact potential narrators, we relied upon our links with refugee advocates—the people who have worked, or are working, with former detainees on a regular basis. Leila Druery, for example, an advocate who was herself running a refugee support organization, has extremely strong links in the Tamil and Afghani refugee communities. Beyond their contacts, a key factor in choosing to work with these advocates is that they act as gatekeepers: they are perfectly placed to help make assessments about the likelihood of a potential narrator being retraumatized, for instance. This helps us create a safe environment and guides us in choosing which narrators to approach. Advocates also mediate the "outsider/insider" dynamic between us and narrators. In many cases, these advocates have formed close friendships with former detainees, meaning that a relationship of mutual respect and trust is present from the beginning of the project. As Dana Affleck said to us:

When I first started visiting asylum seekers in detention, I spoke some Arabic and most of the people that I met were from Arabic-speaking countries, so that was how we broke the ice. . . . At first it is hard to ignore the obvious differences between us—in terms of our lived experiences, the language barrier, and cultural differences—but it didn't take long before those differences were either overcome or become a familiar part of our friendship. However, a difference that could never really be shaken is the difference in our liberties. At the end of a visit, I can leave the detention center and they cannot. I can make plans for my future and they cannot. I have agency over my life and they do not. I can't pretend that this doesn't have some impact on my friendships with people in detention. It is if and when my friends are released that our friendships grow to something beyond the walls of the visitor room. It is such a joy to be invited into the lives they carve for themselves and to share mine with them. Many of these people are my nearest and dearest and I couldn't imagine my life without them.

Honoring Narrators' Agency While Protecting Their Safety

Two central goals informed our planning for Behind the Wire: First, create a collection of engaging and compelling stories that would give readers insight into the reality of mandatory detention and build empathy. Second, enable asylum seekers who have been silenced by the immigration system to tell their stories within an ethical framework that honors their experiences, supports them to feel safe in speaking, and allows them to maintain ownership of their stories. The pursuit of these twin outcome and process goals has influenced every step of our work on the project.

From the outset, we took a very flexible approach to setting a timeline for Behind the Wire. This came down to two factors: one, we were all volunteering on this project, and so we needed to fit our tasks in between work and study; and two, we knew that the process of finding and interviewing narrators would take a lot of time. We thus gave ourselves a tentative timeline in which we would complete our first round of interviews by the end of 2014 (which gave us about eight months from the time the project was first conceived).

Despite what seemed like a relatively generous timeline, we've since found that it has had to be revised. At the time of writing this field report, we were in the midst of conducting and editing our first handful of interviews. This was in large part due to delays associated with questions about legal risk (which we address in detail below), but it was also due to the high level of interest in the project and simply the significant amount of time it would take to "do oral history" in a way consistent with our goals for Behind the Wire.

In terms of research, the gap in our knowledge when we started out was really in the mechanics of conducting oral histories, so we busied ourselves reading as many different examples of oral history narratives as we could find. This initial research proved immensely helpful in giving us an idea of what oral history looks like and what challenges we were likely to face.

We then began to reach out to potential narrators, using our preexisting networks. From the outset, we were surprised by how many ex-detainees wanted to speak with us. The level of interest brought its own challenges. We had always envisaged collecting a small group of diverse narratives. Having five young Sri Lankan men who had all been held in detention together wanting to speak to us complicated that strategy.

We made a decision early in our planning process that we did not want to silence anyone who had experienced mandatory detention. As long as we had a willing interviewer, we would engage with every asylum seeker who wanted to speak with us. This was another important factor that led us to launch the Behind the Wire website, providing a more expansive platform for asylum seekers to tell their stories. Through the website, Behind the Wire has become an open-ended project.

We also found that many of the asylum seekers who wanted to speak to us were currently in the process of having their refugee claims assessed. A large number were in immigration detention. This created one of the challenges—if not *the* central challenge—in our planning process:

how to honor narrators' agency in deciding to speak to us, while at the same time ensuring their safety in relation to the very real legal risks involved in disclosing their experiences publicly.

Applying for refugee status requires asylum seekers to tell the government their life story in minute detail, to make out a case of persecution. Any unexplained detail or inconsistency between the story presented in Behind the Wire and their account to the government could be grounds for the government to reject their case by finding they "lack credibility." Also, because the Australian government is determined to keep what goes on in detention centers secret, asylum seekers who speak out are seen as troublemakers and treated with hostility.

Because we came to Behind the Wire with experience in refugee advocacy, and because we were reaching out to narrators through advocate networks, we were broadly aware of these risks when we started out. Our initial strategy for managing them was quite simple: explain all the potential legal risks to narrators and ensure we have informed consent; give narrators a stake in the editing process; allow them to have the final say over whether we publish their story; and anonymize stories by changing names and other identifying details. As the project progressed, however, this strategy became more complicated.

To start with, we soon realized anonymizing stories could be very difficult. Asylum seekers currently in detention are a relatively small group—no more than a few thousand. Their daily life is closely monitored, and the government knows everything about their backstories. We realized tweaking details and names would not necessarily be enough, particularly for asylum seekers with very distinctive stories. Through seeking legal advice, we also learned there were risks in asylum seekers simply speaking to us, regardless of whether we published their stories. Recording in immigration detention centers is forbidden, so conducting interviews there would require narrators and interviewers to act unlawfully. We were also told that if the immigration department found out about our interviews, our original transcripts could be subpoenaed by the government in any future court case involving a narrator.

Addressing these risks has been a challenging and ongoing process. We have had to confront the deeply troubling question of how much we should defer to narrators' decisions when they are extremely vulnerable. Some of our potential narrators have been in detention for years, with no end in sight, and they desperately want someone to bear witness to their lives—to show that they have not been forgotten. They have said that they are willing to run the legal risks to tell their story. But we also know some are suffering severe depression, and many are desperate. On the one hand we feel we have a responsibility to be protective—to ensure their safety in circumstances when they may be too vulnerable to make rational decisions for themselves. On the other, we don't want to undermine their agency and contribute to their sense of powerlessness by becoming complicit in the government's project of silencing them. "Don't take this from me," said one of our potential narrators, when we suggested it might be too risky for her to tell her story.

Ultimately, legal risks have significantly influenced our criteria for choosing narrators.

To assess risks accurately, we have created a classification system for potential narrators according to their visa status, all the way from former detainees who are now Australian citizens to asylum seekers currently in a detention center. We use this rubric to select narrators who are in low-risk situations, essentially refugees who now have Australian resident visas. We have also categorically decided that we will not interview certain "high-risk" groups of narrators. For narrators who are somewhere in the middle of the risk scale, we make a case-by-case decision. We do not seek these narrators out, but if they come to us wanting to participate, we explain risks and offer them free, individualized legal advice through our refugee lawyer contacts. This discussion has sometimes led to narrators choosing not to participate, occasionally on our advice or the advice of their support network. Ultimately the choice is theirs.

At the same time, we have stood by our decision to engage with every asylum seeker who wants to speak to us, even if they are in a relatively high-risk legal scenario. We understand that for some people, the very act of telling their story may be important, so we've discussed—though not yet had to implement—ways to facilitate that, even if conducting a traditional oral history process or publishing a narrator's story might be impossible for legal reasons. These strategies could include allowing people in detention to tell us their stories through letters rather than oral interviews, or interviewing narrators despite knowing we won't be able to publish their stories until after their refugee applications are finalized. We see this engagement as critical to our process goals for Behind the Wire, even if it does not ultimately feed into our concrete outcomes.

Articulating Discomfort

After our lengthy discussions of legal risks and ethics, we approached our first interviews feeling not only ready to get started but also really excited—in part a mirroring of our narrators' enthusiasm. Osama Diraqi, an Iraqi refugee, says that when he first heard about Behind the Wire, he "was so happy. Because you know, so many people, they don't know anything about refugees." Osama's comment is typical of the response we've received from many former detainees: in a context where silencing and ignorance are the norm, these are people who are eager for their stories to see the light.

Our interviews have tended to take place wherever the narrator feels most comfortable. In some cases, that has meant going to the narrator's home. This feels quite natural and means the narrator is likely to feel more relaxed. It also changes the dynamic slightly between interviewer and narrator, as the narrator also plays the role of host. André, who interviewed Osama at his flat in Melbourne's outer northern suburbs, says, "It was nice to meet Osama at his place because it felt less 'professional'—I was not only an interviewer but a guest as well. When I arrived, he poured me some juice and offered me some Iraqi biscuits—it was a nice way to start the conversation, having a bit of food together and chatting about the weather." On a similar note, we have encouraged our interviewers to share a little bit about themselves with narrators, so that the interview feels more like a meeting of two equals.

Other interviews have taken place outside the home, but still in spaces familiar to the narrator. Michael interviewed Ali Bakhtiarvandi (whose excerpted interview opens this chapter) at the office of an activist group that Ali volunteers with every weekend. Michael says that Ali "lives in Ballarat, an hour and a half out of Melbourne, but he comes down here every weekend to volunteer. He suggested the space. It was quiet and he was comfortable there. He drinks many cups of tea, and this setting had the advantage of a kettle and an ample supply of tea bags."

Aside from picking a familiar location, another method for establishing trust has been to develop a relationship with the narrator that goes beyond the interviewer/narrator dynamic. As Rajith Savanadasa, one of our interviewers, says, "I try to involve them in my life." For Rajith, that went as far as inviting a narrator to his bachelor party (a game of tennis). As mentioned above, the asylum seekers Dana visited in detention became her "nearest and dearest."

However, close relationships between interviewers and narrators can also lead to difficulties. Dana found that interviewing a close friend added an additional level of distress. At one particularly difficult point in the interview, Dana turned off the recorder to take a break. But then the narrator continued speaking, in more detail and at greater length, about some of the particularly traumatizing aspects of his story. When Dana asked if she could turn the recorder back on, she felt that the narrator was a little bit upset with her—possibly because she'd blurred the lines between what he was telling her as a participant in our project and what he was telling her as a friend. In a debrief after this interview, we discussed how such moments might be inevitable when talking to a friend— it's neither possible nor desirable to be able to separate a friendship from a more formal interviewer/interviewee relationship. As Michael said during the debrief, the best we can hope for is to approach such moments in a "spirit of friendship and humanity."

A further complication in Dana's case was her own worry that she was using her relationship with the narrator to take advantage of him. This was a common worry for those who work closely with asylum seekers— as someone's lawyer, or regular visitor, there is a natural anxiety that someone in such a vulnerable position might agree to something they're not completely comfortable with out of gratitude. As Dana told us, when she asked her friend if he wanted to take part, he replied, "I'd do anything for you, Dana." Again, it's not necessarily possible to separate out someone's motivations between gratitude, the desire to tell one's own story, and the wish to change public opinion. In an effort to address this issue, we scheduled a meeting between Dana's narrator and another member of the Behind the Wire team—in the hope that it would bring home the fact that this project exists beyond the personal relationship between narrator and interviewer.

In any case, such relationships with narrators are not always possible—in fact, they will probably always be the exception rather than the norm. Where the interviewer and the narrator don't share a long-term friendship, it has still been important to treat these interviews differently from other types—a journalistic or client-intake interview, for example. This is especially the case when the interviewer has a background as a journalist, as is true for several of us. During some of our interviews, we found that the conversation moved more slowly than in an interview we might do for a newspaper or magazine. In the latter situation the reporter often enters the room with a relatively clear idea of what he or she hopes to hear in the interview and asks questions that will guide the conversation in that direction. In stark contrast, many Behind the Wire interviews were far more relaxed and open ended. We also found that an initial meeting, without a recorder, in which we simply have a normal conversation with a potential narrator, helps to break the ice. Having that first conversation before proceeding also means that we can be absolutely sure that the narrator is taking part voluntarily.

Follow-up interviews have proven to be essential. Rajith says that the first interview is "driven by how open [the participant] is initially." Often, that means narrators have tried to recall the most memorable events during detention in a first interview. Of course, this is only natural—Rajith found that narrators often recounted the most difficult stories in their first conversation, such as details of leaving their homes and other traumatic memories. In subsequent conversations, he actually found that narrators spoke with more ease about their everyday lives. André found that in his initial interview with Osama, that focus on key events meant that he didn't give as many specific details about life in detention. Follow-up interviews are the perfect opportunity to flesh out the details that give stories their richness, details which narrators often skim over when recalling long past events for the first time in years.

Michael's experience with Ali also reflected that need for follow-up interviews—in this case, as much because of the interviewer's shock as what the narrator might have left out:

> In the first interview I was shocked at the awfulness of what he went through. I knew things were bad, but I didn't know about his hunger strike or understand the way the authorities denied him information about his case. I think it rendered me a little speechless, but he steered the interview by himself just fine. And we had two subsequent interviews—before each one I typed the previous transcript and made lists of things that had arisen that I wanted to ask about.

That discomfort Michael articulates has very much been a factor in our interviews. That narrators' stories often left their interviewers speechless is perhaps a mark of how much projects like Behind the Wire are needed. And while these instances of discomfort could make it harder to direct an interview, or to remember what your next question was, they also served as signposts for the moment at which an interview had transcended generalities and platitudes and struck at some deeper, more painful truth.

I Always Found a Reason Not to Start

Thus far, we have found that editing is really about making a series of difficult, case-by-case choices. Again, our two goals could be broadly defined in terms of process and outcome. In terms of process—in trying to honor our narrators' voices, and to remain as true as we can to their stories—each word cut from the original transcript, and each sentence rearranged to another part of the story, takes on a great significance. But it is also important to remember that the end outcome is going to be a book and a website aimed at a general, rather than a specialized, audience—meaning that the stories have to be presented in as clear and accessible a manner as possible.

For Michael, the interview process with Ali was a long one, and the sheer amount of ground covered in their conversations made editing a daunting task:

> We did three interviews, for a total of nearly five hours. They were spread over several weeks, for reasons of our availability. I haven't returned to Ali with the draft story yet, but I have arranged to do so. One surprising thing for me is that once I'd typed out the transcript, I found myself stalling on beginning the editing process. I wasn't really sure why, but I always found a reason not to start—I think it was a combination of not wanting to face such a long transcript, but also not wanting to face the stories of unrelenting trauma that it contains.

Aside from the difficulty of simply getting started, or of wanting to put off sitting down to experience "stories of unrelenting trauma" again, there is the further complication of having to make the decision, for one reason or another, to cut an event or incident despite its emotional power.

Content from an interview may be cut for a variety of reasons. The first and most obvious one is length—our lengthiest interviews have yielded transcripts of up to thirty thousand words. Length becomes an even more acute issue when we consider that these stories will also be published on-line, where the average reader's attention span is necessarily shorter than in print. While in all of our transcripts there are always obvious things that can be left out of the final story—needless repetition, overly general content, and the interviewers' questions—there are many more components that require deeper reflection. In our transcripts, those more difficult decisions included how to represent the mundanity of life in detention as it was related to us. Often, narrators found that rather than specific traumatic episodes, it was actually the sameness of day after day in detention, coupled with uncertainty about their future, that was truly soul crushing. As interviewers, it sometimes felt natural to gravitate toward spectacular incidents—hunger strikes and riots, for example—but even here there was an element of repetition, of sameness. For those detained for extremely long periods, like Ali, these incidents pile up over the years until it is their sheer ordinariness that is paradoxically both shocking and numbing. But in a story format, there is the risk that including each incident will begin to read like a list that, rather than accurately conveying the narrator's experience, only succeeds in disengaging the reader.

This difficulty in the editing stage also stems from the multifaceted nature of Behind the Wire. As discussed above, one of our goals is primarily historical—to document daily life in Australia's detention centers. With that goal in mind, we are inclined toward retaining exhaustive detail, such as lengthy descriptions of buildings or the layout of the center. However, the inclusion of details that may be historically important is not necessarily of interest to the general public, so finding the right balance between detail and narrative drive is important.

Another difficulty has been choosing where to cut back on our narrators' editorializing. Our objective with Behind the Wire is to present these stories in a manner that encourages our readers to lose themselves in the narrative—and in turn, for those readers to be able to make up their own minds about mandatory detention. At the same time, our narrators were often very passionate about Australian politics and society (as would be expected). Leaving out some of those forthright opinions might make for a more engaging story, but to cut them all runs the risk of losing something essential about our narrators' voices. Many of these opinions reflected our narrators' countries of origin and articulated vital political, ethnic, and religious tensions back home—discussions that were difficult for us to place within the context of a more personal narrative about detention.

The question of voice has been a recurring complication. Our narrators all spoke English as a second language. Often that meant that they expressed themselves in novel, ear-catching ways. But it also meant that their transcripts contain grammatical mistakes or difficult-to-understand sentences. In the end, we chose to ask the narrators how they would like to be represented—whether, for example, they would like their English to be corrected when necessary. As of this writing, we have begun to seek funding for interpreters, with the aim of being able to talk to a wider pool of narrators who speak little or no English. This will throw up fresh challenges in terms of preserving narrators' voices, but it will also allow us to highlight particularly marginalized stories.

Ultimately, we've come to realize how much power and discretion comes with the task of editing another person's story. Decisions about what to leave in and out of the final narrative, what titles to give to different sections, and what sentences to modify, however slightly, all have a huge effect on how a story is read. Perhaps the hesitation to begin editing can be seen as a hesitation about having this power and how to use it in a way that leads to a fair, and truthful, representation of the narrator.

A Small Act of Compassion and Defiance

What will Behind the Wire look like as a finished project? To be honest, we're not sure if a project like this *can* end, at least not while Australia continues to imprison those seeking asylum here. In March 2017, we published an anthology of our narrators' stories, *They Cannot Take the Sky: Stories from Detention*, and launched a companion website; but having embarked on this journey with our narrators, it's hard to see it ending with those two publishing outcomes. In part, this is simply because the lives of our interviewers and narrators are so often entwined—they won't stop seeing each other, and being friends with each other, now that the book and website have launched. And in part it's because we all see ourselves as refugee advocates as well, and the same things that motivated us to begin this project in the first place will continue to motivate us to keep it going—to listen to, and share, more stories.

At a personal level, the impact of the project has been profound. The act of sitting down with another person and listening to them—really listening, not trying to force yourself into the conversation—is rare enough. But to do so with someone whose experiences have been so traumatic feels, regardless of wider social impact, like an immensely positive, worthwhile thing to do. For narrators, we hope the act of telling and being listened to affirms that their suffering has been acknowledged and allows them to feel that they are seen and valued as human beings. We have had some early feedback from refugee advocates who have said that our narrators' stories have been shared amongst people currently in detention and that reading the stories of others who have been through the same ordeal has provided some comfort against the hopelessness, and loneliness, of their situations. And for us as interviewers, particularly in the context of ever-worsening policy, each interview feels like a brief antidote to the despair and powerlessness that always threatens to overwhelm anyone who cares about these issues—a small act of compassion and defiance.

Of course, we also hope that Behind the Wire can play a part in changing the minds of Australians about mandatory detention. We hope that when confronted with the reality of what we are doing to other human beings just like them, ordinary Australians will be outraged. And we hope that for advocates and researchers, these stories will enrich their activism and their research. Each one of the stories we've come across as part of this project has had its own unique power, and published together, we hope that these stories have an even greater collective power—to inform, enlighten, and, most of all, to move people to empathy.

Postscript

Since writing this chapter, Behind the Wire has grown as a project and as an organization. The publication of *They Cannot Take the Sky* coincided with a major exhibition of the same title at Melbourne's Immigration Museum. *They Cannot Take the Sky* features the stories of thirty-five narrators, ten of whom are still detained, and was published by Allen & Unwin, one of Australia's largest independent publishers. An audiobook version of the book was simultaneously put out by Audible. The exhibition features over two hours of audio and video stories drawn from the content of the book, as well as a series of photographic portraits. More information about these projects can be found on our website: http://behindthewire.org.au.

In addition to the book and museum exhibition, in January 2017 we launched a ten-part podcast series, *The Messenger*, a coproduction with Melbourne's Wheeler Centre for Books, Writing and Ideas. *The Messenger* is based on several thousand voice messages left between Abdul Aziz Muhamat, a Sudanese refugee detained on Manus Island since October 2013, and one of our coordinators, Michael Green. You can listen to the podcast at www.wheelercentre.com/broadcasts/podcasts/the-messenger.

OG TOLD ME

PENDARVIS HARSHAW

Pendarvis Harshaw is a photographer and journalist who was born and raised in Oakland, California. In 2011, Pendarvis started a project called OG Told Me, in which he photographs and interviews elder Black men in Oakland. About OG Told Me, Pendarvis says, "When an elder dies, a library is burned. This project is about preserving a portion of that library." Here, Pendarvis shares excerpts from the interviews he has conducted, along with his reflections on finding narrators and insider/ outsider dynamics in oral history.

Excerpt from "OG Told Me"

I worked at Sunset Dairy off and on from the time I was nine. I had to carry ten gallons of milk, and I was a lil ol' boy then. But you did what you had to do, you know? When I first got my draft card, I went to my job and told Mr. Collier, who owned the dairy, that I had been drafted and he said, "I'll tell you what I can do, I can keep you out of this army and declare you essential to keep the economy going for the dairy thing." At first I didn't believe him. But he was able to do that, you know?

His two little boys and I grew up together. I'd go to the farm where their dad was. We did everything together—slept in the same bed, went to all his nice cottages up near the lakes and everything, rode in the big boats, ate at the same tables and all that stuff. But anyways, his son and I got into it. And he brought two other boys and three other girls—white girls—up to the dairy in his brand new convertible Buick. He wanted me to stop operations and bring him something, and I wouldn't do it. So we got into it. And as a result of it, I was almost laced [lynched]—but two white women saved me.

And then, Mr. Collier, he said everything would be all right. I refused to go back. He told me, "If you don't be back at work on Monday, you'll be in the army in the next 30 days." Well I didn't think that it could be possible for a man to do that. I mean, we saw that big picture in the post office, Uncle Sam, with the big red-striped thing and the black tall derby on. And they'd say, "Uncle Sam will come and take care of his thing, ya know?" And that was the first time that I really understood who Uncle Sam really was.

Anyway, I went out there and made the best of it. You didn't want to be there, but you did what you had to do. You went where they sent you.

I ended up in Central China and Burma. They sent me off to New York University for some special training before I left. And then I went to Fort Baylor, Virginia, for a little training. And then out here to Riverside, California. And then from here, to overseas. . . . There's a lot of other history between that and there, but I'm just hitting the hot spots.

—Oscar Wright

Methodology

The excerpt above is only the beginning of an hour-long conversation I had with Oscar Wright, a 91-year-old man from Mississippi. During the discussion in Mr. Wright's living room, we touched on topics that ranged from his time as a member on the local school board to his letter correspondence with two American presidents, George W. Bush and Barack Obama.

There were so many six-by-nine framed photos on Oscar Wright's walls that you could hardly see the wallpaper. His worn couch looked like it had been molded just for him. Maybe it had been. After all, he sat on it like a throne. It was smack dab in the middle of his living room. His feng shui was perfect: he was within arm's reach of old photo albums, documents about the well-being of Black boys in Oakland's public schools, and a coffee table (that's where I put my recorder). I asked if it was okay to record, he gave me permission, and then we started.

Mr. Wright has lived one hell of a life. The photos on his living room and hallway walls depict frozen moments of his journey. Black-and-white portraits of family members and friends who've transcended to the afterlife adorn the walls. His photo albums, notebooks, and a couple of framed letters documenting his interactions with high-ranking officials speak volumes about some of the things he has seen. We only talked for an hour. And after that hour-long conversation with that 91-year-old man, I walked out of that photograph-filled living room knowing that I had only touched on "the hot spots."

Touching the tip of the iceberg, or "the hot spots," has been one of the consistent themes of my OG Told Me project. Just the major moments—those are what people remember. Whether it's Oscar Wright or a gentleman in his sixties by the name of Woody Carter, when looking back on their lives, these men talk about the milestones.

The milestones—the major tragedies or life-changing events—those are what come to mind when someone asks you for the wisdom you've gained in life.

I sometimes laugh at the premise of this project.

Imagine: a bigheaded kid with a camera around his neck comes up to you in the middle of the street and asks you: *If you had the chance to tell young people one piece of advice, based on your life's experience, what wisdom would you give them?*

I've gotten all types of responses. Elders have danced for me and they've denied me. I try to make sure my ego doesn't get hurt when they don't speak to me. At the same time, I don't over-congratulate myself when things go well. It's all a matter of how the person I'm interviewing is feeling. Again, imagine that bigheaded kid approaching you on a day where you're just not feeling well. What would you tell that kid? Or maybe it's one of those days where the sun is on your shoulders, and you're willing to talk to anyone, including this camera-toting young man. I don't credit myself with doing anything special or approaching anyone in a particular way that helps them open up to me. I'm nice. I have manners. Before introducing myself as a journalist, I sometimes crack a joke or give a compliment to the person I plan on interviewing.

I use minimal equipment in an attempt to not look intrusive. I use a compact point-and-shoot camera with an interchangeable lens; I've used a couple of different models from the Sony Alpha series. Sometimes I just use my phone to take photos. I use an audio recorder or my phone to record the interviews. To keep a written record of notable quotes, I either use my computer or the old-school pen and notepad. Sometimes I use all of the aforementioned methods. There are rare occasions when I only use video (those are the guerrilla journalism moments). When I interview someone, I try my best to explain to them why I am using a particular recording method. I also make it a point to be clear about the purpose of my project and where their story will end up.

I rarely rush.

Sometimes I can't help but to introduce myself to someone, ask them for a quote, and take their photo. These are truly spur-of-the-moment acts of intuition. In these instances, I use just my phone to record and take photos. They usually aren't the best-quality photos, but the stories are often amazing.

Other times I have to track down someone for an interview. Someone I've seen around the neighborhood a million times. Someone like Oscar Wright.

It's all a case-by-case scenario. There is no "right way" to conduct one of these interviews.

History of the Project

The roots of the OG Told Me project are in the poetry I wrote as a kid. I would be on the bus, at the corner store, or just walking down the street, and I'd cross an elder Black man's path. Often, the elder Black man would say something witty, ear-catching, thought-provoking, or just something that I'd want to remember, so I could repeat it one day and sound as cool as he did. I took note. When I got home, I'd put their quotes at the top of my blank page of paper and then write whole poems or raps about these remarks.

In high school, the idea grew into an album project. The concept was that I'd get quotes from elders, sample the recordings, and then mix the wise words into songs that I wrote. I recorded about six tracks. I had some pretty good interviews and songs in the works, but then I went off to college.

In college, I learned the art of survival within the great indoors. I was beyond broke while I attended Howard University in Washington, DC. I worked as a journalist, teacher, and even as a newspaper delivery boy for the *New York Times*! One summer, I drove a fusion taco truck and sold healthy snacks for a company called Food on the Fly. I think I spent more time making money for college than I did learning in college.

After I left Howard, one class short of graduating, I returned to Oakland with a chip on my shoulder. I hadn't planned on struggling just to come home and struggle more. I was sleeping on my mom's couch (and I wasn't too happy about it) and teaching a class specifically for young Black boys at Oakland Technical High School. The class was part of the Office of African American Male Achievement, the nation's first. It was Oakland Unified School District's latest effort to do something about the underperforming academic record of Black boys in its schools. My class was called "The Lion's Lair," and I loved it.

We practiced different handshakes, did push-ups in between reading chapters from Ralph Ellison's *Invisible Man*, and had a guest lecturer come in and speak to the class every Friday. The list of speakers included Mistah FAB (rap artist), Jesus El (acrobatic slam-dunker and dancer), and

Baba Achebe Hoskins (community activist, actor, magician, and respected elder).

The students, ages fourteen to sixteen, were all from the surrounding neighborhood. So I knew a couple of their older relatives, or at least knew their faces from riding my bike around town. We had a good connection. The only things that stood in the way of learning were tardiness, absences, and students being on their phones. I couldn't combat the attendance problem, but the phone issue was my war to fight.

I started OGToldMe.com during the first month of teaching at Tech. I only had a few interviews posted on the Tumblr-based site, but it was content nonetheless.

When I would catch one of my students on their phone in class, I'd give them a choice: to share what they were looking at (most likely a social network site or a text message), or go to OGToldMe.com and read an entry from my site. The greatest reaction was when one of my students saw an elder's face on the site and said, "I know OG! I see him all the time, I just didn't know his name."

That's when I realized it was working. On a small scale, I was bringing two generations together. Two generations who needed each other. Two generations who are often at odds with each other. I was taking the information from the mothball-scented living rooms of the elders in our neighborhood and bringing it directly to the cracked-screen smartphones of the next generation. As the school year ended, I kept my OG Told Me blog going and haven't really stopped since.

Choosing My Narrators

Mr. Wright lives three blocks away from my mom's house. I'd seen him around town on numerous occasions. I always noted his presence, mainly because of the way he introduced himself. It's not every day you hear someone state their age and race before they say anything else.

"My name is Oscar Wright, and I am a 91-year-old African American man."

That's how he introduces himself at the Oakland school board meetings before he brings forth further evidence of the state-sponsored miseducation of Black men in America.

"My name is Oscar Wright, and I am a 91-year-old African American man."

That's how he introduces himself when he speaks to a group of young Black men, before showing them a collage of their ancestors, the great thinkers and creators they come from.

"My name is Oscar Wright, and I am a 91-year-old African American man."

That's how he introduced himself to me when I made the short journey from my mother's house in North Oakland to his doorstep. He was sitting out front and invited me in. We talked as people typically do. Aside from the fact that I asked for the conversation to be recorded, nothing was different. And that's how most of my interviews are. Mr. Wright differed from my other narrators in one way, though: he is a seasoned public speaker.

The conversation flowed. He showed me photos. Told me stories of old classmates and friends. I asked questions about his parents and siblings. He offered experiences from his first and second marriages, and of course, he talked about his kids. He's proud of them.

The questions about family are usually at the front end of the OG Told Me discussion. No matter the length of the interview, questions about family open doors to who a person is and what they've learned in their life's experience; the family is the first classroom. A brief interview I did with a man I refer to as "Tracy, the man in the pink hat" in downtown Oakland in late 2014 showed that the family question works in both short and longer interviews. "I came out here to find my father," he said. I hadn't asked him anything other than where he was from. He offered the detail about his father.

Anytime someone offers me intimate information, I pose a follow-up question. A person is reaching out, wanting to tell their story. When given an ear to listen, it's amazing what people will say—especially people who don't have much of an audience to hear them out. Maybe that's why interviewing random people on the street is important, given that aspect of the human condition: we all want something but don't always know how to ask for it.

When someone on the street opens up to me, I used to think it meant that there was something *there*, something that made the person want to tell me their story. Now I know that *I* was there. That person wanted to tell their story all along, and I merely presented them with an opportunity.

Who knows how long Mr. Wright had been waiting to tell someone his war stories? Or how many times the man with the pink hat had attempted to speak to someone about searching for his father? I know for a fact that Watani Stiner, a former inmate at San Quentin, wanted to tell his story.

I interviewed Stiner, who did two different stints in prison for charges related to the killings of Bunchy Carter and John Huggins (top-ranking officers in the Black Panther Party's Los Angeles chapter). Stiner's story is amazing. Just after he finished high school, he had a baby with his childhood sweetheart and joined the United Slaves (US) Organization. The US Organization was one of many civil rights groups that worked out of an office in the heart of Los Angeles's Black community. Unfortunately, the groups stepped on each other's toes on multiple occasions, and, with the assistance of government agents who infiltrated these groups, small flames were fanned and minor conflicts became full-fledged gunfights. Posing as activists, the agents sent propaganda and misinformation from one group to the other. These acts were a part of a government-sanctioned plan to dismantle the efforts of African Americans fighting for civil rights. That plan was called COINTELPRO.[1]

---

1. COINTELPRO, or the Counterintelligence Program, was begun by the FBI in 1956 to disrupt the Communist Party of the United States through infiltration, disinformation, and other acts of sabotage. The FBI expanded the program in the sixties to include other domestic groups, including the KKK, the Socialist Workers Party, and the Black Panthers. COINTELPRO operations were discontinued in 1971.

On January 17, 1969, these heated interactions boiled over and left blood on the grounds of UCLA's campus. The Black Student Union held a meeting on the campus, which was attended by members of both the Black Panther Party and the US Organization. It's reported that a commotion broke out between members of each group, followed by a brief squabble, and then a gun was drawn. Shots were fired and people fled, some using the window of a classroom as an escape route. When the smoke cleared, Bunchy Carter and John Huggins were left dead. The double homicide resulted in Larry "Watani" Stiner and his brother, George, being arrested and charged on counts related to the deaths.

The Stiner brothers were sent to San Quentin, where they were prime targets for incarcerated Black Panther members and supporters. Fearing for their lives, the two gentlemen devised a scheme to escape from California's most notorious prison. After a visit from their parents, it's reported that the two used assistance from the guards in order to escape the prison walls, before meeting their ride atop a hill in Marin. The driver got them out of there, and they boarded a plane headed to South America.

The brothers lived in the South American countries of Guyana and Suriname, where Stiner sold crafts, trinkets, and soaps. During his travels, he bumped into Jim Jones in Jonestown, Guyana—an eerie experience, as he writes about in his unpublished memoir. He also had to deal with a military coup in Suriname. The country had some horrid economic woes, which prompted Watani Stiner to take an action that would alter his life, again.

Stiner, who had fathered six children since escaping prison (in addition to the one child he had before being living in exile), decided to turn himself in to the US embassy in November 1993, after twenty years on the run. He wanted his kids to have American citizenship and a better life.

A year's worth of back-and-forth negotiation happened before Stiner was back on US soil and headed to San Quentin to serve the rest of his life sentence. In exchange for a life in jail, the United States had agreed to grant Stiner's kids US citizenship.

When I met Stiner, he had been incarcerated at San Quentin for over fifteen years. He was calm and stoic. He was interested in restorative justice, poetry, and writing for the *San Quentin News*. He was the man behind a section called "From an OG's Perspective." Given my project's aim, he and I were meant to sit down and discuss the intergenerational relationships between Black men, both inside and outside the prison gates.

The conversation with Stiner was a high-water mark for my project. His high-profile crime, his incredible tale of "the bad guy" doing something kind for his kids, and his way of thinking were powerful elements. His comments hit home when he talked about the connection, or lack thereof, between him and his children—namely the young men he had fathered.

At the time, his second-youngest son was in a prison in Southern California for gang-related activities. The questions Stiner had about discipline, peer influence, media, and society as a whole were the ones I found to be the most intriguing.

Although incarcerated in a facility on US soil, Stiner hadn't seen the United States since the late sixties. He had little to no understanding of how society worked, nor about the world of Southern California gangs in which his son lived. Stiner asked me questions about gang warfare, group thinking, and being a follower. I tried my best to communicate what I knew, and I explained how drastically different the gangs in Southern California were from the turfs of Northern California.

He said he also paid attention to whatever popular media the prison allowed in and talked with the young people at the prison. He had gained some ideas about his son's world through his conversations with people of a younger generation, and he was appreciative of that connection. But at the same time, Stiner was at a loss in terms of how to connect with his son, and for that matter, some of the younger men at San Quentin.

The intergenerational connection, or lack thereof: that's what's at the heart of my project. In choosing the subjects I interview, I keep that focus in mind.

Familiarity with Your Narrators

I think it's important that I'm a young Black man conducting this experiment. As I said earlier, the family questions opened doors for discussions. And I believe that it's because the older Black men I interview see me as a young "brother" that I've had such success when it comes to getting people to open up to me.

You can't teach familiarity. It's not an acquired skill set. It's not something I learned at UC Berkeley's Graduate School of Journalism or at Howard University's School of Communications. It's not charisma or charm. I don't even think it's explainable. It's something I was born with.

I'm familiar with my target audience. I'm digging into my own community and exploring something I've noticed time and time again. If I weren't a young Black man, or if I weren't from Oakland, I wouldn't get the same results.

Being able to relate to other Black men is as deep as the shared experiences of our ancestors, and at the same time, it's as shallow as simply having the same skin tone. But both factors add to or take away from how comfortable the narrator might be with the interviewer.

These elder men are helping a younger brother out. And even with all the disconnection between generations in this society, especially in the Black community, this action is still held sacred. The OGs always want to look out for a "young brotha."

An Oral Historian's Power

Power is the ability to define phenomena and make it act in a desired manner.

—Huey P. Newton

These are the powers I was granted: being literate, sociable, a photographer, a patient editor, and a quick thinker—when I'm at my best. Once I gain access, as I've shown with the examples of the man in the pink hat, Watani Stiner, and Oscar Wright, the door opens and things just flow. The questions about family are the first step toward knowing someone.

The questions about love, careers, education, struggles, and successes soon follow.

I talked with Mr. Wright a lot about the racism he faced during his coming-of-age experience. How he reacted to discrimination in the South. How he handled racism in the armed forces, and how his educational shortcomings were the product of a racist system. All of these experiences led to the formation of the 91-year-old education rights fighter I saw before me.

One look at the major events in the course of someone's life gives you an understanding a million times greater of the individual in front of you. It's an amazing feeling to be able to chart someone's story, the major turns they took, the risks and rewards, the habits they kicked, the moves they made, the failed relationships and job opportunities, the wars they fought in, and the legislation that changed their lives. It's interesting. It's a real-life history class.

Mr. Wright's experience bumped up against the Korean War, the Homestead Act, the Title IX decision, *Brown v. Board of Education*, and the Voting Rights Act. All of these were major moments in American history—as well as moments that directly influenced Mr. Wright's story. This is a reminder that I'm not just taking notes from old people bumping their gums; no, this is real.

There have been mistakes all throughout my project. I've gotten better as time has gone on, but I know I have room to grow. What started off as a personal project recording lessons from old men has now gotten press in both local and national media. Even more importantly, some of the elders I've interviewed have seen their pieces. And when they've seen me on the street afterward, they've let me know when I've misquoted them. It's not a good feeling.

I once posted an interview about an elder named Gerald Green who used to hang out at a corner store in North Oakland. Mr. Green had told me a story about achieving balance in his life: being able to hang out with the fellas while still getting his schoolwork done. In retelling his story, I wrote that he'd "always" hang out at the store with his friends. I was wrong. The next time I saw Mr. Green, he made sure to let me know to change the word *always*. He clarified that he would stop by the store every now and then, but that he wasn't a loiterer—and he wanted that to be clear. I apologized and made the change immediately.

People take this seriously. It's a record of living people. For some of the men I've interviewed, it's the only record the world has of them apart from government records (medical, school, prison). They want to be presented in an honest and dignified fashion. This is something I didn't understand at one point. But through doing this project, I've gained an understanding of how documenting the spoken stories of a people is a way to preserve culture. To take these stories and present them on an academic level—that gives more power to the individuals I've interviewed. There is power in this project. I know that now.

Honestly, I didn't take myself seriously until I saw others taking me seriously.

Having a Specific Focus

I have never received a negative word about the overall concept of this project.

If anything, people have asked me why I don't interview men of all races, or why I don't interview women. I tell them that that's not the aim of my project. I'm here to find the wisdom of elder Black men and translate their experiences, good or bad, to the younger generation. I've chosen a specific focus, and that has helped me a lot. I would love to interview people of other races and genders, but I couldn't imagine interviewing every baby boomer with a good story. My voice recorder wouldn't know what to do with all of that information.

I chose elder Black men because I personally wanted to know what their world was like. Fingers crossed, one day I'll be an older Black man. So speaking to them and gaining their wisdom is as much for me as it is for my high school students.

I would love to expand my interviews, geographically speaking. I would love to interview older Black men from New York, Detroit, New

Orleans, Chicago, and Los Angeles. Why stop in Oakland? I think that documenting the experiences of elder Black men across the nation would be an interesting study. They're an invisible group. Men who were looked over when they served in the armed forces, when they became educated, a group that vanished due to the war on drugs and mass incarceration. Preserving the stories and experiences of this particular demographic group is not only important to me, but to America as a whole. What did the men who lived through the civil rights era and crack epidemic learn? What can they teach "millennials"? A specific area of focus has granted me so much in terms of knowing how I want this project to progress.

Forward Progress

This can't be a blog forever. There is a book in the works. A curriculum to teach young people the crafts of journalism and oral history by choosing a specific topic to focus on, a way to cover a given area of interest, and advice on how to go for it. And I might even make this project into a comic series one day—who knows?

The possibilities are vast when it comes to this project. But I think a few things should remain intact no matter what I do: the specific area of focus, the lessons passed between generations, and the feeling of familiarity this project gives people. The last thing on that list is what matters the most to me. If I'm not genuinely interested in an interview, then it will show. If I'm not learning from an interaction, then the audience will not learn. If there is no progression on my behalf, my audience doesn't progress. This is both good and bad. The good side: people know it's from the heart. The bad side: once my heart stops, so does this project. What do I do about it? Keep progressing on my own and look for someone (some people?) to carry on this torch. And that's what I hope to do, soon.

There is no shortage of people out there willing to tell their stories. I doubt you'll find another Watani Stiner, but I guarantee you can find an elder with framed memories all around his living room in your mother's neighborhood. And if all else fails, I'm sure Mr. Wright would have no gripes about introducing himself to another young person: "My name is Oscar Wright, and I am a ___-year-old African American man."

Postscript

In April 2017, selections from OG Told Me were self-published as a coming-of-age memoir about growing up in Oakland and listening to local elders. Several narrators from the original blog are included in the book with photographs and interview excerpts, and the book has been featured in *FADER* magazine and the *Los Angeles Times*.

AFTER THE DISASTER: REBUILDING LIVES AND COMMUNITIES IN FUKUSHIMA

JON FUNABIKI[1]

Jon Funabiki is a professor of journalism and former executive director of the Dilena Takeyama Center at San Francisco State University (SFSU). Guadalupe González and Natalie Yemenidjian are graduates of the journalism program at SFSU. In 2011, Jon helped to organize community events in San Francisco at the Dilena Takeyama Center following the "triple disaster" of earthquake, typhoon, and nuclear reactor breach that caused widespread devastation around Fukushima, Japan. Out of this project and his work as a journalism professor grew the opportunity to take students to Fukushima to gather firsthand accounts of the disaster and its effects on some of the thousands of disrupted lives in the region. In this field report, Jon recounts how he organized an oral history around an ambassador program of SFSU students to Fukushima. He also describes the challenges of bridging linguistic and cultural barriers in seeking personal stories, navigating the possibility of retraumatizing narrators, and finding ways to stand with narrators beyond simply sharing their stories.

Excerpt from "After the Disaster"

When the earthquake happened, in my mind all I thought was that we have to escape and run away from here. Fortunately, I had electricity, and we saw the news—an Iron Wave came to the coast.

---

1. Guadalupe González and Natalie Yemenidjian contributed to this field report.

The next day, March 12, at 6 a.m., we heard sirens. The voice was saying, *"Nigete kudasai"*—"Run away, please."

So I and about twelve neighbors ran away to Baji Park. Most people tried to go to Tsushima, the evacuation site. There's only one way to get there and it was very crowded. So we decided to go to the park.

Everyone thought they could go back the next day—some people didn't even bring sandals. I forgot to bring money. I needed coins to make calls because I didn't have a cell phone. I made a phone call on someone else's phone.

After the earthquake, I evacuated to Iitate Village in Fukushima. My son was in Aomori prefecture. He decided to come to Iitate to pick me up because there was high radiation. It was difficult at Iitate because there was no gas. There was no water. Then, we decided to go to Kashiwazaki [located on the west coast of Japan in Niigata prefecture]. I moved from one side of the ocean to the other.

I think my life is not good. When we watched the hurricanes in the United States, I thought that would never happen to me. We have a lot of earthquakes, but never thought we'd face this situation. I feel different now.

—Ozaki Takako

Finding the Project

This is the story of Ozaki Takako, as told to Natalie Yemenidjian, one of my journalism students at SFSU, in August 2014. Ozaki-san, a 68-year-old woman, was living in a temporary housing shelter in Fukushima. She was among the hundreds of thousands of people who were forced to evacuate their homes when Japan's northeastern coast was pummeled by a triple disaster on March 11, 2011. It was triggered by a monster earthquake and tsunami that wreaked havoc on towns, villages, farmlands, and fishing fleets in the prefectures of Iwate, Miyagi, and Fukushima. And when the "Iron Wave" smacked the Fukushima Daiichi Nuclear Power Plant, it caused a meltdown, explosions, and the release of plumes of radioactivity. Over all, nearly 16,000 people were killed and more than 6,100 injured. In the immediate aftermath, more than 492,000 people were displaced—run out of town because of physical danger, government evacuation orders, and fear.

All of this was covered by the news media. As with many other disasters, the "3/11 disaster" dominated headlines around the world for many months, especially as officials struggled to stave off further catastrophe at the crippled nuclear power plant. As with other disasters, news coverage and public awareness dwindled over time as the crisis appeared, at least on the surface, to subside.

And yet, as with other disasters, the crisis has yet to end for the people of Fukushima. In fact, at the time Yemenidjian interviewed Ozaki-san—more than three and a half years later—more than eighty thousand Japanese men, women, and children were dislocated, many of them living in temporary housing shelters like the one Ozaki-san lived in. The shelters look like pale steel boxes lined up in orderly rows on asphalt parking lots. These are tight quarters—a single small room serves as the living room, dining room, and bedroom. One of my other students observed that the wan and pallid shelters practically disappeared into the sky on gray, overcast days. And for many outsiders, the residents have all but disappeared as well—they are living in limbo.

We wondered, *What has happened to these people? How are they coping in the post-disaster period? How have their lives been disrupted, and what's happened to their communities? What are their hopes for the future?*

"Please Don't Forget Japan"

This was the context of our project After the Disaster: Rebuilding Lives and Communities in Fukushima. It might be dramatic to say that the idea struck us like a bolt from the blue. Instead, it grew like moss over more than a year's time. We were inspired by the notion of capturing the stories of what we came to regard as "forgotten people." People and organizations grew excited by the idea and offered assistance. Opportunities arose, and we took them.

Officially, it was sponsored by the SFSU's Dilena Takeyama Center for the Study of Japan and Japanese Culture, which organizes programs for the campus and community. As the center's director and a professor of journalism, I'm offered opportunities to combine my interests in Japan, journalism, and broader forms of storytelling. I believe that people express their fears, hopes, and dreams through the stories they tell.

From the start, the Fukushima disaster ignited an immediate outpouring of grief and generosity among San Francisco Bay Area residents. Our region has a large Japanese American community and strong business and cultural ties to that country. The school enjoys a large number of exchange students from Japan, and I'll never forget seeing many of them holding buckets and shedding tears as they collected donations on campus for the Japanese Red Cross.

The Dilena Takeyama Center organized a number of disaster-related programs, and one was particularly emotional. We exhibited a series of powerful poems written by disaster survivors in a traditional form called "tanka." I had seen the poems exhibited at the Cathedral of St. John the Divine in New York, and so I asked the organizers for permission to bring them to San Francisco. We displayed the poems in Japanese and English. Written by housewives, college students, fishermen, and other ordinary citizens, they expressed trauma and tragedy most profoundly.

One poem, written by Kato Nobuko, cried out:

> in broad daylight
> the sea rose up and attacked—
> a great tsunami
> unimaginable in this world

Another, written by Tamura Shojin, lamented:

> building these coffins
> filled with sorrow
> for infants
> for one-year-olds—
> how tiny they are

Just days before the exhibit opened in January 2013, the Seattle-based Laurasian Institution asked us to host a group of fifty Fukushima-area high school students who were taking part in a leadership development program. The program was designed to prod the students, some of whom had been directly impacted by the disaster, to become the next generation of leaders who would help Japan recover and grow in the future. The students, wearing their prim blue uniforms, arrived while we were in the midst of mounting the show. We invited the students to read the poems and then write a blessing or message on a piece of paper that would be tied to a bamboo tree, similar to a tradition practiced at Japanese shrines. We could tell that these teenagers were moved that an American university would deem the poems important enough to display in the United States. Many of the students penned messages that haunted us:

Remember Japan.
Don't forget Japan.
Please don't forget Japan.

A few days later, nearly four hundred people—students, faculty, community leaders, artists, business owners—attended the opening night reception. The response affirmed our belief in the strong pull that Japan holds on San Franciscans and the power of the personal story to stir emotions, raise awareness, and encourage empathy among people separated by the Pacific Ocean.

At about the same time, an unexpected invitation came from the International Center at Fukushima University. They asked if SFSU would be interested in sending a group of our students to see firsthand how Fukushima and its residents were faring. They were worried that global news coverage of the disaster and the radiation threat had burned negative images of Fukushima into the consciousness of people around the world. Enrollments at the campus had fallen. The university is located in the city of Fukushima, which is about thirty-six miles inland from the nuclear power plant. The center created the Fukushima Ambassadors Program, which enables students from universities in the United

States and other countries to visit Fukushima for two weeks, offering "a hands-on learning opportunity that focuses on the physical, financial, and social consequences of the tsunami and subsequent nuclear accident in Fukushima."

This would become the vehicle that would enable us to help the Japanese people tell their stories and close that five-thousand-mile gap between San Francisco and Fukushima. It offered us a tangible way to respond to the plea "Please don't forget Japan." The basic outlines of a strategy began to form: our students would use the Ambassadors Program as a way to learn about the disaster and to meet and interview individuals and families to develop stories.

I worked closely with William McMichael, the center's deputy director and creator of the Ambassadors Program, to discuss the changes needed to accommodate our students' reporting needs. The existing Ambassadors Program was a fast-paced tour in which participants galloped from one site to another. In contrast, our students needed more time at each location to get to know people, conduct in-depth interviews, and shoot videos and photos. In the summer of 2013, I visited Fukushima to meet some of the people and visit some of the sites that would be included in our tour. When I saw the scale of the temporary housing developments—one of them had eight hundred or more residents—I realized that they had to become the focus of our students' inquiry. The shelters conjured images in my mind of the internment camps that were built in the United States to hold Japanese Americans during World War II. My own parents were held in one of those internment camps, so the experience of dislocation cuts close to my heart.

Meanwhile, I also began searching for funding to cover students' expenses. As a public university, SFSU attracts many students from families with modest incomes; many of our students are immigrants or the children of immigrants. My goal was to secure funding to ensure that the students' air travel and other major expenses would be subsidized. The Sasakawa Peace Foundation of Tokyo, which had funded other projects related to disaster recovery, stepped in to provide this funding.

A key concern for us had to do with bridging the gap between the American and Japanese cultures. We wanted to make sure that we built in ways to develop trust with the Japanese, who can be reticent to discuss private matters—especially those dealing with emotional or mental health issues—with strangers. In advance of our trip, McMichael spoke to officials at the temporary housing shelters to explain our mission. McMichael modified the Ambassadors Program so that we could make multiple trips to the temporary shelters and also engage in ice-breaking activities, such as joining residents in outdoor exercises and cooking nabeyaki noodles. The extra work created logistical headaches and stress for McMichael, but it also increased the level of trust between the residents and our students. McMichael, who is Japanese Canadian and bilingual, served as one of our main interpreters. Other center staff members and a group of volunteer Fukushima University students who were studying English also helped as interpreters. I recruited Chuck Olson, a classmate of mine when we were both SFSU students ourselves. He had been working and living in Tokyo for more than thirty years. Olson volunteered his time to assist with the interpreting services, and his knowledge of Japanese culture proved invaluable to our students.

Meanwhile, faculty of the journalism department and the Japanese language and literature program helped recruit a "dream team" of students—five advanced journalism students and one Japanese-language student. In addition to Yemenidjian, the team included journalism students Guadalupe González, Gavin McIntyre, Lorisa Salvatin, and Debbie Svoboda, as well as Corinne Morier, the Japanese-language student. The group was as diverse as America: the four women and two men included an African American, a Mexican American, an Armenian American, a Filipina American, and two white students. None of them had previously visited Japan.

To prepare them, we developed a series of orientation seminars. Dr. Stephen Murphy-Shigematsu, a psychologist intimately familiar with both Japanese culture and trauma issues, emphasized the problems of stigma and also advised us to treat people sensitively so as not to retraumatize them.

For another seminar, Yuri Kageyama, a reporter from the Tokyo bureau of the Associated Press, came to San Francisco to describe how she approaches stories in Fukushima. Kageyama echoed the high school students' fears about being forgotten: "I wish there were more interest, because the people of Fukushima are extremely worried about being forgotten. This is an important story, it's probably the biggest story of my life," said Kageyama. "I've been with AP for more than twenty years, and I think it's up to us reporters to make sure that important stories are not forgotten."

During a Skype talk, Nicole Martinez, an assistant professor and radiation expert at Clemson University, advised the students not to worry about overblown reports of radiation contamination that circulated on the internet. As a participant in a previous Ambassadors Program, she had conducted her own radiation monitoring experiment. Using dosimeters, she found that Fukushima participants were exposed to less radiation than ordinary people living in Denver, Colorado.

There were a number of bureaucratic hurdles to leap, which at first seemed minor. Some were caused in part by university officials who were jittered by the thought of college students traipsing through radiation-soaked fields—exactly the kind of stereotypical scenes that the Ambassadors Program was meant to dispel. Whether real or imaginary, the university's concerns over health, safety, and risk led to mountains of confusing paperwork, multiple levels of approval, and other requirements—doctors' sign-offs, insurance policies, safety restrictions, mandatory first aid training, and so on. The weight of the paperwork became threatening as the clock ticked toward our planned departure date. The official OK to purchase our airline tickets didn't come until shortly before departure.

"We All Lost the Same Thing"

That's one of the reasons I can't sleep. When I start thinking about that, I can't sleep. Even if I went back, I know that I can't go back to my old life. There are no young people around, there is no work, I can't grow any vegetables. And my neighbors are no longer there, so even if I would return to a place like that, I don't know what I would do. So now I think about, where I should go next, where I should live next. So it's not a decision that's easy to make.

And my son, I've thought about moving in with my son, but there is no way. I cannot go back to (my former home in) Iitate, because the *butsudan* (altar) is there and the family plot is there. And all my belongings are there because all I took was the minimum of what I needed. And there are community meetings going on for former residents of Iitate, so all those things are still there. And I have to worry about my mother, where she is living, and I don't want to move to a place where I don't know anyone there. So all those things I think about. And on my days off, I go around looking around for housing and things like that, but it seems that is what everyone is doing as well.

As someone who went through this, to realize you just lost your *furusato* (homeland) and to have to tell your daughter that her *inaka* (the place you grew up) . . . our uncles and aunties . . . they've also lost their home. So to realize that is not just you that lost something but all these people as a whole, we all lost the same thing, and realizing that is very hard.

—Takahashi Fujiko

This is how Takahashi Fujiko described the deep sense of loss that she felt more than three years after the disaster. She worked at Ka-Chan No Chikara, a small café that opened in downtown Fukushima to provide jobs for some of the women who have been dislocated by the disaster. You can order grilled fish or noodles for lunch and browse shelves of small handicrafts. Takahashi-san had to move because her home in Iitate falls within the thirty-kilometer exclusion zone that officials drew around the Fukushima Daiichi Nuclear Power Plant. The house itself was not damaged. Unlike many of the other people interviewed during our trip to Fukushima, Takahashi-san did not live in a temporary housing shelter. Instead, she and her husband rented a small apartment in the city. The interview was conducted by Guadalupe González, who had graduated from the SFSU journalism department a few months before the start of the trip to Fukushima.

González and Yemenidjian, two of the six students selected for the Fukushima project, participated in a Voice of Witness "Amplifying Unheard Voices" workshop in Berkeley as part of our preparation for the trip. This came about because of an invitation from Mimi Lok, VOW's executive director. We wondered whether VOW's oral history techniques could be incorporated into our effort. After all, there are similarities between the approaches of the journalist and the oral historian. Both profess to uncover the stories of our subjects. Yet, there are differences, some profound, in technique and philosophy. By tradition and training, the journalist plays the role of an independent observer, or referee, who seeks truth by weighing input from a range of relevant sources. This means that the journalist is detached from the people who are subjects and sources. As we learned in VOW's workshop, the oral historian seeks the truth within the individual, who is regarded as a "narrator," rather than a "subject." This means the oral historian and the narrator form a partnership, and they work together to excavate his or her story. This leads to the most important difference, the power dynamic. In journalism, the journalist is in control; in oral history, it is the narrator. It is, after all, the narrator's story.

Despite these differences, both the journalist and the oral historian need to close the gap that separates him or her from the interviewee. In our workshop, we explored trust-building techniques and strategies that oral historians use, many of which benefit journalists as well. How can you put the narrator at ease? How can you demonstrate that you deserve the narrator's confidence? How can you show that you are being nonjudgmental about the story about to be shared? How can you show patience, compassion, and empathy?

These were some of the lessons that González brought with him to Fukushima. González had met Takahashi-san when our group stopped at the café one day for lunch. Sensing that she might be willing to tell her story, he asked if she would be willing to be interviewed again another day. González brought one of our volunteer interpreters, a student from Fukushima University, with him to the next meeting, which took place during her work shift. On the outside, Takahashi-san seemed cheerful as she sold bento (box lunches) to customers, but she began to reveal her anxieties and sorrow as the interview progressed. Takahashi-san's inability to return to her *furusato* and uncertainty about the future became clear. Sleep had become elusive. "So not knowing how long things are going to last—those kinds of fears and anxiety is a lot to deal with," she confided.

González has concluded that the main benefit of the oral history approach is that it exposes the humanity of the narrator.

"It avoids misquoting, misinterpretation, and sensationalizing what in most cases is a personal topic and allows the narrator to demonstrate their true emotional state," he said. "And sometimes in order to understand a story and the emotions behind it, one needs to hear it directly from the source."

Thinking back on the interview, González said the oral history process made him dig deeper into Takahashi-san's story:

> The hardest part about using the oral history approach in Fukushima was the language barrier. The easiest part was the human connection. I did not need to know the spoken language to understand the stress in Fujiko's voice, to see the anxiety on her face, or the helplessness in her posture.
>
> My assignment to cover the café at first seemed relatively feasible. When we first visited the café for lunch, an employee welcomed us and explained the cafe's purpose. When I met with the manager another day, she handed me pamphlets that explained the mission of the café and broke down its business practices. She gave me general information in a matter-of-fact way. When I finally was able to speak to an employee who was an evacuee, the story changed dramatically.
>
> I decided to pursue the oral history approach for this story because I wanted Fujuko to tell her own story. After all, the story was supposed to be about the café, which was founded for people like her. It only made sense to go directly to the source; I wanted to report on the current condition of the evacuees.
>
> I had a student interpreter during the entire interview, which was great to ask questions, but difficult for me to understand the

narrator's response. I sort of understood that the interpreter was giving me a summarized version of the narrator's responses because she would talk for a few minutes, but he would only give me one or two sentences. Still, I sincerely inquired about her story and listened. Once I returned to the United States, I had a Japanese friend who now lives in San Francisco translate her responses, which I had recorded.

The most surprising moment during this experience was after this interview. As we were leaving the café, the student translator told me that he did not expect me to be so interested in her story. I guess he made this conclusion due to the questions I was asking and the length of the interview. I told him we would only take about twenty minutes at the café gathering information. But because I was unsatisfied with the information given to me and asked to speak to an employee who was affected by the disaster, we were there for over an hour. I spoke to Fujiko for forty-five minutes. I'm glad he got that impression because I was certainly being sincere.

"Dried Earth Frying"

Yemenidjian, whose interview with Ozaki-san appeared at the beginning of this chapter, found that the oral history technique was "perfect for what I wanted to accomplish in Fukushima, which was to give them the 'mic' and the byline and to merely be a bearer of their stories." This became the case again when she decided to capture the story of Sato Kazuya, one of the Fukushima University students who tagged along with our group as a volunteer interpreter. Over the course of the two weeks, Sato-san divulged that he had developed post-traumatic stress disorder and a fear of trains as a result of the disaster. As Yemenidjian retells the story:

> We had a language barrier; however, what made his story the most compelling during my trip was how comfortable he felt with me. He was willing to talk about his anxiety disorder and post-traumatic stress disorder down to the pills he took to keep from having debilitating panic attacks.
>
> We walked from Fukushima University to the train station as I scribbled his story, and he patiently explained that he was on a train when the 9.0 earthquake hit. Shaking, the train stopping suddenly on the tracks and there was fear in everyone's eyes. After it was over,

Sato, who was seventeen years old at the time, spent three nights in an evacuation center with no contact with his parents.

Sato said, "After we went back to my house, I was surprised because there was a lot of garbage in front of our terrace. That view was like a portrait out of a Japanese history textbook, like during WWII with bodies everywhere. The view was similar. A lot of wood was still burning. Some propane gas was on fire just in front of my house. The smell was a very bad smell, it's hard to explain—I think it came from the earth. It was like dried earth frying."

As we waited on the platform of the station, Sato-san moved past the group of people we were with and told me that he had a "deep" fear of trains. I could see it in his eyes that he could hear our train fast approaching.

Sato said, "In Japan, everyone uses a train. In Japan, the mental illness is the problem of yourself, not a disease."

"A Bridge of Understanding"

The fourteen-day program prepared by Fukushima University provided our group a wide range of contrasting experiences. In most parts of Fukushima, life went on as normal. In fact, many of the scenes could have been mistaken for suburban America, complete with busy shopping malls, sports fields, and highways. All along the way, our students interviewed the people of Fukushima to capture their experiences from the disaster and their hopes for the future. All our students used journalistic approaches, while some—like González and Yemenidjian—also experimented with oral history techniques. Each one of us was profoundly impacted. Chuck Olson, our volunteer interpreter, said he was familiar with most of the substantive issues that came up during the tour since he has been able to observe the unfolding story of Fukushima from his vantage point in Tokyo, which is about one and a half hours away by bullet train. But hearing the experiences of the people firsthand was quite different.

"For me, the trip made all that I knew about Fukushima, from reading, TV, et cetera, very real and personal," he said. "I had seen all the horrific pictures, had read the numbers, and even seen people on TV. But that pales beside sitting in front of those ladies in Koriyama telling us about their houses being robbed by people, . . . about trees growing in the family fields, and about the people who did not join the session but [instead sat] in their temporary housing crying every night."

When Olson first volunteered, he said that it was one way for him to "pay back" SFSU for the education he received. After the experience, he commented on the value of being a part of the storytelling process.

"For me, it was not only hearing the stories, but being in the position of trying to transmit all the feeling and nuance to the rest of you," he said. "That was the most powerful experience for me. To become a bridge of understanding like that was one of the reasons I came to Japan forty years ago. And getting to do it for you and people from SFSU was a special treat."

Fukushima University's McMichael commented afterwards that his students gained a lot from observing and working with our students. "The incredible translation and intercultural experience aside, I think our students learned a whole deal from watching the vigorous, skillful, and serious approach your students took to the program," he said. "I also think our students enjoyed the perspective your students brought to the program, as it's not very often our students get exposure to students who are as environmentally conscious and self-aware as students from the US (and especially California) tend to be."

"Perhaps Change Might Happen"

On the seventh day of our trip, we were asked to help a nonprofit organization that coordinates volunteers who want to participate in Fukushima's recovery. This type of volunteer activity has become a standard element of the Ambassadors Program. On this particular day, the target was a rural home. Our assignment was simple: clear the badly overgrown weeds and vegetation that covered the hillside and two small rice paddies. The house was owned by an eighty-year-old man who was evacuated, and it was not known when he might be able to return to the house. We were given weedwackers, clippers, and rakes.

At the start, the assignment seemed almost impossible to accomplish. The students worked quietly, diligently, and without complaint, despite the heat and humidity that marked a typical Japanese summer. Weeds were cut down and raked into bundles that resembled small bales of hay. Some frogs, lizards, and bugs fell victim to the weedwackers. By midday, the students could see that their labors were having an impact. By the end of the day, the land was cleared. Sweat and mud clung to their clothes. The physical activity gave everyone time to reflect on what they had heard and experienced. It became clear to all of us that the task of weeding a hillside home shrank to the size of a dot when compared to the enormity of the work needed to clean up Fukushima, rebuild homes and businesses, and restore the health—physical and emotional—of its people. Consider this one factoid: the government estimates that the amount of contaminated soil that needs to be collected and stored will total thirty million cubic meters. And they still don't know where to put it. This saga, then, could go on for decades.

At the end of that hot seventh day, some of our students wrote short reflections about what was going through their minds. Gavin McIntyre, a photojournalism student, wrote this:

> As part of the Fukushima Ambassadors Program, we were given the task to clean debris from one of these houses. When we got there, the weeds had covered the entire area, and the only visible sign of residency were spiders in their web that had been created since the evacuation. The three-story house could not be seen from the road. Lost in the weeds it seemed as though it would be impossible to make any difference. After hours of chopping and pulling weeds from the path to the house, it started to seem as though we were actually accomplishing something in an area that hasn't had much success in a long time.
>
> On our way back home I found out that the residents wouldn't be coming home for another year and half. In my mind, all I thought was that the work we had done was meaningless, that the weeds that we had just cut down would be back again. But then a thought crossed my mind. Over the last week we have heard about how evacuees are suffering from stress-related deaths because they have received little

to no help to cope with their suffering. So, if my actions—no matter how meaningless they may possibly be—if I could relieve worry from their minds, or just show them that there are people out there who care about them, then it was all worth it.

Several months later, I asked McIntyre what he took away from his time in Fukushima.

"It was a sad and wonderful experience," he said. "I met a lot of polite people who are trying to help the communities. However, a lot of people felt forgotten and didn't know what was next for them. There's still a lot to be done in Fukushima, and leaving felt a little like we were leaving them behind. I thought about my purpose as a journalist. I'm there to witness something, and show it to people who can't, so that perhaps change might happen."

REENTRY STORIES:
LIFE AFTER PRISON AND JAIL

CLAIRE KIEFER

Claire Kiefer, curriculum specialist at Voice of Witness and one of the cowriters and editors of this book, interviewed nine people in the spring and summer of 2014 about their experience reentering society after being released from prisons and jails. The interviews were conducted at a variety of places: almost half of them took place inside a San Francisco County jail, a few of them at a reentry center, and one in the café at Whole Foods. In this chapter, Claire explores themes of accessing potential narrators (largely through connections with a local nonprofit serving ex-offenders), establishing trust with narrators, and vicarious trauma and self-care.

Excerpt from "Reentry Stories"

When I was eighteen, I moved from juvenile hall to prison. I was at San Quentin for about a year or so. From Quentin I went to Folsom for about four, four and a half years. The charges were: three counts of attempted murder, three counts of great bodily injury, three counts of assault and battery, assault with a deadly weapon, being in possession of an illegal concealed firearm, discharging a firearm in public, home invasion. Because I took two strikes in place of more time, my actual sentence was six years and four months. The judge said that if I took no strikes, he'd make sure I did no less than twenty years. If I took one, we could be in the range of fifteen or so years.

I took the two strikes for less time.[1] It was a risky move, but I just had to get real with myself. Like man, is this really how I want to continue living life, forever and ever?

Folsom's pre-release program consists of this: you sit in a room with somebody, you tell them what your plan is, they give you a list of shelters and food kitchens, and they give you a Goodwill voucher for some clothes. And that's your pre-release plan. I had a counselor, but no one seemed to care if I had a solid plan. You have to prepare yourself; they're not gonna do it for you. When they asked me what my plan was, I told them that my godmom had a place where I could stay in Richmond, and that I figured she had a couple job opportunities lined up for me. They were like yeah, that's great, here's your list of soup kitchens and here are your vouchers—good luck.

I was worried about getting a job and reintegrating into society. When you've been away for seven years, things have changed. I sat and thought about it, and just had to weigh it out. What happened to me just showed how serious things could get. I thought, *Is there anything worth risking my freedom and being in prison for the rest of my life?* I felt I was better than that. All my life I've had people say, "You have so much potential!" So I just started thinking, *Man, I'm better than this.*

When I was in prison, I did some work with victim-offender dialogues. There was a fourth dude I assaulted on the day of my arrest. My cousin and I were wiggin' on some ecstasy pills and we saw some random dude on the street, and I jumped him. I stomped him within inches of his life. I didn't know how bad it was until later on. I wound up doing some work through a facilitator named Jack Dyson,

---

1. California's Three Strikes sentencing law was originally enacted in 1994. The essence of the Three Strikes law was to require a defendant convicted of any new felony, having suffered one prior conviction of a serious felony, to be sentenced to state prison for twice the term otherwise provided for the crime. If the defendant was convicted of any felony with two or more prior strikes, the law mandated a state prison term of at least twenty-five years to life. "California's Three Strikes Law," California Courts official website, www.courts.ca.gov/20142.htm.

and I was able to meet Tom, the guy I assaulted, apologize to him, and talk to him. He and I are really close friends now. That was my first introduction to restorative justice.

I guess Tom had been beating the pavement trying to find out how he could get in contact with me. Tom was in contact with Jack Dyson, and somehow they got in touch with my godmom. One day when we were on the phone, she said, "Son, I want you to tell me what you think about this opportunity." And I was like hey, you know, it could be good.

Jack worked with both Tom and me separately for about a year and a half prior to our meeting. The first time we met, I walked into the room and saw him, and we hugged for like five or ten minutes. We didn't say anything. Jack had gotten us a boardroom at Folsom and it was just the three of us: me, Jack, and Tom. After we hugged, we sat down and still didn't say anything for another five minutes, just tried to let everything settle and, you know, collect ourselves.

It was really deep. Jack didn't really have to do anything because he had prepared us both really well. And when I went in there, I didn't even expect any "I forgive yous" or any of that. I just wanted to do it because—you know, when you're in prison, everyone will preach about how they've changed to anyone who will listen. And I was one of them! But I was for real about it, and I was like, *How can I really measure if I've changed? I think I've changed, but how do I test that?* And that was what this opportunity presented for me—like man, have you changed enough to sit down and take responsibility for something so wrong that you've done? Can you handle having someone sit there and tell you how you've screwed up their life and really accept that? Can you sit with that, and really genuinely be sorry? The old me wouldn't have done that; the old me didn't care about, like, anything. So this was big for me.

I went in there not expecting anything. I knew he could just come in and cuss me out, and I thought, *How would I react to that?* I told myself that I'd just have to suck it up and take it, because he suffered lifelong injuries from what I did to him. He's had some memory loss, has problems with motor skills. A lot of stuff, and we talked about that. But by the end we were talking about writing a book together. It felt really good.

Jack put me in touch with Ruth Morgan at Community Works, and when I got out, she hired me as a facilitator. I work with violence prevention, domestic violence, substance abuse, stuff like that. I facilitate those kinds of groups. It made a huge difference having this job and not just flipping burgers or something. I love what I do. I've never really had any issues with domestic violence myself, but I work with cats in jail, I work with cats getting out of jail, and I work with cats who look like me. I was blessed, because who better to work with cats who look like me? I'm not discrediting anyone else's communication skills, but you know, that's just the reality of it.

Here in California, they need to get serious about the "R" they threw at the end of CDCR[2]—that "Rehabilitation" part. Because if the pre-release program I had at Folsom is any indication of what generally goes on, then damn. Just in the four years I was at Folsom, I saw programs get cut like you wouldn't believe. How do you expect people to rehabilitate themselves when you take away the tools? How do you expect somebody to make it when you hand them two hundred bucks and tell them good luck, don't come back?

—Raymond

Imagining the Project

For the past ten years, I've been teaching creative writing classes in prisons and jails as a volunteer. My interest in prison education started while I was in college at Tulane University; I heard one of my professors mention that he'd once taught a class in a prison, and something just clicked for me. I'd always been interested in the US prison system and its failings,

---

2. California Department of Corrections and Rehabilitation.

and the more I learned about the lack of education and rehabilitation in prisons and jails, the more motivated I was to do something about it. By then, I was studying creative writing and volunteering at the Moratorium Campaign, and teaching poetry in prisons seemed to be a perfect merging of my interests.[3] I started teaching a class at the local jail a couple of nights a week, and the experience was powerful—the students were so eager to learn, probably because they hardly had any opportunities to do so while incarcerated. Since that summer, I've taught at a host of prisons and jails around the country but have spent the most time at California's San Quentin State Prison. I've learned a lot about prison and jail culture, and the hardships and challenges of incarceration, mostly from listening to my students' stories.

One thing I've noticed time and again is that there are tremendous obstacles to be faced beyond the prison gates. According to the California Department of Corrections and Rehabilitation, 65 percent of people released from state prisons return within three years. With our prison population growing at a staggering rate and recidivism only getting worse, I've become preoccupied with the problem of reentry in American society.[4]

The development of *Say It Forward* gave me a perfect opportunity to begin an oral history project about reentry that I'd been imagining and planning for a long time. I wanted to know: What were people's fears about surviving (and thriving) in society post-incarceration? What had prevented them from successfully staying out? Were there any constraints of probation and parole that were prohibitive to acquiring jobs and stable housing? Over the years, I'd done plenty of reading about these issues and was encouraged to see more media attention on the subject of reentry, but there was still a dearth of personal stories from people who had experienced it firsthand. Through oral history interviews, I

---

3. The Moratorium Campaign is a national education-based campaign to end capital punishment founded by Sister Helen Prejean.

4. A fundamental concept of criminal justice referring to the rate of relapse into criminal behavior and re-arrest.

could hear from the people most directly impacted by the prison and jail systems who were facing the challenges of reentry.

The first thing I did was contact Ruth Morgan, the executive director of Community Works. Community Works is a nonprofit organization that has programming in prisons, jails, and reentry centers all over the Bay Area. It works to interrupt the cycles of familial incarceration and recidivism through empowering individuals, families, and communities who've been impacted by them. Community Works' programs range from creative writing, theater, and parenting classes in jail, to case management at reentry centers, to policy internships for teenagers with an incarcerated parent. They do necessary and miraculous work.

Capitalizing on my preexisting connections in the community helped smooth the launch of my project. Before joining Voice of Witness, I taught children of incarcerated parents at a public high school in San Francisco through Community Works' ROOTS program, so I knew exactly who to reach out to. I was able to gain access to narrators much more efficiently through Community Works' programs because of those relationships. A project like this would certainly still be possible for a facilitator who was either new to a city or didn't have such connections, but it would take more time to build the network through which to locate narrators and advocates.

Ruth directed me to Teeoni Newsom and Reggie Daniels. Teeoni is a case manager for young men, ages eighteen to twenty-four, who have recently been released from jail, and Reggie teaches violence prevention classes at a San Francisco County jail and provides case management for his students as well. Because Teeoni and Reggie are formerly incarcerated, they're particularly effective with their students and clients; there's an implicit understanding that they've earned their stripes. Teeoni and Reggie's help was essential to the success of this project. They both volunteered to be interviewed as well as to help facilitate my interviews with their students and clients. I think that having gone through the daunting process of reentry themselves, they really believed in the spirit of the project and felt that there was value in exploring reentry and, hopefully, generating awareness about its challenges. I'm incredibly grateful to them for trusting my intentions and methodology.

Reaching Out to Narrators

In March 2014, when I reached out to Teeoni about my project—conducting oral history interviews with people who had recently been released from prison or jail, or were currently incarcerated and soon to be released—she graciously invited me to come in and speak to her group to see who might be interested in talking to me. I came to the Young Men's Reentry Center the next week, introduced myself to her clients, and talked to them about why I was doing this project. I told them about my background in prison education and explained that I thought there was a troubling lack of information about the problems with reentry, and that no voices could better articulate the challenges and needs of people reentering society than their own. Several of Teeoni's clients expressed interest in participating, one of whom was Raymond. Raymond occupies a unique role at the reentry program; he is both a client and a facilitator.

Raymond and I met at the reentry center on a Tuesday, exactly a week after I'd visited Teeoni's group. We had good interviewer/narrator chemistry from the beginning. I think part of that was due to having met the week prior, and a bonus was that I'd also worked for Community Works, so I suspect he trusted my intentions more, knowing that we'd shared a common career trajectory. I also think that being open, honest, and transparent (most essentially at the beginning of an interview) is very important. I've found, both in this interview and in previous and subsequent ones, that if I had an opportunity to inject a little humor into the conversation, that often helped as well. There were moments in our interview where Raymond laughed and I took the cue to laugh with him, or even where I teased him a little bit about something he'd said or done. I think that laughing together helped to defuse the gravity of the topic and allowed us to bond, which lessened the pressure and made the interview experience a little bit more fun.

Because this was my first interview for the project, I hadn't quite figured out the right balance of questions I should ask, or how I should front-load the interview. In retrospect, I think I spent too long asking about Raymond's earlier years, childhood, and initial arrests, because we weren't talking about reentry until much later in the interview. All of the information was very interesting and ultimately useful but perhaps distracted from the more distilled purpose of the project. About an hour into the interview, I realized that we hadn't even gotten to his release yet, so I tried to steer the conversation in that direction. This is something that came up in almost all of my interviews for this project: we talked for much longer about the narrator's early life than I anticipated.

This is one of the challenges of doing oral history: often, the story's focus ends up being different than what you intended. I went into the interview assuming that the crux of the story would be Raymond's release from prison and reacclimation into society, and while hearing about Raymond's reentry experience was really interesting, the most powerful part of the interview, for me, was his story about reconnecting with his victim, Tom, and the restorative justice process they embarked on together. I was in awe of the bravery and strength it took— on both their parts—to generate the kind of healing that resulted from the process.

Not all of my interviews were as dynamic as Raymond's. When I began interviewing Lamont, a couple of weeks after my interview with Raymond, I quickly realized that Lamont—only twenty-one years old— had never been to adult jail or prison (he'd only done a brief stint in juvenile hall). Ultimately, that wasn't really what I was looking for, since reentry is a much different experience when you're a juvenile. I figured I'd go with it, though, and conduct the best interview I could, and that at least I'd get a perspective on the problems specific to juvenile reentry. Certainly, being arrested, incarcerated, and released as a child comes with its own set of challenges. About reentry, Lamont said: "I was just glad to be out of jail, really. I wasn't in there too long, but it felt so long. Jails need to do rehabilitation. They need to actually have programs that help people not come back there. People need to be shown examples of what they're doing to people, like with restorative justice."

Hearing Lamont, whose experience was so vastly different from Raymond's, mention restorative justice just cemented what I already knew: alternative approaches to punishment are desperately needed to interrupt the destructive cycle of recidivism. I didn't hear a lot about reentry from Lamont—at least not in the direct way I'd anticipated—but it was encouraging to hear him echo some of the same sentiments about the prison and jail system that I heard from many of my narrators throughout this process.

Establishing Trust

I tried to make my interviews with Raymond and Lamont as comfortable as possible by chatting with each of them first, explaining the project and its intentions, and offering them food. After my interview with Raymond, I bought him lunch at a local café. It was really nice to share a meal together and talk about something other than his incarceration and release; it made the experience feel less formal and, I believe, deepened our investment in the project. My interview with Lamont was later in the afternoon, so I brought a selection of pastries for him as a gesture of thanks. I found that small gestures, such as offering food or drink (or even just ensuring that someone is comfortable), can be disarming for both the narrator and the interviewer and really set the tone for a more open, connected interview.

My next set of interviews took place inside a San Francisco County jail, however, which precluded a lot of those gestures. I had to get a special clearance to even bring in my audio recorder, and due to my equipment clearance only extending two weeks, I had to be prudent about scheduling interviews quickly and getting several done each day that I was there. This made for a couple of very long days of back-to-back interviewing in a small interview room inside the jail, but that's one of the first lessons you learn when working inside jails and prisons: make do with what you've got.

Reggie invited me into his RSVP (Resolve to Stop the Violence) class to talk to his students about the project. He teaches violent offenders to become accountable, analyze the male-role belief system many of them have long held, and use emotional language to express themselves, repair harm, and minimize recidivism. RSVP has been incredibly successful in rehabilitating offenders and reducing recidivism in San Francisco. Like the other RSVP facilitators, Reggie went through the program himself during his own incarceration. Having the opportunity to introduce myself, talk a little bit about Voice of Witness and my reentry project, and explain the process to them was very helpful in developing trust and understanding, particularly given the harrowing ambience of a jail setting.

Reggie's students were inquisitive and interested. Several of them signed up for interviews during that initial class meeting, and I arranged to come in the following week. Community Works facilitated my jail clearance, which made things a lot easier. Working with a nonprofit was beneficial in so many ways, especially since I was dealing with the notoriously difficult corrections department. Furthermore, nonprofits or community organizations that are doing similar work often have access to narrators that may otherwise be challenging to locate.

At Voice of Witness, we talk a lot about developing trust and facilitating comfort and connection in order to experience an oral history interview as a "mutual sighting," as Alessandro Portelli calls it—a scenario in which both the interviewer and narrator really *see* each other, an interaction built upon empathic listening and human connection. This is a really crucial part of the process, and one that can be difficult to manage within a jail. Some of the men I interviewed at the jail were meeting me for the first time. Others had heard me talk a little bit about Voice of Witness and my reentry project in Reggie's class but hadn't really gotten a chance to know me. Agreeing to be interviewed under these circumstances required a particular bravery and trust, especially considering the obvious power differential between incarcerated person and free person.

Confronting Power Dynamics

Power dynamics can be scary to talk about. It's hard to acknowledge your own privilege or lack thereof, and it can be even harder to bring it up with the person you're interviewing. There is almost always some power imbalance between the interviewer and narrator based on differences in social identifiers such as race, ethnicity, gender, economic status, ability, sexual orientation, religion, age, and other factors. I found the most effective way to deal with power imbalance was to be as straightforward and upfront as possible when speaking with my narrators about my project and its intentions. At the beginning of each of my interviews, I explained to my narrator that I was doing this project because I felt that there was a troubling lack of awareness about the problem of reentry in our country, that I believed that their voices needed to be heard, and that I hoped that creating awareness about reentry could potentially help provoke change.

Of course, being honest and upfront doesn't negate discrepancies in power or social capital. The reality is this: I'm a white, middle-class woman whose job affords her the luxury of pursuing her personal interests through an oral history project of her own design. More than half of the people I interviewed were incarcerated, and the other half had felony criminal records. Everyone I interviewed was a person of color, and all of them had to shoulder the burden of living in a society that punishes ex-offenders. But ultimately, I think that most people can detect sincerity. When they trust that you're asking them tough questions because you really care about what they have to say, they're much more likely to be willing to open up to you. I think that's true for almost all of us.

I haven't been in jail or prison myself, and my life hasn't been deeply impacted by familial incarceration. What I had going for me as an interviewer was persistent curiosity coupled with a passionate concern about prisons, probation/parole, and reentry in American society. I couldn't promise any sort of tangible change; I couldn't assure any of my narrators that their lives would specifically benefit from talking to me. In a way, though, I think that acknowledging that uncertainty deepened the trust between my narrators and me because it meant that we were embarking on this journey together, both taking a risk and hoping for the best possible outcome.

Perhaps my past experience teaching in prisons and jails afforded me a bit of trust from some of the men (and the one woman) I interviewed. It still must have been quite a leap for them, to open up to me, but I suspect that they could intuit some level of commitment on the basis of my decade of teaching behind bars. This isn't to say that someone with no prior experience within prisons or jails couldn't conduct a similar project, however. I think that above all else, the interviewer's transparency and sincerity are the most important contributors to success.

Making Room for the Unexpected

One of the joyful surprises of oral history is learning that as an interviewer, you didn't even really know what you were looking for in the first place. I intended to focus very pointedly on the moment of someone's release from prison or jail and the aftermath. But as I conducted my interviews, I realized that my narrators' childhood stories, the stories of how they ended up in jail or prison in the first place, and the accounts of their experiences while incarcerated were just as important as the parts dealing with reentry. At Voice of Witness, we're often asked about the differences between oral history and traditional journalism, and I think that one of the distinguishing factors is oral history's focus on the whole person (as opposed to just the isolated story a journalist is seeking). For instance, this is what Marion, a man I interviewed at the jail, had to say:

> A lot of people in my neighborhood, they get trapped and never get out, because they don't know how to. Street life, doing crimes— that's what they grow up knowing. So how are you gonna know what it's like to walk a straight path? Not being prepared to get out [of jail], without being given another avenue to do something differently once you do get out, you're not really going to benefit from jail. People lock you up and think you're gonna change, but you're gonna get out and do the same thing.
>
> It's like a rat running around in a cage. I haven't had a rat or any little animal in a cage before, but I bet it's gonna walk around all four

walls that never go nowhere if the walls never come up. And if the
walls do come up? I doubt that they're gonna know what to do.

The challenges associated with reentry exist because of all the problems
that precede it. What Marion said about people getting trapped and not
knowing how to emerge is something I heard over and over during my
interviews. I began to realize that for me to tell a collective story about
reentry without also telling stories about early childhood trauma and
incarceration would be incomplete. Oral historians do much better work
when they remain open to possibility, to meandering off the path.

As I got deeper into my project and conducted more and more interviews, I began to recognize the "aha" moments more readily. For me, the
"aha" moments were when a narrator said something particularly resonant—
something that served as their story's climax. As an interviewer, I got a
little adrenaline rush each time this happened; it was evidence that I was on
the right course. This happened for me when Marion said that "if the walls
come up, they won't know what to do." In essence, he was able to put into
words that which I'd been trying to understand and articulate for months:
one of the most crippling problems with our reentry system is that people
are not set up to succeed outside prison and jail walls, and that they simply
"don't know what to do."

Like many of the other people I interviewed, Phillip spent time in
juvenile hall and the California Division of Juvenile Justice before being
arrested as an adult.[5] Eventually, he was so institutionalized that functioning on the outside seemed impossible. About his release from jail,
Phillip said, "I didn't want to be on the streets no more. I figured, *Okay,
jail's going to be my life. I love jail. I want to be a criminal all of my life.* So I
went out and did a theft. I wanted to be back in jail because of the comfort and being supported."

---

5. California's Division of Juvenile Justice (DJJ), formerly known as the California Youth
Authority (CYA), houses and provides treatment to people under the age of twenty-five
who have serious criminal backgrounds and intense treatment needs. Juveniles and young
adult offenders are referred to DJJ from both juvenile and superior court. DJJ also houses
youth under the age of eighteen who have been sentenced to state prison.

The harmful cycle of arrest and reentry manifests in many different ways. A felony record or parole status can prevent a person from acquiring a job or an apartment. Probation and parole often have a curfew mandate, which can interfere with many people's jobs. In most cases, the conditions of parole require that the parolee return to the county in which he or she committed their crime, which often means that they are surrounded by old friends and habits, and are sometimes the targets of criminal retaliation. On the personal side, family members often tire of supporting someone who continues to get arrested and released, which leaves the parolee without family support or housing. Phillip's caretaker, his grandmother, allowed him to live with her several times after he was released from jail, but eventually she and Phillip had a falling out, which left Phillip sleeping on the streets near San Francisco's Embarcadero. The criminalization of homelessness contributes to recidivism in a very direct way, and Phillip's desire to be arrested again so that he could return to his only support system—fellow inmates—speaks to the hopelessness and internalized oppression that many people coming out of jail or prison face.

Vicarious Trauma and Self-Care

Talking to people at length about their traumatic experiences can be emotionally draining. Self-care is hard for people like me, who immediately go to the "I don't deserve sympathy when they're the ones who endured trauma" place. It's important not to ignore vicarious trauma, though, as it can be insidious and destructive. Having worked with prisoners for over a decade now, I've developed some coping mechanisms, but I still found myself shouldering some deep sadness during the project. These kinds of stories often stick with you. I found myself coming home and thinking about the conversations I'd had that day or that week, mulling over the impact (or lack thereof) that my interviews might have on the people I spoke with. Was my project actually helping to effect change? Had the people I interviewed experienced any sort of catharsis; had their lives been enriched in any way?

Bearing witness to painful stories is difficult. I certainly don't have all the answers, but I found that being aware of the dangers of vicarious trauma was generally helpful and prompted me to be intentional about doing things to release the stress I was drawn to carry. Doing things like gardening, jogging, and watching funny shows on TV helped to provide balance. None of these things erase vicarious trauma, of course, but for me, giving myself structured time and space to do something relaxing was helpful.

In the introduction to her book *Trauma Stewardship*, Laura van Dernoot Lipsky says this about the long-term effects of vicarious trauma: "I finally came to understand that my exposure to other people's trauma had changed me on a fundamental level. There had been an osmosis: I had absorbed and accumulated trauma to the point that it had become part of me, and my view of the world had changed."[6]

Van Dernoot Lipsky goes on to describe how decades of doing trauma work has caused her to view everyday experiences differently. As she and her family reached the precipice of a cliff in the Caribbean, she stood gazing out at the ocean and thought about how many people had killed themselves by jumping off this particular cliff. Often, people who work with survivors of trauma develop hypervigilance, having grown accustomed to confronting a worst-case scenario or having to mitigate a crisis at any moment. I don't know if there are any definitive answers or solutions to managing long-term vicarious trauma, but being aware of and acknowledging these feelings, and their connection to trauma work, can be useful.

One morning at the jail, I interviewed a man named Roland. Roland is sixty-seven years old, has lung disease, and has spent a great deal of his adulthood behind bars. During our interview, I kept thinking, *He wants so badly to do well, but for whatever reason, he just can't.* Roland told me about how he grew up in poverty, how disappointed his brothers and sisters are in him, how he's been rearrested every time he's been released, how he's shuffled from halfway house to homeless shelter to temporary hotel. I could sense the embarrassment he felt as he described his petty crimes

---

6. Van Dernoot Lipsky, *Trauma Stewardship*, 1.

to me. But I could also tell that just being listened to meant a great deal
to him, and that's what kept me going.

I would argue that one has to be empathic to be a good oral historian. In fact, it's often empathy that drives oral history projects. We are
curious because we care so deeply. It's tricky, though, as the same empathy that moves us to listen to people can be debilitating. In oral history
interviews, we ask for details, descriptions of emotions, and often the
specifics of a heartbreaking situation. While those details and specifics
are what make a compelling story, they're also the thorns that stick in
the interviewer's side for weeks and months after the interview. We are
bearing witness to these people's profoundly important stories, but we
can't necessarily do anything to fix their hardships, and that can be a
heavy burden to carry.

And yet, it isn't always sorrow that sticks with us. During one of my
reentry interviews, a narrator challenged my comfort zone in a way I
hadn't anticipated. Over the years, I've taught and interviewed incarcerated men and women who are in prison or jail for all kinds of crimes.
In general, I don't even ask what they were accused or convicted of,
and I genuinely don't think it makes a difference. Ultimately, doesn't
everyone have a story that matters? I was there to facilitate a story's
telling, not to determine its worth. During one of my interviews in the
jail, though, I faced a situation I'd never dealt with before: my narrator
began to describe his crimes as a pimp of underage girls. He told me
about how he would troll online chat rooms in search of emotionally
vulnerable women (many of whom were underage teenagers), promise
them love and security and money, and sell them to johns for sex. He
also admitted that he had sex with them himself, and that he had physically abused them when they performed poorly or somehow violated
his trust or honor. As he spoke, I felt a deep conflict: by continuing to
listen to him, was I condoning his behavior? As an oral historian, must I
remain neutral and unbiased?

The truth is, none of us are truly unbiased. I can't deny bias against
child sex traffickers. It doesn't mean that I don't think they have rights,

or dignity, but I am not without bias. Therefore, it was challenging to keep going, to be an empathic listener and to focus on my goal of conducting a thorough interview, as he described scenarios that made me feel angry and sad. Ultimately, I deferred to my duty as an oral history interviewer and tried as hard as I could not to exhibit judgment, because despite my personal feelings about his crimes, I realized that he is a whole person—more than just the worst thing he's ever done—and that I was there to listen to his story, whatever it was. But as we so often say at Voice of Witness, these skills are a practice. I am still practicing.

When I left the jail after that interview, I recognized immediately that I needed to process my feelings about it with someone. I called Cliff, who was at the Voice of Witness office, and asked if he could meet me for lunch. At a café down the street from our office, I told him what had happened, described the interview, and talked through some of the ways in which this experience had challenged me. Looking back, I don't think I was looking for advice or validation that I was "right" to feel disturbed; I just needed someone to listen. This was a very simple and instinctual act of self-care that allowed me to address the feelings of secondary trauma and move on.

Where Do We Go from Here?

The most formidable question I've had to contend with throughout my project is this: What good will all this do for the people who shared their stories? This is something I've thought about continually from the conception of the project through its current status. Would my narrators be disappointed if they weren't able to see concrete change? Could telling their stories be a revolutionary act in and of itself? I'm still not sure. I am still thinking through how I can best share these stories. Were time not a factor, I would love to continue collecting stories about reentry and compile them in a full-length book. In the meantime, I will share the stories with Community Works, as they may be useful in arts programming or funding appeals.

When I asked Reggie what he thought about this experience, he said:

I think storytelling has the potential to change lives. I think it does change lives. It's compelling; it's essential. When I tell my story—when I speak about when I got shot, when I speak about prison—all of the sudden, I'm not a facilitator in a program trying to push information at you, but I'm a dude who suffered like you suffered. It not only changes the way [my students] see me, but it gives them the potential to change the way they see themselves.

What Reggie is talking about, I think, is solidarity—the unifying bond that sharing stories offers people. If we can see someone in a new way, if we conceive of them as a more whole person, if we can understand them a little bit better, maybe the result will be deeper connection and empathy. I hope that my narrators feel a little bit braver having shared their stories with me, and I hope that they feel empowered as a part of the greater narrative about reentry. At this point, I don't yet know how far-reaching the impact of my project will be or what form it will take next. I don't even know what the connection between my oral history project and policy reform will be. Can these stories be used as political advocacy? Should they be? Whatever happens, I do know this: my inquiry is just beginning.

UNSETTLED:
RELOCATING AFTER KATRINA

ERIC MARSHALL

Eric Marshall was a student at Hampshire College in Amherst, Massachusetts, when he set out to develop an oral history project for his senior thesis. He was intent on working in oral history after reading the books of Studs Terkel and Isabel Wilkerson and falling in love with oral history for the way the author didn't interfere with the narrators' "experience and connection to the story." Eric is from the South and ultimately decided on interviewing people who had been displaced by Hurricane Katrina. In this field report, Eric describes some of the early trials and challenges of developing his oral history from scratch and without any training, other than that available from his favorite books. Ultimately, he learns he has the most success when he's able to let narrators set the terms of the interview themselves.

Excerpts from "Unsettled"

[Jimmy]: The game warden, who had come by in the boat, came back in the morning. [Merri]: We got in the boat and the man drove around the corner and got a couple, an elderly Black couple that had lived behind us. She had diabetes and he was blind. [Jimmy]: We went by Baptist Hospital where helicopters were on the top of the roof, evacuating. And also, we first came into contact with these big old high-tension electrical lines that were literally about as big as my arm. And we had to lift them up over the boat so that we could get through. And I was in the front to lift it up and hand it back to—what was his name? I can't even remember the man's name. . . . The driver, then he gave it [to] Merri. And I thought, if it's alive, my problems are over, 'cause when I grabbed it I figured I'd just be cinders. 'Cause this is one of those real high-tension . . . you know those metal poles way high up in the air. Well we got by that. And in the meantime you're floatin' and you're lookin' down on top of cars. And I thought, I don't mind cars, I just hope I don't see any eyeballs lookin' back up at me. That was really gonna freak me out if I saw someone drown.

—Merri Pruitt and Jimmy Littleton

The thing is it was almost like you had absolutely nothing, not even clothes. So churches would have giveaways where they would have clothes and stuff like that. You'd go and get that. For a while ATMs were locked up, you couldn't really even get to your money. . . . So it really was survival mode. And then when the apartment came through I remember us coming in and it was brand new—no one had ever lived in it, because they had just built it. But we walked in with the bags that we had and the apartment was empty from floor to ceiling. And you know you realize this is where I live now, and I need a dustpan, I need a garbage, I need everything. Then it was literally survival mode. Making sure that our daughter was fine. My dad, he's eighty-five now, so he was like seventy-five around that time, and making sure that he was healthy, we were stressed to the max—blood pressure probably as high as who knows what.

—Deneen Tyler

The Story's Beginning

More often than not, the task of a historian is to find the beginning of the story—the first sign of revolution, the first voice to speak out. However, for the purpose of this study, I was not investigating the beginning of the story, but the end. Since 2005, documentation of Hurricane Katrina has focused mainly on the destruction of the storm, the government's mishandling of the rescue and recovery, and the rebuilding process. I wanted to look at how Katrina was still relevant in the lives of those who chose to relocate away from New Orleans after the storm. *When did they make their decision to relocate? How has it affected their relationships with family and friends? How has their relocation affected their relationship with New Orleans? What is their relationship with their current city? Has Katrina affected the way they conceptualize their own space?* I wanted to expand my own understanding of the scale of the storm, and I wanted to add to the available documentation. To do that, I needed to ask questions that pushed the discussion forward and into the present.

At my former school, Hampshire College, every fourth-year student is required to complete a yearlong thesis project. I started out as a writing major, but by my third year I was taking almost exclusively history classes. This is where I first became exposed to oral history. I read *Hard Times* by Studs Terkel, Isabel Wilkerson's *Warmth of Other Suns*, and Paul Thompson's *Voice of the Past*—books that showed me the kind of storytelling possible with oral history. I was drawn to the honest and humble nature of oral history, how the author did not interfere with the narrator's experience and connection to the story, and how it can be used to learn about communities and stories left out by traditional histories. By my fourth year, I was intent on compiling an oral history for my thesis.

Being from the South, and Houston more specifically, I knew I wanted my thesis to be relevant to my home. While reading for a class during my third year, I came across an article by Stephen Sloan that discussed the relationship between oral history and Hurricane Katrina.[1] Sloan writes:

> The consequent mass of media coverage and ongoing political discourse surrounding the storm have brought their power to bear in shaping the larger narrative and collective memory of the event, but

---

1. Stephen Sloan, "Oral History and Hurricane Katrina: Reflections on Shouts and Silences," *Oral History Review* 35, no. 2 (May 30, 2008): 176–86.

all have failed to provide a clear depiction of the impact of the hurricane. Fading media coverage post—Hurricane Katrina has reinforced
its inability to provide an authentic and enduring portrait of the
storm and the lives and communities it changed.

This statement made me think about my own experience during Katrina
and my own memory of the storm. In 2005, I was an eighth grader at Lani-
er Middle School in Houston, Texas. At fourteen years old, I didn't understand a lot of what was going on. I remembered hearing about the storm everyone was calling one of the largest ever and watching the news coverage
of a flooded New Orleans. I remembered playing video games with a family
from Louisiana that my church had put up in an apartment. Looking back, I
don't think I understood how Katrina impacted them beyond moving their
lives to a new city, and I didn't fully realize how it had affected Houston and
my own life. As time passed, I had only vague memories of the storm. I was
right alongside the general public in my understanding of Katrina.

In his article, Sloan suggests that "a profound way to begin is to try
to appreciate how the storm manifested itself for an individual, for a
family, for a community—and one of the most effective and powerful
ways to capture that is oral history." Looking at the oral history work
produced on Katrina, I noticed the framing of the storm was limited to
analyzing and collecting firsthand accounts of the storm and its immediate aftermath. The stories started with the window panes shaking, or a
description of their preparations in the days leading up to the storm, and
normally ended when they either returned home to view the damage or
escaped the flooded streets of New Orleans. I knew that there was more
that needed be recorded and added to this collection. Traumatic stories,
such as those that I planned to collect, often take time to become available to the narrators themselves, and subsequently to the public. Reading Sloan's article inspired me to look at my own understanding of the
storm and how I could add to the existing collected archive. By the time
I began collecting interviews, it was eight years after the storm. I hoped
enough time had passed and enough healing had occurred that my narrators could share thoughtful and in-depth reflections in our interviews.

It Seemed Like It Would Be a Simple Process

Before I proposed my project as my senior thesis, I did some background research on Katrina's diaspora. I looked for some solid numbers on how many people were still living away from New Orleans. The journal articles and books I found contained the initial numbers that FEMA gathered after the storm. A few surveys by the US Census Bureau focused on the repopulation of New Orleans, but they did not differentiate between new residents and former residents who were purchasing new property. As a result of the unorganized efforts to evacuate people from the city when the storm hit, we lack an accurate account of the initial displacement. There is currently no archive available that accounts for each person who evacuated, relocated, or returned to New Orleans. Oral history does not require such an infrastructure in order to succeed. Not having to deal with this challenge is what made oral history a natural fit for this subject.

When I proposed the project to my thesis committee before leaving for summer break, it seemed like it would be a simple process. I thought that I would find individuals displaced by Katrina and interview them about their relationship with New Orleans and their new city. Because I am from Houston and so many people had relocated there after the storm, it was not hard to find people who fit these criteria. I began talking with friends and family, telling them to get the word out, and within a few weeks I had six potential narrators. Three of them were in Houston, one in Baton Rouge, one in Nashville, and one in Baltimore.

My friend's mother gave me a lead on a couple—Scott and Alison—who owned a bookstore in Houston. I sent them a short email explaining my project, and what it would mean if they decided to participate. I spent hours writing the email, making sure that I described my project as concisely as possible. I explained that I was a fourth-year college student starting a yearlong oral history project on people who were "permanently displaced" by Hurricane Katrina, and that I was interested more in their experience after the storm than in their experience during the storm itself. The reply came quickly, but it took me a year to understand what their response meant about how they understood their situation.

Their email was two sentences long, and read,

We weren't displaced. We simply left as of late December 2007.
—Scott

My immediate reaction to the email was, *Well, Katrina came through the Gulf Coast, and then two years later they left—of course they were displaced.* Maybe it took a little longer than others, but surely Katrina was the reason they ultimately left New Orleans.

Wanting to explain myself, I immediately emailed back and asked if I could come by their store. While talking with them in person, I explained that one of the goals of my project was to add to the existing archive and record the stories that were left out of previous oral histories. This was a bit confusing for Scott and Alison. During our first interaction, I realized they had a lot of assumptions about what the project was about and just why I wanted to record their story. After the storm, a lot of attention was placed on those most directly impacted by the storm. Scott and Alison were skeptical of the motive of my project for this very reason. I do not think they believed their experience fit within the frame of my project. They had lived comfortably in New Orleans. They didn't see their experience as extraordinary. They lived between Houston and New Orleans for the first two years after the storm, before they sold their business and left. It was hard for them to understand why I wanted to collect their story. I continued to explain the intentions of my project as best I could, but because they were my first potential narrators, I was not as confident and comfortable with explaining my proposal as I should have been. I was in the midst of trying to figure out what my project was at the same time I was trying to explain myself and the project to them. I was not prepared for the question, *Why us?*

At the end of our first meeting, they didn't exactly agree to be a part of the project, but they didn't say no. It was obvious to me that I needed to tighten up my language specific to the project so that I could better explain its intentions and scale. I needed to be comfortable explaining the project so that they could be comfortable participating in it. I took some time to get organized after speaking with them and emailed them back with an updated proposal. After I provided them with a clearer picture of what the project was going to require, everyone was more comfortable moving forward.

When I got back to school in the fall, one of the first things I did was set my schedule for the project. In the first two months I would find my narrators, conduct my initial research, write my interview questions, and finalize a narrator release. Over Thanksgiving break I would conduct the first set of interviews while I continued my research. By the end of the first semester and winter break, I would write a literature review, revise the project goals and interview questions, complete all my interviews, and begin the transcription process. After transcribing the interviews by the middle of February, I would begin processing the interviews and planning the direction and form of the final paper. In the final month and a half I would complete the project and write the paper.

Once I had my schedule in place, my professors advised me to keep the number of narrators between five and seven. Since I would only have a year to complete the study and wanted to limit the number of participants, I chose to restrict my study to former residents of New Orleans who were now living in Houston. My final group of narrators consisted of six individuals, two of whom participated in a joint interview:

1. Scott Parker, 70s, white, born in Sonoma County, California. Moved to New Orleans in 1976. Former resident of the French Quarter. Stayed, then relocated to Houston in 2007.

2. Deneen Tyler, 50s, African American, born in Boston, Massachusetts. Moved to New Orleans in 1970. Former resident of Gentilly. Evacuated to Houston.

3. Devyn Tyler, 20s, African American, born in New Orleans, Louisiana. Former resident of Gentilly. Evacuated to Houston.

4. Merri Pruitt, 60s, white, born in Indiana. Moved to New Orleans in 1976. Former resident of Broadmoor. Stayed for five days, evacuated to Houston within the week.

5. Jimmy Littleton, 70s, white, born in Alabama. Moved to New Orleans in 1968. Former resident of Broadmoor. Stayed for five days, evacuated to Houston within the week.

6. Lisa Carnley, 30s, Vietnamese American, raised in Houma, Louisiana. Former resident of Jefferson Parish. Evacuated to Mississippi. Moved to Orlando, then Alabama, before relocating to Houston.

All but one of my narrators began their relationship with New Orleans after Hurricane Betsy, a devastating storm that hit the city in 1965. Those not born in or around New Orleans still could say they had lived there for more than thirty years. They represent a wide range of the city's cultures and generations. Each of the narrators left the city at a different time. They all started their relationship with Houston for different reasons. Even though I only used a few narrators, within a limited frame, the content of their interviews was even more than I could handle. Having only a few narrators allowed me to better focus my attention on connecting the other forms of research I gathered.

A major problem with Katrina research is that New Orleans gets the majority of the attention. The strongest part of the hurricane missed New Orleans, and the research has left out the Mississippi Gulf Coast and certain areas of Alabama.[2] I understood that by focusing on just former New Orleans residents, I wouldn't be showing the true spectrum of experience. In order to make readers aware of this problem, I added a "research limitations" section explaining my decision. The main reason for these limitations was time. It was always my hope that, in the future, I could expand the frame of the project to include more of those stories that have still gone unrecorded.

I wanted to get the facts of the storm correct before I started my interviews; it was just as important to me to understand the different emotional reactions to the storm. *What were people saying about New Orleans? What were they saying about the residents of New Orleans? Were the residents aware of what was going on and what was being said about them? How did the reporters make sense of the situation in New Orleans? As outsiders, did they*

---

2. The flooding of New Orleans was a manmade disaster caused by the breaching of the levees. The strongest winds and heaviest rains were to the east of New Orleans. It is common to hear that Katrina "missed" or "turned away from" the New Orleans area.

understand the true impact of the storm? It was important for me to figure out not only how the residents of New Orleans experienced the storm but also how the larger nation experienced it.

The first book I read for my background research was *The Great Deluge,* by Douglas Brinkley. Brinkley's book is a firsthand description of the days leading up to and the week after the storm. His narrative is supported by newspaper articles, transcripts of press conferences, analysis of government documents, and interviews he collected himself. Brinkley's sources came from all over the world, and from every communication medium. The diverse footnotes section in the Brinkley book provided a good foundation of varied sources that helped me throughout my project. In every project I've ever worked on, there has been a book like *The Great Deluge* that has served as the first axle to build around. The book doesn't have to have all the information, but it can tell you where to look. For oral history, oftentimes you are building your own archive, index, glossary, all at the same time. You can only rely on what is available to you; a resource that can serve as a switchboard of sorts is vital.

Starting the Interviews

After I completed my initial research, I began writing my interview guide. This document included a short description of the project, a contract agreement including where and how the project would be available to the public, and a sample set of interview questions.[3] While writing my interview questions, I made sure I covered different subject material than previous oral histories. I used a couple of oral histories as reference—*Voices from the Storm*, published by Voice of Witness, and *Voices Rising: Stories from the Katrina Narrative Project*, published by University of New Orleans Press. It was necessary to ask background questions like: *Where were you born? When did you first move to New Orleans? Where were you living in New Orleans at*

---

3. Narrators could also choose if they wanted to use their real names or a pseudonym. This is for their protection and privacy. Although my full project will only be made available through the Hampshire College library, it was an important part of the process for my narrators.

the time of the storm? Did you evacuate? But after those questions, I wanted
to move beyond previous histories and ask questions such as: *New Orleans
has gone through a lot of changes since the storm. There is a lot of new construction,
a lot of new residents. When you went back, what kinds of changes did you notice?*
and *After the storm a lot of former residents ended up in cities like Atlanta, Houston, Baton Rouge, and Dallas. In your experience, did impromptu communities of
people from New Orleans form? Did you have much contact with evacuees in Houston?* and *When did you decide to relocate? Can you walk me through what you were
thinking? What factors caused you to make your decision?*

When scheduling my interviews, I sent my potential narrators a short
email with a brief description of who I was, what the project was about,
what their participation would require, and what the interview process
would be like, and asked them to let me know if they had any questions.
If they responded and wanted to know more, I sent them a copy of my
interview guide to look over so they could have a better understanding
of the kinds of questions I was going to ask. I wanted to give them time
to prepare for the interview as well. After that, I would ask if there was
a time that we could meet, either just to talk, or to do the interview if
they were ready. These same steps applied for phone interviews as well. I
wanted them to feel comfortable, and to show them that they could trust
me. How could they tell me their story if they didn't know who I was? I
didn't want them to worry that I would interview them and disappear or
just stop contacting them altogether.

The whole time I was trying to set up these interviews, I was at school
in Massachusetts. I made sure to be in regular contact with them—at least
an email every month or so. Most of the time it was just small talk that
pertained to the project. I asked them if they knew anyone else who would
be interested in participating, or if they had any more questions, or if we
were still confirmed for the date of the interview. I wanted them to know
that I was accountable and still interested and engaged in the project.

I wanted to make sure I gave my narrators an opportunity to speak
for themselves. I wanted their story to go beyond just a logistical retelling—something more than, "After three months we left. Our friends

helped us find an apartment in Houston . . ." Around Thanksgiving, just before I started my interviews, I realized what the Parkers meant when they said they weren't displaced. The storm may have been a root cause of their relocation, but everyone who decided to move also had the choice to stay. Describing their situation as "displacement" took away their agency and limited their ability to explain their experience as accurately as possible. Oral history gives the narrators the agency to tell their own story. I wanted my questions to be as open as possible so as to not constrict their answers.

During my interview with Deneen Tyler, we started to talk about place. Deneen made the comment: "I was trying to survive. I didn't really give a crap. I was glad to be alive. . . . I was in survival mode and maintaining mode and sustaining mode. And it took a couple of years before it was sort of like—okay, we're living here, we live here now, you know. It took time to get to a point of comfort." This moment struck me during the interview. "Point of comfort" is a beautiful description of such an important feeling. After she answered that initial question, I asked if she remembered talking about her "point of comfort" and Houston.

I found the interviews to be an incredibly rewarding part of the process, as well as the most frustrating. When I interviewed Lisa Carnley for the first time, I met her at the Cajun restaurant she owns in Houston. I showed up toward the end of lunch, got my food, and sat down. She came over shortly after, and I interviewed her while I ate. It was one of the best interviews I've ever had. She was engaging and opinionated, smart and funny. Once I got home I immediately downloaded the file onto my computer, only to find out that my recorder had not been on. I felt lost and overwhelmed. Lisa had taken the time to meet with me and entrusted me as a caretaker of her story, and I let her down. Since I was nervous, I had assumed that the blinking red light meant that it was recording. I even considered taking out my second backup recorder, but thought that might intimidate her. It took me a day or so, but I emailed Lisa and apologized for taking up her time and asked if she would have time for another interview. She was incredibly understanding and helped me laugh about the situation. I knew talking about Katrina was traumatic for her, and I was grateful she met with me again. When we met for the second time, I shared a story a good friend of mine once told me about Studs Terkel—how he would always act like he didn't know how the tape recorder worked and just sort of fiddle with it for a moment and say something like, "Oh well, it either gets it, or it doesn't." Sharing my own anxiety with her helped me relax and give a more focused interview.

I also found interviews could be physically demanding as well. When I interviewed Scott at his bookstore, we had to do the interview at the checkout, and while he had a place to sit behind the counter, I had to stand. Because it was one of my first interviews for my thesis, I was very nervous and didn't want to ask for a chair. So I stood there. I did my best to lean up on a bookshelf, but after three hours, they were getting ready to close, my knees were hurting, and we hadn't even gotten through half of the questions. It is always great when you interview someone who is willing to talk a lot. They can get off topic and ramble on, but I have always felt that this is a sign that they are comfortable and trusting of you. It does, however, create a problem when you feel the need to ask a follow-up question. Interrupting them might shorten their future responses. So instead of asking my question, and disrupting the interview, I simply wrote down the question so that I could ask them after they finished, or if we didn't get to it during the interview I could follow up either over email or during another interview. This method worked in another way as well. By writing down the questions I didn't want to forget, I had more questions to ask in future interviews.

As I moved through my interviews, I gradually became more confident in my understanding of the project. The biggest change that happened during this process was learning what to expect from each interview and using information from the previous interviews to prepare for the next. One element of the interviews that I worked on improving the most was my own reactions to their questions. I wanted to make sure that I wasn't interrupting a narrator's thought process. I worked on internalizing my reactions and preparing follow-up questions instead of constantly interjecting. The more I allowed the interview to grow in front of me, the more I was able to respond and analyze and most importantly—listen.

Find a System That Works for You

From the five interviews I collected, there were about seven and a half hours' worth of audio recordings. The transcription process took me a little more than a month to complete.[4] While transcribing, I made sure to keep a summary log for each transcript. The summaries included the subjects covered and their corresponding time. This helped immensely once I began writing. I know that some people get others to help them with their transcription. The process can be draining, but I think it is necessary to have an organizational system in place that you created and implemented yourself by the time you start writing. There are books on oral history theory that can provide detailed organizational systems.[5] These can often be complicated and at times unhelpful, but if you take a "Goldilocks" approach, you can find or create a system that works for you. The goal isn't to duplicate someone else's process or arbitrarily choose an organizational system just because it works for someone else, but to create a system that will allow you to access your research reliably and efficiently.

By the end of the transcription process, I had picked a few themes to focus on. Rather than include the interviews as a whole, I separated my paper into three chapters—integrating the interviews into an overarching narrative. The first chapter outlined the events leading up to and including the storm. The second focused on the narrators' transition to Houston. The third looked at the impact of the narrators' relocation on their lives in Houston and the impact on the city of New Orleans.

---

4. I used the free program ExpressScribe along with a foot pedal. The foot pedal, especially, helped cut down on the amount of time that I spent transcribing my interviews.

5. One text I found helpful was Valerie Yow's *Recording Oral History*, 2nd ed. (Lanham, MD: Rowman & Littlefield, 2009).

For each of these three chapters I assigned labels and tags like those you would find, for instance, with a YouTube video of a dog playing fetch—"dog," "playing," "dog trick," and so on. I gave tags to my interviews and research that would later become the topics of paragraphs and pages within the chapters. Each tag received its own color. I assigned a tag for the debate on the word *refugee*, one for the *change* in New Orleans, and another for *Houston traffic*. All of these topics appeared in my background research as well as the interviews. And for every time they appeared in the text, they received their corresponding label. When I wanted to find where my sources talked about displacement, for example, I just looked for the yellow tab. This organized my thoughts and helped me start writing.

Once I finished my paper, I presented my project at a symposium with several other students who had also completed their own oral histories. There were about forty-five to fifty people there, most of whom were family and friends of the presenters. I spoke about my project, the work I had done, and what it meant to me as a Houstonian and a resident of the Gulf Coast for these people to trust me to record their stories. After I finished there was a short five-minute question-and-answer session. A woman near the back of the room raised her hand. She introduced herself as a former resident of New Orleans who had moved before the storm, and said that one of her best friends died during Katrina. She did not have a question to ask me. She simply thanked me for the work I had done. To me, as the collector of an oral history, this simple comment meant everything. The story I told was not my own. It was my narrators' story, and the story of the people of New Orleans. My goal was to use their interviews to provide an honest account of what happened to those individuals who relocated from New Orleans after Hurricane Katrina.

When I started this oral history, I knew very little about Katrina. I lived in its periphery. I had my own ideas about how the displaced were living, how they were feeling. I tried to understand what happened during the storm and what followed. You start with your idea for the project—something that is completely yours. You bring in research, and interviews, and experience. You listen. By the end of the project, it may be your writing, but it is not *your* project anymore. The ideas I brought to this project served as a great starting point. I followed my narrators' lead to stay true to their experience. When I finished the project, it was clear: I was not the author but the caretaker. The relationship between Hurricane Katrina and the people of New Orleans and Houston is not over.

OUR TOWN, OUR STORIES: A SCHOOL/COMMUNITY COLLABORATION

CLIFF MAYOTTE

Cliff Mayotte, education program director at Voice of Witness and one of the co-writers and editors of this book, cofacilitated a school-based project that explored using oral history to "bring the school into the community and the community into the school." The Our Town, Our Stories project was created in collaboration with MetWest High School in Oakland, California, in the spring of 2014. Part of the project's mission was to connect school and community in meaningful ways and to seek out stories from students, faculty, family, and community members that challenged or disrupted the dominant narrative, or "single story," of Oakland. In this chapter, oral history becomes a focal point for a multifaceted look at education, community, and how students grapple with the day-to-day realities of navigating their own sense of place within the classroom and beyond it.

Excerpt from "Our Town, Our Stories"

There are plenty of stereotypes that come with Oakland, right? I was part of this program called Amigos de las Americas when I was in high school. A foreign exchange program, right, you do community service in another country, and so I went to Costa Rica. I was in this program with all of this training I had to do in order to go, and in the trainings . . . I was one of three Latina people. Everybody else is white, and I was like, *How is it I hardly ever see any white people in East Oakland, but in this program, a great opportunity for youth, and the only youth I see are not people of color?* And so that was one of the moments I didn't understand why that was, and then when I finally got to Costa Rica, right, basically this program has chapters, people from all over the US go to meet up, and I was one of the very few people of color. Then I remember being in this group doing icebreakers, and talking about ourselves, and I said I was from Oakland. And they were like, "From California?" Yeah, Oakland, California. And they were like, "Isn't that the place with all the murders?" And I'm like, "YES." I guess, if that's what you want to think. It's also the place with all the diversity, also the place I call home, where my family lives. When you go from one place to another, see people's cultures, right, but all they knew was that's the place with all the murders. And that it's dangerous, right? My struggle with that was what they were associating with me. I noticed they kind of gave me the side eye. I don't know, it was just different.

—Ana Villalobos

Beyond the School Community

Many people with a stake in education—students, teachers, parents, and neighbors—struggle to create tangible connections between schools and the communities they're a part of. While all schools are a part of their communities in a literal sense, these connections can feel remote and abstract. Schools operate with their own schedules, mandates, and unique needs, creating school cultures that can be completely disengaged from their neighborhoods, and the world at large. Mandatory testing, outmoded disciplinary models, graduation requirements, and the everyday demands of teaching and learning can all derail a school's intention to connect student learning with the community outside the school grounds. This is, of course, deeply ironic, as much of a young person's education is based on how they learn to interact with and engage in their community once they leave school. As a longtime educator and parent, I have heard schools refer to themselves vaguely as "the school community," as if it's some kind of rushed afterthought, with no intention to explore the deep connection that exists between what students learn in the classroom and how to apply that learning beyond the four walls of the school. As famed teacher, minister, and community builder Jack Shelton said, "In my mind, a school that is not part of the community does not fully exist; it's almost an abstraction. I think for the school's own benefit, it needs to be engaged with the place where it exists; and it needs to use the tools and strengths it has in that place to make a difference there."

The inspiration for the Our Town, Our Stories project was to use oral history as a way to bring the school into the community and the community into the school, and through the process, to help students develop the academic and empathy-based skills that would sustain them in college and beyond. As an initiative of the Voice of Witness Education Program, our particular interest was to facilitate what oral historian Alessandro Portelli calls a "mutual sighting" between narrator and interviewer and to expand this idea in a larger context—namely the school community and the Oakland neighborhoods that surrounded our project partners at MetWest High School.

The project was intended to create a platform and audience for students to uncover and share multiple stories from Oakland—stories that went beyond the dominant narrative of Oakland, which has become synonymous with homicide, gangs, police brutality, and more recently, displacement and gentrification. Our Town, Our Stories would create an opportunity for students to seek out the stories that swirled around them every day but were rarely shared with a wider audience.

Our Town, Our Stories was originally designed as a two-week summer enrichment program for students from all over Oakland. We did a fair amount of outreach (albeit a bit late) that included mailings, social media outreach, and visits to a handful of Oakland schools. Ultimately, our outreach methods proved to be too little, too late, and only a few students enrolled in the program. So, with a few weeks to go before the program was to begin, we had to cancel it. While this was a setback, it proved to be a crucial learning opportunity and a blessing in disguise, as it paved the way for the program's reincarnation at MetWest High School.

One of the few students who had signed up for the program, MetWest senior Donzahniya Pitre (Donzah), was very disappointed about the program not going forward. We had connected with Donzah through Robin Levi, board member at Justice Now and coeditor of the Voice of Witness book *Inside This Place, Not of It: Narratives from Women's Prisons*. Robin was serving as a mentor to Donzah through the Students Rising Above program, which is devoted to creating opportunities for low-income, first-generation college-bound students in the Bay Area. To honor Donzah's enthusiasm and commitment, Claire Kiefer and I met with her to discuss the ethics and practicalities of oral history. Our meeting covered the various steps in the oral history process, which included contacting potential narrators and conducting, transcribing, and editing an interview. Donzah had expressed interest in interviewing friends, family, and community members in Oakland. It was during this meeting that Donzah suggested we run the Our Town, Our Stories project as a class at MetWest High School during the school year. An inspired idea, and based on Donzah's description, it seemed that the structure of MetWest might be ideally suited to the program.

Part of the mission of MetWest High School is to "prepare young adults to recognize and take advantage of all resources to further their personal well-being and the well-being of their communities." To this end, the school employs a unique framework in which teachers act as advisors, helping students navigate their various academic needs as well as assisting them in arranging internships with different local companies, agencies, and nonprofits that align with the school's mission and the desires and interests of the students. Clearly, the MetWest mission was committed to bridging the gap between the school community and the community surrounding the school. Donzah put us in touch with her advisor Sonia Hansra (who also teaches English). Sonia became our point person and our main faculty collaborator at MetWest. This was how

Sonia described the unique relationship between adults and students at the school:

> We're their counselor, and sometimes their older sister, we are their internship coordinator, and we're their main contact at school, so if there's any sort of issue it's the advisor that is contacted. It's a strong relationship. . . . Sometimes it's a struggle though because, I mean at the end of the day, I'm also giving them their grade, right?

The flexible structure at MetWest made it possible for members of arts and education organizations to teach classes over the course of a school year. This was exactly the kind of structure suited to Our Town, Our Stories, and a workable model for school/community engagement. In a stroke of luck, Sonia was very familiar with Voice of Witness, and her hoped-for learning goals for her students were well aligned with the Voice of Witness Education Program goals of developing communication, critical thinking, and literacy skills. In reflecting on these skills and outcomes, Sonia poses an essential question for teaching and learning through oral history, and education in general:

> I guess a question for me is just how do you develop genuine curiosity? You have to have that to be able to have an authentic interview or conversation, right? You've got to be curious enough to ask those follow-up questions and show some interest. That's just a struggle with all content areas, you know? I'm super passionate about what I teach, but how do you build that in the learners?

More to the point, how do you build that in anyone? From our initial conversations and throughout the project, Sonia and the rest of the teaching team would strive to connect curiosity and empathy with the oral history process. We also explored learning goals in relation to the social justice underpinnings of the school's curriculum, which examined oppression, justice, and reconciliation. This was a good match with the Voice of Witness mission, which places a high value on listening as a key component of social justice. After some connective tissue was established, we began to discuss the logistics of the project, the content, and how to reach out to potentially interested students. Both Claire and I felt lucky to be working with Sonia. Among other details, we decided that we would meet twice a week for about two months, and hold a culminating public event at SoleSpace, an art and retail gallery in downtown Oakland.

While drafting program content, we became very interested in giving students the opportunity to develop their visual storytelling skills to go along with their verbal and written skills. We envisioned our final product as a photo essay that combined the oral history narratives with photographs that were thematically linked to the stories. The combined approach of stories and images can be very powerful, as well as take pressure off students to manage large chunks of text—which can be a real hurdle—especially for students who are building their literacy skills and encountering oral history for the first time. During the initial phases of developing content for the project, we were fortunate to collaborate with Sita Bhaumik, a photographer and visual arts educator we first met through 826 Valencia, a writing and tutoring center in San Francisco. Luckily for us, she was available and happened to be in the midst of teaching a photography course, so she had a lot of great curricular content to share. Sita had done several projects that incorporated visual art with written narratives, and we had some very inspiring conversations on the relationship between the two. Sita was very facile about this relationship. Here's an example of her thought process related to the project:

> *When is a photograph too much and when is it not enough?* This became a central question. During this two-month project I facilitated the creation of photographic narratives by students. Each student selected a narrator they would interview. They were then tasked with representing this story in written and visual form. These stories were intensely personal, often dealing with racism, violence, abandonment, and/or abuse. If these stories were challenging to hear, they were even more challenging to represent. However, it was through the sharing of these stories that students ultimately became accountable not to us as instructors or facilitators but to their narrators.

As Claire, Sita, and I were developing our curriculum, the school was preparing to roll out this new class to students. Through a series of school town hall meetings, advisor discussions, and individual recruiting sessions, Sonia was able to put together an initial group of twelve students to help birth the Our Town, Our Stories project. The group consisted of seniors who would use the skills developed during the project for their senior portfolio requirements and sophomores who had either expressed interest in the class or were suggested to us by their advisors as students who would potentially benefit from the experience. As with any collaborative project, individuals were participating with varying levels of interest and for very different reasons. These dynamics, and others (including time), shaped our collaboration throughout the project.

Launching "Our Town, Our Stories"

Our first class meeting took place during the second week of the spring semester. We covered some of the logistics first, to make sure we were all on the same page in terms of meeting times, days of the week, duration of the project, and what specifically students would be graded on, which we were informed was important to cover during our first meeting. In hindsight (especially as newcomers), this felt like a crippling power dynamic to introduce on the first day. It was a bit like saying, "Hi, you don't know us, but trust me, we're pretty cool, we're adults, we hold the power, and we're going to grade you." During this meeting, we also spoke a bit about oral history and Voice of Witness, but ultimately decided for us not to talk too much, and engage with oral history methodology and practice over the next two classes. This initial class was a way for us to explore community stories—what shapes them, where they come from, and how they're shared. The class then began a written reflection and discussion of several of the essential questions of the project:

- What is the dominant narrative, or "single story," about Oakland?

- When you mention Oakland to people who don't live here, what is their initial impression of the city?

- When you turn on the television and there's a story about Oakland, what's it usually about?

There was also a second prompt of the written reflection and discussion addressing the following question for the project: *What do you feel are some untold stories in Oakland that deserve to be heard?* Student responses to the questions of the first prompt related primarily to violence: police brutality, gang violence, homicide, robbery, et cetera. Responses to the second prompt centered on Oakland's strong sense of community, its diversity, and good neighbors. One description used the term *deep Oakland*. Both of these overall responses would prove to be significant as the project unfolded.

Sita then introduced a brief photo activity to inspire students to begin thinking about how images can communicate a sense of place. She asked students to use their phone cameras and walk around the school campus to "take a photograph that feels representative of, or tells a story about, MetWest High School." At the end of class, we were able to have a brief look at and discussion of the photos. The images represented a range that reflected as much about the student's developmental process as it did about how students wanted to represent a sense of place through photography. Some images were literal (such as a photo of the MetWest logo), and some expressed individual students' sense of place at the school and their contribution to it—one such photograph was of a mural that a student painted. From this first class meeting, it was apparent that while students were interested in exploring the unheard stories of Oakland in a general sense, they were (rightly) much more interested in figuring out how their stories either reflected a sense of their own place in the ongoing narrative of Oakland, or what placed them outside of an Oakland they were still trying to figure out. The first class concluded with a homework assignment to think about five locations that epitomized students' perceptions of Oakland and to read a short poem by Bertolt Brecht called "Questions from a Worker Who Reads." The poem communicates how history is shaped by high-profile, dominant culture figures such as generals and presidents, and how everyday experiences by ordinary people are part of the historical narrative but rarely shared. We wanted to create an opening for students to see themselves as participants and not bystanders in their own histories.

After this first meeting, it was important to take a deep breath and acknowledge some of the factors that would impact the project: a noisy room that had more than its fair share of foot traffic (being close to a refrigerator where students retrieved snacks); our being newcomers/outsiders to the MetWest community; and students navigating complicated interpersonal relationships (across ages and grade levels), dealing with varying communication skill levels, and basically figuring out what they'd gotten themselves into. In my experience, these are factors that confront all community oral history projects (with the possible exception of the noisy refrigerator). This first class, and the next few that followed, manifested the many moving pieces that constitute oral history projects.

As is fairly standard with oral history projects, time expands, contracts, and scatters. In our case, some of this had to do with the culture of high school—student field trips, mandatory testing, student illness, and soccer matches. The activities and circumstances may be different, but these variables impact most oral history projects and ought to be factored into the process and timeline. Life moves forward when you're trying to pause and share stories about your life. In our particular case, some of these circumstances included student challenges in just trying to get to school every day, coping with unstable home environments, needing to care for siblings, managing transportation issues, and other more immediate concerns. Because of these factors, and a feeling that we had not built in enough time to get to know the students and for them to get to know each other, we ended up adding several class sessions to the project. As an oral history educator, I took this as a reminder that projects of this nature usually take more time than you originally planned for. This doesn't speak to a lack of organization, but more to the fact that storytelling projects require openness, trust, and vulnerability, as well as especially creating space for these things to be nurtured. For these reasons, oral history projects are hard to rush. Our students also needed time to process and digest new information—whether it was a Brecht poem, a story from our book series, a visual storytelling concept, or a basic oral history question. As visiting educators, it was easy to forget that students have other classes and commitments beyond what's happening during our seventy minutes together twice a week. For my part, this felt like a beginner's mistake.

Following the first class meeting, the next several were opportunities to learn more about each other and get some hands-on practice with learning the basics of oral history and visual storytelling. We were hampered somewhat by the issues already mentioned, as well as issues of fluctuating attendance. It wasn't that students weren't showing up, but these first few classes saw new students arrive and others disappear without explanation. This is a phenomenon of many oral history projects, and it's hard to explain but not unusual. The issue of time is a constant factor, and with other commitments, it's difficult for people to commit to what is ultimately a time- and labor-intensive process.

During our classes, we read excerpts from the Voice of Witness book series, discussed potential narrators, engaged in various photography / visual art activities, and went about the business of scheduling interviews, in addition to conducting several rounds of practice interviews. These interviews were fun but also challenging, as students struggled to establish common ground with each other. Some were veritable strangers to each other, owing to the class split between sophomores and seniors.

Initially, many students had broader ideas about whom they would interview for the project—local shopkeepers, activists, or other long-standing community members. The truth is that many of these suggestions came from the adults in the room. The three of us were interested in hearing these stories, and students were either not interested or reluctant to reach out to people they did not know—even though the school worked hard at promoting these kinds of communication skills. It was easy for us to project an experienced, adult mind-set about this aspect of the project: *All you have to do is reach out to the woman who runs the restaurant and ask her if she'd be willing to be interviewed.* Even when students had a narrator in mind, it could be a challenge to schedule an interview. Some of this is a matter of persistence, and some has to do with school and "real world" schedules not meshing.

One of the students, Frances Berumen, summed up the nature of this challenge: "First of all, you're really enthusiastic about interviewing that person, and that person doesn't have the time, so that was really difficult scheduling an interview, and then if you need to do follow-up questions or meet up with that person again to take pictures—I mean, it's difficult."

Ultimately, the students' range of narrators was determined by several factors: desire, access, expediency, and, interestingly, age. Some (but not all) of the students felt uncomfortable interviewing their peers, as we observed during our practice interviews. Students gravitated toward narrators who were older family members or trusted school faculty and staff. My feeling is that this group of students wanted to establish their connection to Oakland through the family and caring adults that surrounded them. For example, Donzah's reflection about the interview process with her aunt expresses her desire to use the oral history process as an intergenerational learning opportunity:

> I like interviews, because I'm a very open person. It takes a lot to be open, but as y'all saw with my auntie, I think being open can really change people's lives, because if a young girl goes through the same struggle that you went through, and you're open about talking about it, that same person will come to you for help, and y'all can create a bond and help her get out of that situation.

One of the project narrators, faculty member JoJo McGathon, had this to say about the mentoring aspects of her interview with a student: "I guess I helped guide her, because I could tell she wanted to figure out how comfortable I was at the beginning. And once she felt I was comfortable answering those more serious questions or going into more detail, she started asking more questions that she didn't pre-prep."

Our original ideas about the unheard stories of Oakland or the decentralized narratives that we would hear—deeper and beyond the media sound bites about homicide and police brutality—ended up, in many instances, to be assumptions on our part. The stories that students were collecting were filled with fresh twists and unexpected details about life in Oakland but were also related to violence, racism, and gentrification—all dominant Oakland narratives. It's not that the other stories were not out there, but the prevalence of the dominant narratives was a reminder of a quote by writer Chimamanda Ngozi Adichie about the danger of the single story and stereotypes: "The problem with stereotypes is not that they are untrue, but that they are incomplete." So these stories were very present in Oakland, and just because we were less interested in hearing them didn't mean they weren't representative of the day-to-day experiences of our narrators and students.

Nurturing Oral History in the Classroom

As we got deeper into the project, we dealt with the usual high school challenges of a lack of follow-through on assignments, scheduled interviews that did not happen, and in a few cases, not being able to upload interviews onto a computer. This definitely slowed down our transcribing and basic editing tasks. This part of the oral history process can be hard in the best of circumstances, and there were many instances when the most reliable school computers were either occupied or were unable to read the interview files. We also had a hard time uploading photographs, even though Sita diligently set up an easy-to-use platform to do so. Even with these technological challenges, the students maintained their diligence and patience; they really wanted to work on their interviews and images, and were very tolerant of these difficulties. Sonia had several useful comments about how students might have experienced this part of the process:

> It was a struggle for them. Having the discipline to sit, and listen, and type. That's not easy and it's not fun, but maybe there's something you gain from the transcribing process. I was thinking that would be good to do because it's not just about getting that quote down; it's about maybe you'll learn something more when you're listening to it over and over.

While the students were the first ones to acknowledge the challenges of transcription, they were also very savvy about its benefits. Frances had a unique perspective about transcribing: "I think it was meaningful, because once you're speaking, you pay attention, right? But you don't really remember what the person said. Once you're transcribing, you're really going deep into the answers that the person gave you and the follow-up questions you asked to understand the situation better."

As the time of our culminating public event at SoleSpace approached, we began to make some practical adjustments in the hopes that we would be able to get the project to the finish line. After a particularly challenging class, Sita suggested that instead of trying to do all the work as a group, we split up and spend the majority of our time working one-on-one with students. It was an inspired idea, and as soon as she proposed it, it seemed essential and obvious. It definitely generated a higher level of connection and productivity, and also a greater sense of expectations.

It was during these last few classes, where we focused heavily on the one-on-one approach, that the majority of the editing of text and photos took place. While some of the students did not have any formal editing experience, they all had a clear sense about the parts of their narrators' stories that would be compelling to an audience. One of the questions we posed frequently during these sessions was, "If the person reading this story has never met your narrator, which parts of the story do you think they'd respond to?" Sita used a similar approach when working with students to create and select images that would visually capture the essence of their narrator's story: one of her particularly productive questions for this was, "What are five words that best describe your narrator?"

With the final event just days away, the stories and images finally began to take shape. Students were beginning to get excited, as they could not only see the finish line (and a grade), but they also got a much clearer sense that what they were doing might have value beyond the class itself. Part of this excitement came from their newfound confidence that their narrators would appreciate how they were being represented through the stories and images students had carefully curated. If the narrators were going to be present when excerpts of their story were publicly shared, then addressing issues of representation was a critical priority. Voice of Witness advisor Rick Ayers frames this issue of representation with the question, "Who is the looker and who is being looked at?" Sita also describes this kind of representation in visual terms:

The process of photographing asked students to consider how their narrators could be represented. Even if we didn't talk about it in those terms, it dealt directly with the politics of representation and the politics of representing Oakland and its residents. In reflecting on the project, I remembered an early question that Cliff had asked me, "How does a camera listen?" Culturally, we refer to "shooting a photo" or "taking a picture." But the camera can also be a listening device.

Our last few meetings were full of the beautiful chaos that accompanies projects when a public event is looming. Organizing events of this kind guarantees the stories will be finished on time, and the stress students feel can be daunting. Producing off-site public events serves as a lesson in integrity for everyone. The flyers have gone out, the invitations have been sent, and the space has been booked, so postponing or canceling is not an option. It was at this point that our group really came together. Our bonding went beyond collaborating to handle the deadline crunch and transformed into a genuine excitement about having these stories shared and students' work being seen "out in the world." The earlier class divisions of sophomore and senior seemed to melt away—whether they were genuinely appreciating each other or were just too busy to worry about it was not entirely clear. After a reminder that one of the learning goals for the project was to become more comfortable with public speaking, several students volunteered to read excerpts from their oral histories during the event. Just in case, we reminded students what time they needed to be there, and that if they didn't show up for the event, they wouldn't get a grade! This last-minute bit of power-wielding paranoia proved to be unnecessary. Everyone showed up, and some of them even arrived early to help set up.

The event itself featured an enthusiastic crowd of students, parents, friends, family members, faculty, and two of the project's narrators. Jeff Perlstein from SoleSpace was very supportive and made everyone feel welcome. Claire, Sita, and I chatted with the students, met some of their parents, and mingled with Sonia and other MetWest faculty and staff. Once everyone was settled, we began the program. Claire and I introduced the project, spoke a bit about the collaboration between Voice of

Witness and MetWest, made sure the students introduced themselves, and made a special point of thanking Sonia, Sita, Jeff, and both narrators in attendance. The students who had prepared to present their stories came up and stood next to where their photos and narrative excerpts were being projected, then they read portions of their narrators' stories. MetWest staffer Malik Edwards heard an excerpt of his story about early childhood in Louisiana, presented by student Guadalupe Serrano Lopez. It read: "In those days everything was segregated. You couldn't go to the library like you wanted to, and our schools were all segregated. We went to all-Black schools, and although we had some fantastic teachers, our schoolbooks were usually handed down from white schools and sometimes the books would have pages missing and be scratched up and written all over."

It was clear from how narrators responded to these stories with smiles and nods of recognition that they felt seen and appreciated. In the days before the event, Claire, Sita, and I half-joked that the students who had not volunteered as presenters would change their minds at the last minute and would jump up and read their stories. During the presentation, it seemed this would not come to pass; the non-reading students seemed pretty intent on not reading their narrator's stories. And then something interesting happened—one by one, students volunteered to read their stories, and before we were finished, all but two of the students had come up in the front of the audience to share. One of these students, Ruqayyah, surprised herself by reading from her grandmother Linda Zareef's story, which features the following excerpt:

> Afro-American males are viewed as troublemakers. For example, my son Asad, right? A lot of people view him negatively because he wears the new clothes that all the youth wear, so people view him as being a troublemaker, without even getting to know him. Black youth can walk down the street, and non-Blacks, they'll cross the street or say, "Don't take my phone!" That's what happens to my son all the time.

After all the presentations were finished, there was a short Q&A in which students, narrators, parents, and other audience members shared their thoughts in what felt like a "story circle" of sorts. Many spoke of the experience as a great way to celebrate and learn about one another, shedding light not just on what connects us all, but also on our generational differences. Many shared their appreciation for the opportunity to bring these stories into the community instead of just keeping them under the gaze of a grading teacher. Sonia's reflections on the event really captured the essence of the evening:

> I remember loving the fact that we weren't at school. I was thinking, *This is such a great idea; we need to do more of this.* There's just something about it, something cooler. It just felt like a special evening for the students, like a very atypical evening for them. To see storytelling as a form of art and a form of sharing. We don't do a lot of that here. We don't at all. Our exhibitions are very academic, research based. "What did you learn about this issue, what's your research, how do you prove it?" So yeah, I feel inspired to do more of that type of work. I don't feel like it's given as much credit as it deserves, you know? Not just as a form of art, but as a form of action. Now that you know this person's experience, then what do you do with that information?

Sonia's question opens up a powerful mode of inquiry for teaching and learning with oral history at its center. It can also serve to illustrate the symbiotic relationship between schools and the larger communities they're a part of. I have described this process as "a community talking to itself." I have experienced it as part celebration and part respectful interrogation between participants. Like most generative learning experiences, it begins with an inquiry into the status quo, and then blossoms into dialogue. For the Our Town, Our Stories project, our questions led us to an exploration of MetWest High School as a community and the community of Oakland as a school. What connected the two were the stories that were collected and shared, and the relationships that grew out of the experience.

CYCLES OF DOMESTIC VIOLENCE

ASHLEY JACOBS

Ashley Jacobs first partnered with Voice of Witness when she shared her story with Claire Kiefer for the collection Inside This Place, Not of It: Narratives from Women's Prisons *(2011). Ashley has taken part in numerous oral history workshops and trainings, and offers the perspective of someone who has both shared difficult memories as part of an oral history project and helped others share their own stories. In 2013, Ashley began a project recording the stories of survivors of domestic abuse. Her ongoing project requires the utmost sensitivity, and in this field report, Ashley reflects on the importance of building a relationship with storytellers by listening to the "voice" behind the story being shared.*

Excerpt from "Cycles of Domestic Violence"

I come from a long line of women who pick men who hit them. My grandmother's first husband had money. He represented stability for the kids, so she took [the abuse] because she didn't think she could take care of the kids on her own. He was the provider. He was very controlling, and he was verbally and physically abusive. I remember her telling me a story about how he threw her out of a second-story window because she did not prepare his dinner correctly. He used fear to keep her at home. He told her, "You know, if I see you with another man, I'll kill you." He would. She knew he would kill her if she left.

She was afraid to go places without him. He would interrogate her for hours and hours about where she'd been and who she was with. He was really jealous of us kids, too. Once I got into an accident— I was hit by a car. I broke my arm and leg, and my grandmother carried me home sixteen blocks from the hospital with casts on my arm and my leg. She carried me. She didn't have a car, never had a driver's license. When she had to leave the house, to go to work or grocery shopping or whatever purpose, she would leave me home with him. I remember having to use the bathroom, but he would not take me. He hated us because of how much she loved us.

It was a generational curse—my mother was the same way. She would get older men who were like father figures because her dad had left when she was little. They were all the same: they had money, they were controlling, and they wanted her to stay home and cook. Whenever she got that wild hair to jump up and go out with her girlfriends, when she'd come home, they would beat her, slap her down on the floor. My mother was a gangster—she could fight!— but she wouldn't hit these men back because she wanted to remain in their good graces. She wouldn't hit back until she knew she was ready to go.

I remember she had a fight with my dad at my grandma's house. I don't know what it is about second-floor buildings in Chicago, but we were on the second floor then. They got into a fistfight with each other. They were not together but would get together just to see us. They came to my grandma's house to see us and ended up in a fight. From the bottom of the stairs I could hear them fighting with each other. I remember my dad telling my mother, "You gon' poke my eye out, let my eyeball go." She had her fingers in his eye. They were entangled in the hallway and they were fighting and they fought till they both rolled down the stairs.

My grandmother had to break it up 'cause she was like, "Y'all still act like y'all in gangs. Like teenagers." She was like, "You know, you shouldn't let your kids see this, if y'all got to do this, go home."

You know, I *saw* that. I could tell you what kind of clothes they had on—my dad had on all white. He has red hair, sandy red hair. So I remember what he looked like, and I remember my mother being so defiant. She stood up for herself. She let him know she wasn't gon' take it. It was because he wasn't nobody to her, you know, he wasn't nobody she loved anymore or wanted to be with. So she got up, she went her way, he went his.

I was wired differently than the rest of my family. I don't know how. I think I'll blame it on God. I think God kept me. God kept me in my head, to see things that were bad and do the opposite. I never had to learn from the bad because I always had examples. I constantly had the bad examples of what would happen.

God taught me that mentality that I'm no exception to the rule in that case. So, I just never had the desire to test it.

You are not a product of your past. What your family has done, what happened to them. It isn't automatic that it happens, or should happen to you. You can change the course of your life just by one word and one action and one decision. That will break the curse right then and there. Just think boldly enough to make that decision. You are your own most prized possession, not anyone else. You are the most valuable thing you've got, right now. There's always time to turn around, to walk away. There is always, every minute, there's an opportunity to get out. Every moment you inhale and exhale, that's an opportunity for escape. To every woman, a striving survivor of domestic violence, you are my hero. Those who have gone because of it, you are my ancestral heroes, because you took it until you couldn't no more.

—Hazel

From Narrator to Interviewer

I first came to Voice of Witness as a narrator. My story, which is included in *Inside This Place, Not of It: Narratives from Women's Prisons*, is about my experience with the prison system and the injustice that took place inside it. In my narrative, I described how I was pregnant and shackled to the delivery table in prison and forced to have a C-section. It was a difficult story to share. When I think about how I felt the day that Claire Kiefer first came to my house to interview me, I remember being nervous, scared, and a little skeptical of what I was getting myself into. I wondered what she would look like and what she would say. *Will she be judgmental? Will she take my story and use it for her own personal gain? Am I making a mistake by opening up to this stranger?* Those were some of the questions that I remember replaying in my mind. When she knocked on the door, I felt butterflies in my stomach, as if I was getting ready to face God himself. I opened it and finally put a face to the voice that I had heard so many times on the phone.

Claire walked in through the door and gave me a hug. And she had brought pastries! I immediately felt like I had known her forever. She didn't immediately start questioning me. Instead, we spoke about how close her family lived to me and how she had grown up in the same area. She laughed with me and played with my son. I dropped my guard immediately, and I was able to fully trust her because I saw that she was an honest person who cared about what I'd been through. I knew immediately that a lifelong friendship had begun.

When we sat at my dining room table to start the interview, I was nervous but at peace that everything would be all right. I was still scared that digging up my pain might not be a great move. I always thought, *out of sight, out of mind.* But once I started answering Claire's questions, I felt like I was going through a healing process. Toward the middle of the interview, I actually felt some relief from all the crying. I realized I needed her more than she needed me. At that moment I didn't care whether my story was chosen for the book or not—I had finally gotten a chance to open up to someone who listened to me without any judgment. After sharing my story with Claire, I felt like a huge burden had been lifted.

From the moment I first shared my story, I knew there was more left for me to do. I didn't have any fear about speaking about what I went through. I actually wanted to speak to others in hopes of making a difference in someone else's life or preventing them from going through the same storm that I did. I started working with SPARK Reproductive Justice NOW, an organization based in Atlanta that was trying to address reproductive rights for women in prison. We worked to get a bill passed to prevent prisons from shackling pregnant women while giving birth. I started to love myself again. I realized that I was not a victim, but a survivor. Standing in front of the capitol in Atlanta, I realized how powerful my voice was. They may have judged me walking in, but once I walked out, the panel members were holding copies of my narrative in their hands, and some of them told me they thought I should never have been in prison in the first place. I knew then that I was making a difference.

Telling my story gave me confidence to stand up to the many obstacles I had yet to face. Previously, I had feared applying for jobs because of my conviction. The first job I got, as a chiropractor's assistant, came from when I talked about my story during a few therapy sessions following a car accident. My story made me more than a line about my charges on a résumé. Sharing my story was making a real difference in my life. Later, I decided that I wanted to help other survivors experience the same feeling of having their burden lifted by sharing their stories. I decided to begin interviews for my own oral history project.

Choosing a Project

My decision to address domestic violence for my oral history project came about in October 2013 during a conversation on the football field with another mother named Jennifer. It was my son's homecoming game, and I had set up a booth to raise money for my son's team by selling crawfish rice and jambalaya. Jennifer's daughter cheered for my son's team, so she stopped by the booth to purchase a dinner. She began telling me about this event that she helped set up for women who'd been through domestic violence, and how an organization she worked with was trying to give survivors a voice. This was their first year putting on an event where women who had survived domestic violence were invited to speak and share their stories. I asked her how she got involved with the organization, and she told me she had gone through some difficult things with her husband. I saw the passion in her spirit and immediately knew that I was also interested in helping these women.

Over a bowl of crawfish rice, I told Jennifer about my work with Voice of Witness and my oral history experience. We had an immediate connection. I explained to her how Voice of Witness gave me a voice to explain my situation and also help other women like me. I told her that if she would introduce me to a few women that she worked with, I could help those women share their stories. I told her that I thought it was important that the stories go deeper than just a retelling of abuse. She agreed. Jennifer eventually became one the four women I spoke with for my project.

From the start of the project, I was interested in understanding how domestic violence can be a generational curse. I'm a strong believer that we all come into this world with a clean slate. Somewhere along our journey, we are taught our ways of living. We learn right from wrong, what is appropriate and what isn't, the proper way to behave, and what's expected by society. My belief is that people don't just decide to be beaten or become an abuser; some of us are taught that this is a way of living.

My goal in this project was to explore the whole lives of individuals who had experienced domestic abuse. I wanted the women I talked with to open up about their lives as children, so that they and everyone who heard their stories could better understand why domestic abuse continues throughout their lives. I wanted to hear how they got out of their situations, and how they planned on breaking the curse that had been passed on throughout so many generations, in hopes of them not passing the torch to their kids. I realized as a narrator when I agreed to share my story that I knew the problem and the solution; I just needed someone to listen to me and give me an opportunity to be human. I wanted to be the one now who was listening.

Finding Narrators and Establishing Trust

After meeting Jennifer and speaking to her, God started sending many amazing women my way. I never had to go out and look for individuals. I relied on a network of women who knew and trusted other women to make introductions, and I would always wait to speak about the details of my project when I felt the time was right.

In some cases, just speaking about what I was doing and what I desired to come from my research was enough to get individuals to share their stories. A lot of times people want to be heard, and you just have to be that outlet. For example, one night I went to a poetry event where I met a great friend of mine named Ms. Wright. She explained to me that she knew a woman named Mona Lisa who had a really inspiring story. So I reached out to Mona on Facebook, explaining who I was and that I would love to meet her and speak to her. She quickly agreed. When someone has agreed to allow you into their lives, it is important to be honest about who you are and the reason you want to speak to them.

Mona was my first interview. I was nervous about interviewing her because I knew she was a history professor and a poet, so when I spoke with her on the phone, I told her I wanted to do her interview first so that she could critique me and give me input on how to make it better. She said, "Not a problem." At that moment, I'm sure any doubts she had were erased, because she began to think of this as not just an interview, but as a possible teaching moment. That was my way of opening the door to have a successful interview. I never wanted to come off to any of the women I spoke with as if I were better than them—I wanted to seem human. It's always important to find a connection of some sort with a narrator. To let them know that they have something to teach you; that you don't know it all. I ask about who they are today before asking them to open up about who they used to be.

I drove to St. Petersburg, Florida, where I met Mona at her beautiful house. I arrived with a copy of *Inside This Place, Not of It* to give to her so that she knew she was not in this alone and that I was with her.

I've found that in doing oral history interviews, there is no set interview format that works best. This time, I didn't go in with questions written out. I remembered when Claire interviewed me how I felt so open, as if I had known her for years. So I wanted to do the same as an interviewer. Mona, because of her background as a professor who actually teaches history, was easy to speak to and already understood what to expect and how the interview might go. I explained to her what I was hoping to learn from my project and informed her that I would keep her updated on everything that came out of it.

Mona told me about how she had never really moved beyond her past. She hadn't had a relationship since her last marriage over ten years ago, because of her experience with domestic violence. Mona had experienced violence all her life and, like me, believed it can be a learned mind-set. She grew up in the army life, where she watched her dad abuse her mother. Mona's dad abused her, too. She then married into the army life, where she was constantly abused. She spoke about how she thought she never had a voice, because her husband made her believe the army was on his side. So she lived in fear.

Mona and her husband had a daughter, and when Mona decided to leave the relationship and try and get out of the marriage, she took her daughter with her. Not long after, Mona's husband came to get the little girl, and he told Mona that he'd gotten custody papers and that she'd never see her daughter again. Mona didn't know what she could do. She left, and he moved. Mona would call, and her ex-husband would never let her see her daughter. He got remarried and had more kids. When her daughter got to an age where she started acting out, he called Mona to get her; Mona didn't respond, because she had never had the chance to form a relationship with her daughter.

Mona's daughter was a grown woman by the time of our interview. The first time Mona reached out to her, it didn't go so well. Her daughter was angry, and her father had never told her the truth about her mother. Her daughter grew up thinking her mother did not want her. She also didn't feel wanted by her father, knowing that he'd kept her to hurt her mother.

After our interview, Mona asked me if I thought she should reach out to her daughter again to tell her the truth. She explained that her daughter's father was on his deathbed and still hadn't told their daughter what had happened. I told Mona I believed she owed her daughter the truth, if she would listen. What happened was unfair to the both of them, and it was important for her daughter to know the truth so she could move forward in her own life. She did reach out to her, and they set up a time to meet and talk about their history. This was the sort of moment I hoped my project would help bring about—a chance for healing on the part of the storyteller.

Mona also spoke about going on to fall in love with a marine who had thought he could be her savior but eventually became abusive himself. She got pregnant, and one day he punched her in the stomach and caused a miscarriage. They separated after that but eventually got back together. She became pregnant again, this time with twins. He denied they were his, and she ended up raising them as a single mother. She had also become estranged from her father, who was the first man who abused her. Thinking back on her childhood, she told me, "You know, just those moments where I would be like, *Why, what compelled you [to abuse me]?* I was a good kid. I got good grades in school. I was very obedient, and I behaved, I helped my mother, I cleaned the house, I did everything a parent could expect of a child, and yet he felt the need to beat me up when he was angry. I always thought maybe it was because military men feel so protected."

Throughout my interview, I caught myself getting angry but had to quickly remind myself not to be judgmental. In oral history, because you are dealing with actual people, it's easy to get caught up in what they went through or wonder what you would have done if you were in that situation. In reality, there is no way to know what you would do; you may have never been in that situation, so you listen and learn. There were moments when I cried while speaking to Mona, because of the tears she had from the struggle of losing her daughter and not knowing how to mend that relationship. Being there to listen to her meant the world to me. Our interview ended with a moment of reflection from Mona:

For the abused person, I would say that it's not the end. There is something on the other side of it. And, you have to have enough faith in
yourself to get through it, to come out on the other side. For the abuser,
take just one moment in time and put yourself in that other person's
shoes. Just for a second, just for one split second. Physically, emotionally, psychologically, spiritually, any way you want—your choice. One
moment in time, to be on the other end, and tell me that that would
not change who you are. Don't judge. Ask questions, get information.

I knew at that moment that Mona felt she had been heard. She was giving
hope to the individual in her situation. Letting them know that they are
not the first and will not be the last—that is the reason I love oral history.
Always remember that if you can touch or change one life, you have ac-
complished a major movement in the right direction. After an interview,
you should almost feel like you had been in the situation with the person
you were interviewing. That, to me, is what makes a great interviewer.

My second narrator, Hazel, was participating in a poetry reading as part
of an event that I was involved in. I met Hazel through another woman who
would become one of my narrators, my friend Ms. Wright. We had great
conversations the night of the event, and I set up a time to speak with Hazel.
Hazel and I did our interview over the phone since she lived four hours
away. We spoke several times about the project, and she was very open to
sharing her experience. Hazel grew up witnessing domestic violence, but
because she had seen what her grandmother, mother, and sister had gone
through, she found a way to avoid it herself. She shared with me some of
the things she had been through, and how they helped make her stronger
in some ways. Her story is excerpted at the beginning of this field report.

I also interviewed Ms. Wright, who had been physically and emotionally abused as a child. As an adult, the tables turned and she began to be
the abuser. Ms. Wright's story showed me that abusers have stories, too.
They could also be victims of abuse, and for some, it's the only way they
know to love and protect themselves from being abused and hurt. That is
why I believe it's important to listen to and understand everyone's struggle. It doesn't make people's actions right, but they may need help, and
sharing their stories honestly is one way to help themselves.

After speaking with the women I met at the event, I circled back and spoke with Jennifer, the woman I met at my son's football game. Jennifer had been adopted into an abusive family. Jennifer told me that having been adopted, she already felt the abandonment of not being loved. "I have gone through some sexual abuse as a child at the hands of my adopted father. I know that the enemy's busy, and I know that it was more of a spiritual thing than him really actually wanting to do that. I don't know if he had gone through child abuse himself, but I know for sure that I went through it. So that played an intricate part in how I was in different relationships with other people."

During my interview I picked up on the fact that she was still very hurt by her experience. I also understood that because she'd trusted her story in my hands, I had to make sure I honored her wishes.

Oftentimes with journalists or other media, the journalist will take pieces of others' stories and fit them into a story the journalist is trying to tell. The story is not about the individual, but the interviewer's goals. A few weeks before my interview with Jennifer, she had done a story with her church in which the media came to interview survivors of domestic abuse. Some journalists had spoken with Jennifer about her experience. Even though most of her abuse had been psychological, they just wanted to know details about "domestic violence" as they saw it, asking questions like, "Did he hit you or not?" When the story was published, Jennifer read it, and she was so upset. She felt that they had portrayed her as just a victim, and that bothered her. It was as if she had not overcome anything. They only wanted to hear her story of abuse, but they weren't listening to her *voice*.

One thing I loved about my experience sharing my story with Voice of Witness is that they showed me the story after it was complete and made sure I understood that it was my story and that I had the power to correct any mistakes, or to add anything I wanted or take out anything I didn't like. I had the opportunity to say, "No, this needs to be fixed." It was about my goals in sharing my story—not just the interviewer's.

At the time of our interview, I reassured Jennifer that I wasn't interested in doing what the journalists had done. I knew that Jennifer trusted me, because she already knew me as an individual. I spoke to her about my own experience and gave her a copy of my book, as I did with all my narrators. I explained in detail the relationship that I had with Claire. Sometimes it relaxes the narrator to not just trust you, but to trust the team of support you have in your corner. I saw how relaxed she was when I spoke about my relationships with the people who had listened to my voice and shared it with others. Also, she follows me on Facebook, so she was also able to see the opportunities it had opened for me. She was confident that I was listening to her voice, and not just taking a part of her story.

Her life revolved around her family and children. Jennifer was a nursing student and was determined to finish school. So throughout her marriage and raising her three kids, she was finally able to finish school and wanted to become more independent. She also wanted to pursue modeling, which triggered her husband's abuse. He would tell her that she was no Beyoncé, or that she wasn't pretty enough. When she was fed up with her husband's psychological abuse, she decided to leave, and he was not okay with that decision. "The physical abuse came at the end when I decided I was gonna leave the situation. I had gone through so much verbal abuse and he would use the Bible to say, 'You can't leave me, because it's in the Bible, this Scripture says this,' and, I was like, no."

Finally, Jennifer stood up for herself. She told me she was packing her bags when her husband grabbed her and started choking her. She knew staying would not be good for her or her kids, so she had to leave. That's exactly what she did, and she never looked back. Jennifer told me, "God kept me. Through that marriage and through all I went through, it was God that kept me, so I would say that you would have to reach for God. That He's your pillar, He's your rock, and, just search for your love of God, and when you experience God's love, then you won't tolerate anything less than that."

I also had the opportunity to speak with Jennifer's daughter, who says she loves her mother and father. She didn't understand everything that was going on, but she knew her mom was not happy then, and she is happy that she was able to move on in her life. At that moment, I realized this little girl has a chance and that the cycle had been broken.

What I've Learned

I think being on the other side of this process made it easier for me to understand the uncertainties and caution that are part of sharing a difficult story. I remember first hearing from Claire by phone and telling her I would think about being part of the project and would give her a call. Claire understood and gave me the time I needed to feel comfortable enough to speak to her. She answered any questions I had honestly. She explained how if my story got chosen, I would be able to help someone else, but also to allow others to see the injustice of the system. So I did the same with my narrators. I always let them feel in control of the interview—steering them in the right direction on occasion, but mostly just allowing them to speak, while remembering that I'd edit the stories but ultimately allow the storyteller to choose what was important.

Oral history, I learned, is not something that can be rushed. Some individuals experience a lifetime of pain. We are complete strangers who are digging up situations that have been buried a long time ago. So we are opening a locked gate, which can be hard. I never wanted to leave an interview feeling that I didn't lift a burden that this individual had been carrying.

For the interviewer, it is important to never be judgmental. The way you dress, how you speak, should convey respect and interest. I need to show that I'm human and that I'm not judgmental. When you're going into these interviews, you need to put yourself into a place where you're humble, and where you can connect with whatever it is that your narrator is going through.

Take the time to invest in their lives to learn what they like to do now. If they feel that they already know you, your interview will go very smoothly. I remember Claire asking me what I wanted to eat, or giving me the opportunity to choose where I was most comfortable doing the interview, and most importantly showing interest in who I was as an individual. I will never forget the day she called me and said, "I want to get the kids gifts for Christmas." The relationship that you can give your narrator is important. Don't treat them as just a story in a book, but as a fellow human who has a struggle to bear, just as we all do. It's in this way that you'll reach a narrator's true voice and not simply hear a part of his or her story.

RESILIENCE:
ELDERS IN EAST HARLEM

LAUREN TAYLOR

Lauren Taylor conceptualized her project as a way to preserve the stories of East Harlem residents who are sixty years old and older. Here, Lauren explores how her two decades of experience as a clinical social worker have informed her interviewing style in her conversations with men and women at the Leonard Covello Senior Center, a community hub that serves as "a vibrant place for older adults to socialize and learn." Throughout her interviews, she has noticed many emergent themes, the most commonly recurring of which is that of her narrators' inspiring resilience. In this field report, Lauren reflects on the relationship between the interviewer and the narrator and the power dynamics and unexpected moments that surface in oral history interviews, and concludes that "narrative, with its capacity for meaning making, brings significance to the experience of both the narrator and the listener."

Excerpt from "Resilience"

It was the end of the day at the Leonard Covello Senior Center in East Harlem and most of the seniors had gone home. The only people left in the lobby were the young Latino man who sits at the reception desk, the custodian—a Latino man in his fifties—an African American senior named Malcolm Prince (referred to respectfully by the others as "Mr. Prince"), and two Latino elders sitting on the periphery. Mr. Prince was talking to the receptionist. I had just come downstairs after interviewing another member of the center. I became a participant-observer, an "insider-outsider," as I both joined the conversation and recorded it, with permission:

Mr. Prince: Down in the army it was segregated. It was all-Black companies and all-white companies. And when I had my first furlough leave, it was like 250 of us going from Tallahassee, Florida, to Jacksonville to catch the mainline to go up north. And the colored wait room could only hold fifty people. And there was—it was only a train coming in, special train coming in to pick us up, at Tallahassee to take us to Jacksonville. It was about eleven at night. And some of the white waiting room, there was nobody sitting over there. I went over there, and a sergeant told me to leave. I said, "You don't know my name. You address me as soldier." And we were fighting Germany and Japan. He took his gun out, put it to my head, and said, "I ain't got time to go to court, filling out papers for killing a nigger." Now, don't ask me a stupid question like, "Did I get up?" Did you think I got—of course I got up. I mean, you talking to me right now, aren't you? There you go. So I got up.

Lauren: So what about race relations in this neighborhood? I was told once that it was rough around here. How was that for you?

Mr. Prince: It's rough everywhere. There's been some incidents. But like I was saying, the difference when I was talking about the army, there was a lot of racism. Well, it was an Italian neighborhood. Basically Italian. I didn't have a problem—race—"Man, you know, you like the girls. You want Spanish girls? You want Black girls? It's all right. But you don't fool with no Italian girls, all right?" Well, I wasn't thinking about fooling with nobody anyway.

Lauren: Do you miss anything about the old neighborhood?

Mr. Prince: I don't miss anything in my life. I miss—what do I miss in my life? A question like that, what do I miss in my life? I think I had a very interesting life.

Lauren: So what do you think is the biggest challenge you've faced in your life?

Mr. Prince: Biggest challenge? I look at life not as a challenge. I don't look at life as a challenge. I look at life—just like this gentleman told me upstairs. It's a journey.

Mr. Prince then turned to me and said: "You know what you should ask people? You know the question you should ask people? You should ask them what they regret." (I had, in fact, asked him that question earlier, and he had said he had no regrets. He had answered, "Just like the man upstairs on the second floor said: 'Life is not a dress rehearsal. It's a play in progress.'") Then the receptionist said, "Mr. Prince, what *do* you regret? Tell us what you regret." Mr. Prince used his hands to make the imaginary form of a woman, and said: "You guys heard of Cialis?" The receptionist and the maintenance man said they had not. Mr. Prince swaggered up to where he pictured the imaginary woman standing, and said, "You know, you can see this beautiful woman. 'Hey baby, you want to . . .' [He made a gesture with his body.] But then you get there and nothin' works." The receptionist and the maintenance man seemed perplexed. One of the two older men on the side said, "Viagra." Then the others understood.

At that point I went out on a limb and asked the receptionist, who had a computer on his desk, to look up the "36-hour Cialis" video on YouTube. It's a takeoff on a commercial for this medication, and features a tall, smartly dressed African American man with an enormous erection, which knocks into things, causing all kinds of havoc. The last scene shows him in an embrace with an elegant woman in an elevator, and the door closes on his erection. All the men in the lobby gathered round and laughed at what they saw on the screen. Afterwards Mr. Prince said to me, "So you're not who I thought you were. I thought you was one of them church ladies. But you ain't no church lady!" I said: "That's right, Mr. Prince. You got it!"

Getting Started

Later, reflecting on this experience, I couldn't help but think: *How did I, an upper-middle-class white girl, who grew up in a suburb on Long Island, end up shooting the breeze about sex with a group of Black and Latino men in East Harlem?*

For the past two decades, I have worked as a social worker with older adults and, more recently, as an oral historian. Over the course of my interconnected careers, I have heard hundreds of life stories. These stories were sometimes stories of suffering and despair, sometimes stories of joy and happiness; they were always stories of survival and resilience. As a social worker I can only choose to preserve these stories in confidence, changing names and details so that their subjects are unrecognizable. As an oral historian, with permission from my narrators, I have the freedom to share their stories publicly. Oral history provides a way of making concrete one's subjective experiences of the aging process and of creating from it a wealth of ideas and information. The major part of my work in clinical social work with older adults has also been about reminiscence and narrative.

I have always loved listening to stories. When I was a small child, my father spun a yarn every night before I went to sleep. His tales of Mrs. Fufnick's boarding house, with Mr. Snachit, the India rubber man, and Jane Turvey, a little girl who did everything upside down and backwards, captivated me and were every bit as real to me as if they had not been invented. My maternal grandmother, who lived to be ninety-eight, was the family historian. Much to the good fortune of the family, one of my cousins had the foresight to record her stories. My relationship with my grandmother was among the factors that drew me to work in the field of aging. My passion for listening to the stories of elders was the driving force behind the conception of the project described in this chapter.

The Community and the Senior Center

They drop jewels on you. You learn a lot from your elders.

—Yiorkanny Ponce, receptionist at
the Leonard Covello Senior Center

I conceptualized the project with the vision that it would help give voice to elders of an underserved community and foster a deeper understanding of the experience of aging in a neighborhood of older people living independently. It would also provide insight into the resilience required to make a life worth living, even when one has faced multiple losses. The individuals who were interviewed are older residents of East Harlem, many of whom receive services through the Carter Burden Center for the Aging, a multifaceted not-for-profit social service agency that provides a range of free programs for people age sixty and over in New York City. Its mission is to help older adults remain in the community and live safely and with dignity. One of the communities served by the Carter Burden Center is East Harlem.

East Harlem is one of the most underserved neighborhoods in New York City. Almost 12,000 people between the ages of sixty and seventy-four live in this neighborhood. Over 13,000 residents are sixty-five and older, representing 11 percent of the total population of 120,511. Of these elderly, 48.7 percent live at or below the federal poverty level.[1] Many of the people benefiting from Carter Burden's services have survived the challenges of war, displacement from their home countries, physical and emotional difficulties, and the loss of loved ones.

In January 2013, the Carter Burden Center took up sponsorship of the Leonard Covello Senior Center in East Harlem. After extensive renovations, made possible by the generosity of government, corporate, and community organizations, and with the help of hundreds of volunteers, the center has become a vibrant place for older adults to socialize and learn.

---

1. New York City Department for the Aging, *Profile of Older New Yorkers*, February 26, 2010, 24, available at www.nyc.gov.

I have been providing supportive counseling for seniors at the Carter Burden Center since 2008, under the auspices of the Service Program for Older People, a not-for-profit mental health clinic for older adults. Because the clinical services at the Carter Burden Center represent only one small part of their purview, the Carter Burden / Leonard Covello Senior Center proved to be a better alternative and an ideal place in which to help older adults in East Harlem tell their stories.

Finding the Narrators

Recruiting for the project was done by announcements in the lunchroom of the center and by distributing flyers in English, Spanish, and Mandarin. These are the languages spoken by the majority of members of the Covello Center. I was concerned about language barriers, as I speak only elementary Spanish and no Mandarin, but the center offered to provide translators as needed. This did not prove to be a problem, as all those who volunteered to be interviewed are bilingual. The majority of the people I interviewed grew up speaking both English and Spanish. Although I have some knowledge of Spanish, I do not have the fluency necessary to conduct an interview in Spanish. What I do bring to an interview is what my colleague Lynn Lawrence calls my dual "bilingual" roles as both therapist and oral historian.

When I first began recording oral histories, I struggled with the desire to comment on, or interpret, what the narrator was saying. Over time I learned to use phrases such as "That must have been very hard for you," which are standard in a therapeutic context and more judicious when doing oral histories. My skill as a therapist has helped me as an interviewer in establishing rapport, in listening to trauma narratives, and in intuiting when it is time to end an interview. Regardless of the "language" I speak, my work involves bearing witness to the story, which is perhaps the most important part of my work.

I have led a sheltered life in comparison with most of the people I interviewed for this project. My training has made me sensitive to the potential impact of racial, ethnic, age, gender, and class differences between interviewer and narrator. I feel it appropriate to let people know I am doing the interviews as a volunteer, as I do not want the narrators, many of whom are economically disadvantaged, to think I might be making money from their stories. Cultural sensitivity is critical in the interviewing process, but the need to tell stories is universal.

In *Doing Oral History*, Donald Ritchie posits that just as the race and gender of the interviewer and narrator affect the interview, whether an interviewer is a member of the community may also make a difference.[2] I'd add age and social class as factors as well. When I first conceptualized the project, I was worried about the insider-outsider issue. My concerns were dispelled the moment I set foot in the Covello Center, where I was greeted with warmth and acceptance. Everyone from the maintenance man to the director of the center helped me feel welcome. Now, when I step inside the building, I feel very much at home.

Although my years of experience as a social worker may have given me an advantage in oral history interviewing, at the start of an interview there are usually two anxious people in the room. Some narrators are concerned at first that I might ask questions they cannot answer. I explain that I will not be asking a list of questions but rather asking them to tell me something about their lives and their experiences growing up in the community of East Harlem. I tell people that the ideal oral history interview has only one question: "Where were you born?" I start by describing the project, and letting narrators know that I will be giving them audio copies of the interviews. Narrators are asked to sign release forms for subsequent use of the materials "by researchers and the public for educational purposes, including publications, exhibitions, World Wide Web, presentations, and promotional purposes."[3] The interviews were digitized and transcribed, and will serve to form an archive of living history for the agency and the public.

---

2. Donald Ritchie, *Doing Oral History* (New York: Oxford University Press, 2015), 246.

3. Wording of release forms provided by the Carter Burden / Leonard Covello Senior Center.

The People

The older people remember East Harlem as a strong community. Despite the rivalries between different ethnic groups, within their own spaces people felt at home. And in the center of the neighborhood was a large open-air market that served as a community meeting place. Many of the older residents recall with nostalgia La Marqueta. Jenny Rodriguez describes it:

> We do miss what they call the Marqueta on 111th to 116th Street because that used to be a big part of our life. I don't know if you've heard of that. It's an indoor market. It's right under the train. And shopping on Saturdays was the biggest thing in this place. It was run by a lot of Jewish people. Everybody that had their little stands were Jewish people. And my mom used to take us all every Saturday over there and do our shopping for food, for house, for clothing, for school, for shoes, everything. And that was a real big part of our life. And they still have a little area of it open, but it's not the same like it used to be back then. A lot of people shopped there because you could get nicer prices there. And fresh food, and vegetables, and meat, and housewares. Everything was there. Everything was there. And for years, that *marqueta* was like a big part of our neighborhood.
>
> Tell you the truth, it just disappeared, like . . . after so many years, I think as I got older, then it just started to diminish because a lot of the people retired. And then nobody else wanted to take the stands over. Because mainly all the stores that were in the neighborhood were really owned by Jewish people. And everybody got along with them. It was the most wonderful thing. Oh, it was a real community. A real community.

But the neighborhood also had gangs, which instilled fear among the residents. Felicita Gonzales learned at a young age how to avoid trouble:

> Now, when I lived here as a child, we knew that they were two places you couldn't go to. Third Avenue had an el and a trolley car.[4] From Third to Second to First was where the Italians lived. And they had a gang called the Red Wings. And we couldn't go over there—that is, the Latins. On Fifth Avenue headed toward 110th and north was where the Blacks lived. So we couldn't go over there.

---

4. The Third Avenue El (elevated) was the last elevated train to operate in Manhattan.

So our gang here, in this middle section, was called the Latin Lords. I never belonged to any gang, because I worked. I was in the candy store. And if I wasn't in the candy store, I was in school. But I would hear about it. The Latin Lords are fighting with the Red Wings, the Red Wings are fighting with—but I knew all about that.

Emergent Themes

As I continued to speak with older residents, a few themes seemed to emerge in nearly every interview. If there is one word that keeps coming to mind when I listened to the stories of older residents of East Harlem, it is *resilience*. Many of the seniors I interviewed for this project were immigrants or the children of immigrants. The majority grew up poor, often needing to forgo education to help support their families. Despite sometimes-overwhelming odds, the people I interviewed demonstrated remarkable resourcefulness and resilience in making their ways in the world. After his father died, Mario Repollet, who was born in Puerto Rico, came to East Harlem hoping to make money to send home to help support his siblings. By his own admission, he fell in with the wrong crowd and ended up selling heroin on the street. He was arrested and spent five years in prison. He speaks openly about his experiences and says he blames no one but himself. While he was in prison, he decided that when he was released he would change his life for the better. He wanted to become a role model for others and give back to his community. It was a struggle to overcome his past, but he succeeded. "My mama can look down and be proud of me now. It wasn't always like that."

Like many of the narrators, Felicita Gonzales learned resilience from her mother. Here she describes how her mother supported her and her siblings after the death of Felicita's father, when she was only seven years old:

> The welfare worker came and told her, well, now you have to send your daughter to the factory, so she can support the family. And my mother told her no. My mother said, "My daughter wants to be a nurse, and she's going to be a nurse. I'm not going to let her go to the factory. If anyone would go, it would be me, not them." So she told her, "Do me a favor. Get the hell out of here. And don't ever

come back." She came back a week later and said, "Oh well, we're not going to—"

She said, "I told you already. I don't want welfare, and I don't want your help. I am going to do it on my own."

Resilience does not occur in a vacuum; it develops in the context of relationships and community. Many of the people I interviewed attribute their resilience to their community, East Harlem.

Another important theme was the ways East Harlem has changed over the course of residents' lives. Only the older residents can tell us about what it was like in the "old days." Gentrification is driving the rents up and changing the complexion of the neighborhood. More white people are moving in, new restaurants are springing up everywhere, and there is a large shopping mall where there were once small, family-owned businesses. The majority of the people I interviewed see the changes as positive but also feel resentment about the rising prices of housing and about lack of respect among young people for their community. Most everyone expressed pleasure that people of different races and ethnicities are now living together more harmoniously in East Harlem than when they were growing up. They care deeply about their community and are proud to be residents of East Harlem. According to resident Wendy Ferreira:

> Oh, I love East Harlem. I love it. The only thing is that the rents are going sky high. You can't live here no more. Got to stay where you are. I live in Franklin Plaza. And every time they raise the rent—oh, god. It's supposed to be a co-op. And the rent goes up, up, up. I don't like that.
>
> Oh, the neighborhood is changing. It's changing a lot. I don't know, it's too much—before it was so nice. You could leave the windows open . . . not anymore. It's changing too much. It's awful. It's awful. It's a different generation. This generation that's coming up nowadays, it's not like when we were coming up. They don't respect. . . . They want everything free. They don't want to work for it. I don't understand. It's very hard for me to understand things like that. Because when I talk to my friends, we are all the same age and we talk about it. Because we respected.

Oh, god, you couldn't say nothing to an old person. No, you had to respect that person. And that person went to your mother and said something. Your mother would come to you. But no, nowadays you can't say . . . you see a kid doing something bad, can't say nothing because the mother curse you out. It's a big difference.

At the end of each interview, I asked the narrator for a "message" to young people going forward. Over and over I heard the same message: "Stay in school! Get an education!" In the words of resident Perita Greer:

That's a good question. Young people going forward. What can I say? Stay in school, I guess. Get a good education. Just try to stay away from trouble. I know it's hard out here. There's so much to distract you. You have all these sneakers and—I mean, it is just so much going on.

Really, stay in school. Focus. I wish I would've finished . . . I don't know. It's hard to say, because their parents' backgrounds, or you don't know what goes on in people's lives. Just tell them to focus, and your dreams will come true.

Making Meaning

The Oral History Association describes oral history as "both the oldest type of historical inquiry, predating the written word, and one of the most modern, initiated with tape recorders in the 1940s."[5] In the early days of recording interviews, the interviewer kept an objective distance from the narrator, and there was little consideration for the intersubjective relationship that develops between interviewer and narrator.[6] Over the past few years, a change has been occurring in oral history, with the focus shifting to the relationship that develops in the meeting space between the interviewer and narrator. The story becomes a

---

5. "Oral History Defined," Oral History Association, www.oralhistory.org/about/do-oral-history.

6. For an excellent history of this process, see "Practices of the Oral History Research Office," Columbia University, www.columbia.edu/cu/lweb/digital/collections/nny/overview.html.

co-construction, even when I am "only" the listener. Most importantly, the story is heard and honored.

Most of the people I interviewed for this project began by telling me they had lived "ordinary" lives and did not think they had anything particularly important or interesting to say. Once I turned on the recorder and asked them to tell me something about their birth and the circumstances of their growing up, the stories flowed unselfconsciously.

A wonderful moment for me is when, at the end of an interview, I put my headphones on the person I interviewed to allow the narrator to hear what has transpired. At first there is the silence of intense listening, and then, inevitably, a broad smile appears. Many of the people I interviewed have never heard their own voices on a recording, and there is the recognition that yes, perhaps that individual's story is worth telling and preserving after all.

Narrative, with its capacity for meaning making, brings significance to the experience of both the narrator and the listener. It provides us a lens through which to understand the subjective experience of aging. Telling one's story is a means of structuring the memories that make up the lifetime of an individual and the history of a community.

Planning a Storytelling Event

When I first thought about doing an oral history project at the Covello Center, I envisioned an informal storytelling event would eventually take place in the community room of the center. When I mentioned this idea to the director of the Burden Center, the parent organization of the Covello Center, I received an enthusiastic response.

I met with Funmilayo Brown, director of development, and Amadeus Alonzo, the health and wellness coordinator. Funmilayo began the meeting by asking, "What, who, how, where, when?" The discussion around these questions required a careful examination of the purpose of the project and planted the seed for a larger, long-range project. Answering these five simple questions proved to be more complicated than I had imagined. Setting the parameters for the type of event was the first order of business. I had not thought about how many participants there would be, nor how the program would be organized. Funmilayo suggested we have no more than six participants, and that I create a storyline, so the narration would flow seamlessly from one topic to another. We discussed how long each narrator would have to speak and what kinds of questions I would ask. We decided that narrators would be asked in advance to bring photos to illustrate their stories. These photos would be projected on a screen during the event. The event would be filmed and become part of the archive at the Carter Burden Center. And, of course, there would be music and food!

The next subject for discussion was the audience. Who would be invited and how many people? Funmilayo suggested we start with a smaller event—friends and family of the narrators—because, as she pointed out, the narrators may never have spoken in front of an audience before. Provided that the event is a success, she would then like to repeat it for a wider public, by "taking the show on the road" and bringing it into the community. I suggested going into the public schools, as Covello has a program in which school kids come and help out at the center. She was enthusiastic, and we agreed that fifth graders are an ideal age for such a program. She said she would invite the city councilwoman for the district, who has been a great supporter of Covello, but not the press, for the same reason that she did not want a bigger audience. As we brainstormed, I suggested I could teach the kids how to do interviews, and they could interview older people. The meeting opened my eyes to the complexities of organizing an oral history event, but we all felt excited about moving forward with this project. We are calling the event *Resiliencia!*, the Spanish word for "resilience."

Postscript

The Resiliencia! event took place in August 2015. There was a full audience, made up of members of the Covello Center and friends and family of the speakers. Because many of the members of the audience were native Spanish speakers, one of the participants volunteered to translate the responses into Spanish. When the event was over, several audience members expressed a desire to be interviewed. The project is currently planning another event through a partnership with the Covello Center and neighboring public schools.

DREAMERS TESTIMONIANDO

SHELBY PASELL

As a student at the University of Pittsburgh, Shelby Pasell became interested in testimonio through her Latin American literature classes. According to Shelby, this genre of storytelling "is an urgent act to re-center the narrator as a person of authority and change the situation being exposed." Shelby's field study explores testimonio and oral history through the lens of immigration, as she reflects on the process of collecting and sharing the stories of undocumented college students in Minnesota. Her oral history project sheds light on power, privilege, and agency, not just from her perspective but from those of the project's narrators as well. These themes resonate throughout the chapter in the interactions between project participants as well as reflect on how genuine social change is possible within the sometimes-contradictory world of "the academy."

Excerpts from "DREAMers Testimoniando"

It's not over, but definitely great things are happening in Minnesota, and it feels good that it's happening in my own home state, and that I was part of the movements in one way or another. When the Prosperity Act was making progress, I attended a lot of events and spoke about my story in public places.[1] I don't know how people reacted

---

1. Minnesota's Prosperity Act went into effect in July 2013. This legislation made undocumented students eligible to receive resident tuition as long as they met the state's requirements.

after hearing my story, but it felt good to know that they could put a face to the issue, instead of people rejecting immigration reform just because they don't believe that those "illegals" can or should have the right to citizenship.

—Irma

I'd get out of the shower, and the first thing I'd do was put on my shoes in case I had to run. In the back of my head, there was always the thought that something could happen that could chase me away. My parents did a good job, which is kinda ironic now that I'm sharing this . . . but they did a good job of saying don't tell people that you are . . . you don't know who's out there and what they might want to do, and it's just not something they need to know. So I grew up with a secret that I guess a lot of people have experienced.

—Gus

In college I relate to people from different countries, they kinda know where I came from. Some of the Hispanics are not documented, and they talk about it like it's not a big deal around me, so I feel like I belong there with them, but they don't know about my stories, I keep my things personal. When they tell about it I'm like, "Oh yeah, that must be disappointing." I don't tell them, "I know how you feel." Now with Mexican jokes or stereotypes, I don't take them to the heart, but when I was younger I actually did. That's why I didn't want to show any side of my coming from Mexico and being undocumented, because most of the kids in middle school would say, "Did you cross the border?" That was a topic in geography class; they talked and showed a videotape about building a border between Mexico and the United States. Then one kid behind me, he'd be like, "That's probably how you came through," and stuff like that. So for me I've been hiding that, because in the area where I'm from . . . not anyone is like that.

—Norma

I had heard from other people who had gone on to college that a lot of people have these assumptions about you. That if you look brown, you might be foreign, you might be studying abroad or you might need a little bit of extra support. That kind of stuff. Or they don't feel they can have the same conversations with you as they would have with their peers. So I guess I was a little bit prepared for it. There are some students who are willing to talk to a minority in class to work on an assignment, but if you go out of the class, it's a little bit different, it's just like a "hello, goodbye" thing. Trying to engage in a conversation about, you know, why is the grass green? You don't have something going on like that. That's kinda upsetting to me, but at the same time, it's kinda cool, it's just another challenge. I've tried talking to some people and it hasn't gone so well. But with the people that I have come to be more connected with, it's really rewarding for me.

—Oscar

Getting Started

I spent the summer of 2013 carrying my voice recorder around the Twin Cities to have conversations with four undocumented college students and graduates. Meanwhile, in buildings very separate from the coffee shops, academic buildings, and gyms we were meeting in, decisions were being made that would change their experiences. Deferred Action for Childhood Arrivals (DACA) was celebrating its first anniversary, and the Prosperity Act (a state-level DREAM Act) was passing in Minnesota.[2] What wasn't changing was the decade-old stagnancy on a national

---

2. The DREAM Act, a bipartisan piece of legislation introduced in 2001, was intended to give undocumented immigrants who were brought to the United States as children (known as "DREAMers") access to higher education, financial aid, and ultimately, a pathway to citizenship. DACA, an executive order signed by President Obama in June 2012, gave the DREAMers nonpermanent legal status and access to work permits. In September 2017, President Trump rescinded the program, deeming it unconstitutional

DREAM Act that would create a path to citizenship for undocumented children who were brought to the United States by their parents. In the midst of all this, we compiled a collection of their stories.

One day that summer, I pulled up to the curb of an Augsburg College academic building in Minneapolis and waited for Oscar to come out from his scholarship meeting. I caught his eye and waved him over to the car, noting that once again he had outdressed me. He considered our meetings professional engagements, often sporting a tie and using formal language to confirm our meeting times. I was more likely to wear jean shorts and communicate with the help of smile emojis. As he got into the car, I felt a bit embarrassed to be picking him up in my mom's luxury-brand SUV and clarified immediately that it wasn't mine. En route we talked about the upcoming year: we were both gearing up for the fall, he with scholarship meetings and I with meetings like the one we were about to have to talk about my undergraduate thesis. After stopping for lunch we drove to the beach, where I laid out a blanket and watched the lake while he read, for the first time, his testimonio alongside the others in the collection I was compiling.

I start with a story like this not because it was exceptional but because it was ordinary. As an undergraduate I compiled a work of testimonio as my bachelor of philosophy (BPhil) thesis in nonfiction writing, Spanish, and global studies. At the University of Pittsburgh, a BPhil isn't related to the field of philosophy but rather focuses on one or more other disciplines, and it is an honors degree that requires the student to complete master's level work as an undergraduate. I embarked on a collaborative project with four immigrant college students and graduates (Irma, Gus, Norma, and Oscar) in Minnesota, where I grew up. I chose to use testimonio after learning about the genre in my Latin American literature classes. Testimonio is a literary genre defined by scholar John Beverly as a "narrative told in the first person by a narrator who is also the real-life

---

and leaving it to Congress to pass new legislation, which has created widespread uncertainty about the future of the DACA program and for DREAMers around the country.

protagonist or witness of the events he or she recounts."[3] Most testimonio is the product of collaboration between a narrator (usually someone who has witnessed a form of oppression) and a compiler (usually an "intellectual" and part of the privileged class). As a genre, it self-consciously attempts to project the personal as the political. Rather than attempting to entertain or simply inform the reader, testimonio is an urgent attempt to re-center the narrator as a person of authority and change the unjust situation being exposed. When successful, it enlists a coalition of nonprofits, universities, advocacy groups, and other entities to combat the injustices presented in the text. Because the work functions as a call to action rather than biography, the narrator shares with the public only what they deem important to the cause, and only what feels empowering rather than exploitative. At the end of the genre's most famous example, *Me llamo Rigoberta Menchú y así me nació de conciencia*, narrator Rigoberta Menchú states: "I'm still keeping secret what I think no one should know. Not even anthropologists or intellectuals, no matter how many books they have, can find out all our secrets."[4]

As testimonio has gained popularity, its definition has broadened, as has the conversation surrounding what defines the "privileged class." Chicana writers have adopted the genre even when they occupy positions of moderate status within the university and society, with one scholar arguing, "A group identity and group marginalization continues to exist in academia even when we have attained a relatively privileged status."[5] In our collaboration, the narrators and I held similar positions of power

---

3. John Beverley, *Through All Things Modern: Second Thoughts on Testimonio* (Durham, NC: Duke University Press, 1991), 1.

4. Literal translation: "My name is Rigoberta Menchú and this is how my consciousness was raised." The book was published in English under the name *I, Rigoberta Menchú: An Indian Woman in Guatemala*. Rigoberta Menchú and Elisabeth Burgos-Debray, *Me llamo Rigoberta Menchú y así me nació de conciencia* (Havana, Cuba: Casa de las Américas, 1983).

5. Dolores Delgado Bernal, Rebeca Burciaga, and Judith Flores Carmona, "Chicana/Latina *Testimonios*: Mapping the Methodological, Pedagogical, and Political," *Equity & Excellence in Education* 45, no. 3 (2012): 363–72, www.tandfonline.com/doi/full/10.1080/10665684.2012.698149.

within the academic world. Irma, who is involved in activism and speaks authoritatively on the subject, had already completed her own thesis on the gay rights movement and its connection to the immigrant rights struggle. Still, my possession of a social security number could not be ignored as an identifier of difference.

For me, immigration was a macro-political issue that needed widespread change. For the narrators, their difference manifested in small, everyday instances of going to the doctor, faking knowledge of the financial aid process, or applying for jobs. I was confident that their experiences would lead them to be invested in politics, but that was only true for one narrator, Irma. It shocked me to learn that some narrators didn't know names of prominent politicians or that a Minnesota Dream Act was being passed. I approached the project as an urgent testament to the need for immigration reform. Over the course of the research, I realized the process of *testimoniando*—the "-ing," gerund form of *testimonio*—was more important than the completed product. The collection is an urgent call, particularly in its mission to foster dialogue and solidarity among DREAMers and allies. I share my experience with testimonio here by giving one small example of how we faced the process.

Building Interview Routines

Working with four different people meant that in the summer of 2013, when the bulk of the collaboration took place, I fell into four different routines with their own meeting locations. With Irma there was a place that served good coffee in downtown Minneapolis near her office. For Norma, it was easiest to meet at the Life Time Fitness where she worked out. Gus preferred my apartment or his, usually late nights, usually involving food. Oscar and I explored the city, learning we shared a favorite taco shop on Lake Street. After getting over the initial jitters of our introductions, I looked forward to the meetings just as I would look forward to seeing a friend. Our conversations were generally comfortable, and I left feeling energized and happy. It may seem like I'm describing my social life rather than my work life, and it's true that I often didn't see much difference between the two (not counting, of course, the hours spent transcribing hundreds of pages of interviews). I share this not as an advertisement for oral history, to describe it as "work that won't feel like work," but as a subtle warning, because beyond the pleasures of friendly meetings with interviewees, this field of work offers serious challenges. There is nothing straightforward, efficient, or predictable about oral history. Before entering a project in this field, I had to let go of all expectations and be prepared to let the process shape both my final publication and my own understanding.

At the end of one meeting, Oscar pointed out that I knew "almost everything about [him]," but he knew almost nothing about me. He asked if we could switch roles, which I agreed to do. He was able to stump me with his first question: "I still don't really get it. Why are you doing this project, why do you care about this?" I struggled through an answer for him, though I didn't feel satisfied with it, and I'm sure he didn't either. How did a fourth-generation white American from a comfortable suburb of the Twin Cities become interested in the lives of undocumented college students?

It was a valid question, especially considering that when I arrived to the University of Pittsburgh as a freshman I didn't know what the DREAM Act was or what it meant to be undocumented. Then one night, friends took me to a meeting run by Jóvenes Sin Nombres (JSN), a student-immigrant art collective / activist organization. We talked about the mural the group had just completed, made plans for future projects, and asked immigrant members to share stories of discrimination or frustration. One female member told us about a time someone asked her why she bothered going to school when she was "just going to be a maid anyway." On the way home I had to ask my friend what the DREAM Act was. He explained it to me on the most basic level: many children are brought to the United States when they are very young and grow up undocumented without any say in the matter. They attend American schools and contribute to their American communities and neighborhoods. When it comes time to consider college, though, their situation is very different than that of their citizen counterparts. If they lived in a state where getting accepted to college was even a possibility, there would be no in-state tuition available to them, no financial aid, and very limited job opportunities even if they were to graduate. As Gus put it, it's "really difficult to explain to someone that I'm a mechanical engineer with a degree from the University of Minnesota who's bilingual, who's been a straight-A student the majority of my life, and can't get a good job." Their hands are tied—they could go "home" to a country they likely haven't seen since childhood and start over with a ten-year ban on entering the United States, or they can stay in the United States and hope they find some sort of opportunity. The DREAM Act, introduced over a decade ago, would give these young people—"DREAMers"—access to higher education and financial aid, and after two years in school or the military, a pathway to citizenship. It has yet to pass, though President Obama's DACA order made small progress by giving the DREAMers nonpermanent legal status and access to work permits. Just a few hours after leaving that first JSN meeting, I began my four-year membership.

It's hard to pinpoint what kept me going back to JSN meetings. I can't say that new friendships and pizza weren't part of it, but I can say that the lofty thoughts and conversations I had been having about equality and opportunity felt concrete in the work JSN was doing. JSN was an outlet for me to work actively for justice—which before then had usually seemed abstract and unattainable—in ways that fit my talents: art and community building. Together they had painted the first Latino mural in Pittsburgh. When I joined, we began work on an experimental short documentary about the experience of being undocumented in the United States. We spent endless Saturday nights in the computer lab, working up to the last minute before premiering our work at the Carnegie Mellon Faces of Migration film festival. I became passionate about the immigration debate in the United States, and the summer after my sophomore year I worked for a pro-immigrant think tank in Washington, DC. Though the issue was important to me, I felt the office work was disconnected from the movement, and I went back to school with a desire to work with DREAMers directly. Through JSN, I connected with Dr. Marco Gemignani, who ran a psychological clinic for Spanish speakers at Duquesne University. Over coffee, he told me about a patient who wrote letters to lawmakers that she never sent, and about the importance he saw in such actions. I don't know why she chose to keep her letters to herself, but Dr. Gemignani felt that the writing itself was a claim to agency, even without a recipient. From that conversation and many others, I decided that my best way to work for the cause I believed in was to create a space for DREAMers to speak and an outlet through which academics and policymakers could learn from what they had to say.

The criteria for participants were minimal: I was looking for college students or graduates in Minnesota and hoped to have an equal representation of men and women. Through NAVIGATE, an organization dedicated to building power in the Latinx community in the state of Minnesota, I put out a call to participants, one person responded to the call, and the others I met more organically, mostly through mutual connections. I benefited from the small-community feel of my home state, usually finding a mutual acquaintance with each participant, which helped ease some of the stress of a stranger asking about a very controversial topic. One of the narrators was a friend, but we had never before discussed their immigration status. Some had shared their stories through other mediums, and others hadn't told even their closest friends. I often worried that the project was just an added stress to the already-busy lives of the narrators, so I was careful to be very casual about time frames and accommodating when they had to cancel. In many ways I felt like I was asking for a lot and giving nothing in return, but they had volunteered to participate and never complained about the time it required, for which I was grateful.

I connected with the narrators through emails or phone conversation before interviewing them. In most cases, the initial interview was our first face-to-face meeting. We followed a loose process spanning two interviews, prefaced with instructions to speak in whichever language they felt most comfortable. Only one interview happened in Spanish—to provide privacy from housemates in the next room—so very little translation was involved in this project. For the first meeting I had prepared an interview guide with standard questions, though admittedly I sometimes veered from that and, for instance, asked Norma about the best places to salsa, or Oscar which Spanish soccer team he cheered for, or I simply posed follow-up questions when it seemed natural. As much as possible, I tried to ask questions the same way I would if there were no oral history project or audio recording, and I made a point to follow my own genuine interest and to linger on topics that seemed to produce more candid or excited responses from the narrators.

It may have created a more "professional" feeling if I had met all the narrators in the same place, with the same amount of privacy, but being flexible about location was the only way to make the meetings possible. Only one narrator had a driver's license, so being able to drive them or meet them where they already were spared them long bus or bike commutes. I saw this as a positive aspect of the project; for example, picking up Irma from work meant that we got to talk about common interests (which sometimes included me asking for career advice) before getting into the interviews, which she approached very formally. I was asking difficult questions, and anything to diminish the discomfort helped. Since I myself was a twenty-one-year-old undergraduate, Irma, Gus, Norma, and Oscar were more like peers than research subjects.

Conducting the Interviews

Though I started each interview feeling nervous, as I'm sure they did, eventually narrators and I would settle into a more conversational mode, and I would stop thinking so much about the questions I had hoped to ask, letting their answers naturally guide the flow to topics they felt were relevant. Sometimes this worked great, like the time I paused and Oscar chimed in, "How about I tell you something else?," or the time Gus had me resume recording at the end of our first interview so he could tell me a story. Of course, the unpredictability would lead to frustration, too; sometimes the questions I thought would be most provocative would fall flat, and other times we'd veer so far off topic that it was hard to get back. It was difficult to reconcile my desire to get specific questions answered with my desire to have the narrators determine the themes and focus of their story. I found the best way to handle this was to let the conversations happen as organically as possible, then go back and identify recurring themes. Norma and Gus consistently brought up their family's importance. Norma repeatedly said things like "A lot of my motivation comes from my parents. . . . I want to help my parents when I can so they can have a better future. I want to give them something small for the incredible amount they've done for me."

Oscar focused on his culture, and the responsibility immigrants and Latinos have to each other and themselves:

> Culture is my way to understand who I am, on top of some science-y stuff. . . . If I want to work in medicine, I'm going to be working with people who identify me with their own ethnic group. If they come into the hospital and tell me something in Spanish, tell me something they miss about Ecuador, if I'm not able to have a conversation about that, I feel that I'm failing them as a doctor and as a person of their ethnic group. I don't like to fail a lot.

By identifying and tallying references to themes such as these, I hoped to counteract some of the authority that stemmed from my creating the questions.

What was sometimes difficult was that our project required a level of intimacy, and intimacy takes time. The first time I talked to each narrator yielded much less material for the final product than the second, as at that point we just weren't as comfortable with each other. In an ideal situation I would have spent even more time developing relationships with each of them. As it was, I began with the basics and moved toward the more personal. I tried not to bring up their undocumented status until late in the first interview. Some of the participants never said the word at all, replacing it with references to their "situation" or wordy phrases like "I wasn't able to tell them something really important about myself." Though I wanted to feel and show that we were equals, there were moments that made it impossible to ignore the great gap between our experiences. All of them brought up their desire to travel, and I listened knowing about my study-abroad semester and other trips. I drove them home after listening to their reasons for not having a license. No matter how friendly we were, I couldn't erase my privilege or do anything to shrink the gap. Oscar told me a story about how a white male approached a group of minority students talking about their experiences, asking if he could join them. The group politely declined, telling him it would change the dynamic. Listening to that story, I found it hard not to wonder what gave me the right to ask the questions I was asking. The only answer I could give myself was that it was important for other conversations to happen solely between them and other immigrants, but that this didn't invalidate the importance of what we were doing. My conversations with the narrators created a different dynamic: it was important that I listen as an outsider and that we form our own kind of communion.

My desire to create intimacy sometimes clashed with how the narrators wanted to be represented in their testimonios. At the beginning of one second interview, I chose to turn the recorder off so that we could privately talk about how different they became when we were recording. I then turned it back on, saying, "I'm going to record what you're saying, but don't worry about it," referring to the recorder. The narrator responded, "Okay, I am going to worry about it. Do you want me to just talk to you?" So I turned the recording back off and we had a discussion about tone and how they wanted to come across versus what our unrecorded conversations sounded like.

It wasn't fair for me to ask my participants to be completely candid when it was their own reputation we were dealing with. Norma was straightforward about her editorial choices: "I dunno if I'd be comfortable with my friends reading it, but I'm sure it would be fine, as long as it doesn't have so much intimacy, which I haven't said . . . personal stuff. I have said a lot of what I've felt, and what has happened throughout my life, which I don't think is wrong, and nothing embarrassing. It's real stuff. Real deal. Everyone goes through something." In many ways this attitude mirrors Menchú's statement on the narrator keeping certain things secret from the interviewer and the reader. Irma, who was used to talking about her experience, often connected personal stories to her political beliefs, which yielded a more formal testimonio: "I hit my breaking point in January 2010 when I found out that I couldn't be in the nursing program. . . . So that's when I became more political about it; that's when I took my frustration into telling people to be more organized about it, telling people to care about the DREAM Act, putting my story and truth out there so that others knew my struggle."

As much as friendliness helped make the process more comfortable, these choices on the part of the narrators were important to the mission of the testimonios. Had our interviews been purely conversational, it would have been more difficult to identify what message each narrator wanted to get across. With my focus on building intimacy and their focus on being purposeful about what they shared, I think we achieved the necessary balance.

That being said, anxiety was an inevitable part of the process. In Gus's case, recognizing his own anxiety forced him to adjust how he shared his story in the second interview. At one moment near the end of his first interview he had talked about his parents and their achievements: "Holy shit, my parents, coming from nothing, got us a house. Yeah, it's awesome." When we read this quote together at the beginning of the second interview (I always brought the transcript of the first interview to the second interview so the participants could also give input on what was missing), he pointed out that he hadn't sworn at all during the rest of the interview, because he had been trying to keep things "buttoned up," but this part felt more powerful because he had let go. Then he told me, "I think if we were to redo this interview, which I'm sorry because it would be a lot more work, but I would stop trying to be so, I guess, scholarly with my answers." We proceeded to look through his previous answers and think about what was missing. In the first interview he explained picking engineering in practical terms, because of his skill set, but in the second he added that people respected engineering and recognized its difficulty. He said that probably subconsciously affected his decision: "It's pretty cool to say, 'Look at where I came from and look at the degree I have.'" In the second interview we added depth to our conversation. The same developments, though less explicit, happened with each narrator as we became more comfortable with each other and with the recorder.

Putting It on Paper

I transcribed all of the interviews verbatim, and the next step was to take what averaged around a hundred pages of transcribed interview per narrator and convert it into a readable written document. This meant shortening it drastically, to around fifteen pages. The process was a bit different for each narrator, but I followed certain principles for all of them. I did not grammatically correct or "standardize" the sentences, meaning not all four testimonios read the same, though I made modifications, specifically to aid in transitions. I identified the themes that recurred throughout one narrator's interview and shaped the narrative around those that were most prominent. Irma repeatedly returned to politics, Norma and Gus to the importance of their families, Oscar to his community's successes and challenges. It was important to me to eliminate moments where the narrator seemed particularly guarded. If they wanted to keep certain information private, I tried to respect that boundary. For example, there was a topic one narrator was always very guarded about. In the interviews, I pushed a bit and got some answers that could have aided the testimonio. During that conversation they told me directly that they didn't see the relevance of my questions, at which point I immediately changed the subject, disappointed but mostly uncomfortable with the knowledge that I had pushed too far. In the editing process this led me to skip the subject all together. Some of my questions were ineffective—either unclear or irrelevant. I removed attempted answers to these as well. The process of compiling the narratives often felt like completing a puzzle: searching for the pieces that fit together to create a whole that I hoped would be satisfying to both the narrators and future readers.

Once I completed the drafts of the testimonios, I met with the narrators again so that they could edit them. I told each of them that in order to ensure that the final product was something they were happy with, they should consider themselves my boss; that was the only appropriate

approach at this point in the project. They each approached this part of
the process in a different way. Irma, Gus, and Norma took to marking
up their pages with grammatical edits and sentence rewrites—moving
their drafts in a more polished direction. Oscar made his edits verbally
(telling me which parts could be left out or which should be added) but
didn't want to correct his language. He felt it was more authentic to stay
with his original phrasing.

Questions about the ethics of fact-checking in testimonio have stirred
debate, which grew more heated after statements were found to be false
in *Me llamo Rigoberta Menchú*. I chose not to fact-check anything my narrators said. Taking on the role of "verifying" what the narrators said would
have worked against their authority over the project. Still, narrators ad-
justed some facts in the editing phase. In one moment, Gus called his
dad to clear up a date and found his original statement had been off by a
few years. Such mistakes are to be expected in any project dealing with
people's memories.

I then edited the final drafts to fit what the narrators wanted. It was
important to me to make every effort for it not to feel like I was taking
their story and making it fit my expectations. The project was meant to
highlight their own agency, and prioritizing my literary ideals wouldn't
have aided in that. The project could only be successful if it represented
the narrators in a way they felt was right. I wanted them to keep control
over their final product and feel proud of what they had said, especially
since some of them had never talked about these things before.

Finally, each narrator read all four testimonios and shared their reactions with me. Though I took vigorous notes during these conversations, I chose not to record them, so that we could be more candid and
informal. I had learned through the process that although the recorder
is invaluable, some of the narrators vastly change their speaking styles
the minute it is turned on, and I wanted to prevent that from happening
in their reactions. My favorite example of this was when Irma, midway
through reading Gus's testimonio, looked up at me and laughed, ex-
claiming, "He's just fucking swearing!"

All of the narrators had spoken of their isolation in their interviews, and in reading each other's stories they all stopped to note the similarities: Irma had given the same reason that Gus gave for not having a driver's license (that they were caught driving without one and had to wait until they were eighteen), soccer had been important for Oscar and Gus both, and they all noted that they were the oldest siblings in their families. They were also quick to point out their differences. Gus and Oscar both felt that, though there were many similarities between them, the other had a more privileged situation. Gus envied Oscar's connection to other Latinos and felt he had a great advantage over the other three, who were raised in Anglo communities. Oscar felt that Gus's Catholic school education was a great advantage. Both were adamant that the other was lucky, and both were right.

It was also revealing how the narrators responded in different ways to each other's stories. For instance, in Gus's story he recounts the moment he interviewed at MIT, and how upon learning he's undocumented, the faculty member expressed surprise, "Really? And you speak English?" This angered Irma and Oscar in a way it hadn't Gus: both stopped reading and commented to me about how terrible that person was. For Gus, the person was an ally. He was angered, conversely, that Irma stated she wasn't interested in interacting with people who didn't care about immigration. He told me, "I have friends who say 'Fuck illegals.'"

All of them pointed out the importance of having parents who encouraged and pushed them, and they noted it as a common theme in each other's stories. They also placed themselves on a continuum of experiences: Gus felt tied very closely to Norma. Irma saw Norma as a representative of where she was a few years ago. Oscar pointed out that he was the youngest and said reading the other stories felt like going through a time machine. "This is just motivating me even more!" he added.

Oral History as Collaboration

For me, the collaborative work on the project was the most rewarding and the most natural. It wasn't my plan to create the informal atmosphere; I just didn't imagine being able to do it any other way.

What I should have anticipated, but didn't, was how much the narrators would shift the goals of the collection. When I began this testimonio project, I wanted the written final project to provide an argument for a change in US immigration law. Over the summer, I realized that the process itself was the value of compiling oral histories. Policy was not an explicit interest of most of the narrators: some were only vaguely aware during our interviews of the ongoing political changes for DREAMers. What *did* capture their interest was the prospect of no longer being overlooked or disregarded. "Until now, nobody has interviewed me to hear my story," Norma told me in our second interview. Later she added a story of when she told her friend about her experiences in school and how that helped him to face his own situation. She also recognized the parallels between that moment and what we were doing with the project: "Without having any idea, just telling him my story, he said I helped him understand that he wasn't the only one like this, that's different. I know that there are other people who feel low, or bad about themselves, so I would like to tell them that yes they can do it, to have faith and a positive attitude."

At the end of each interview I asked if they had a message for the reader or if there was anything they wanted the reader to know. I had assumed they direct their messages to politicians, or people who were against immigration reform, but all four of them spoke to DREAMers or other people going through difficult situations:

> **Irma:** It's a message to other DREAMers out there; I hope that other DREAMers have the patience to heal from all of the experiences that we've had.

> **Gus:** That's a loaded question especially when you ask someone like me. . . . I think regardless of your situation, just don't stop. Here's the big thing, because even I did this to myself: don't make excuses

and place barriers in front of you. A lot of times you are your biggest obstacle. And you need to make sure that doesn't happen.

Norma: Never, never stop looking to the top of the stairs, to see what is there that you can't see from the bottom. Not having a document or residency stops you. I felt invisible, I felt like I wasn't part of any culture, even though I was in the United States. I didn't feel like I was part of the US, but little by little, looking at the gifts I've been given (like permission to work), that's something. So I would like to say: don't stop having the faith that you can study, travel, or whatever it is.

Oscar: I would say one word: *nova*. Many people don't even know what the definition of that is. It's a star that all of the sudden projects a lot of light, and then the light just kinda fades away. The star goes back to its original brightness. . . . So get full of yourself sometimes, but then remember you're not all that. At the end of this whole life, we're all the same. Remember your roots, and don't get too full of yourself. Just nova, nova.

These answers were especially powerful knowing that none of the speakers had a strong group of DREAMer friends, even if they were involved in politics. When they read each other's stories and when they made these statements, I saw just how isolating their experiences had been and how important it was for them to feel solidarity.

I had been sure that to "be political" meant to influence local and national politics directly, to affect the larger system. The responses of the narrators gave me a much more localized view. Hearing the narrators' responses to each other's stories, as well as to their own, helped me to realize that the political power of this work was present in the process, perhaps more so than in the product. The political change happened within our interactions: in the telling of their stories and their experiencing and commenting upon the stories of their peers. This fit with how I witnessed each narrator defining political power in their own experiences. Each of them had a role model who changed their lives in much more explicit and arguably important ways than a politician could, as well as supportive parents who stressed the importance of education. More than arguing for national policy changes, their stories represent the importance of individuals in a person's life and the importance of sharing one's experience—the importance of feeling heard.

There were practical reasons for the shift to a more localized focus as well. Originally the project was to be a collaboration with NAVIGATE. The plan was for student members to design a book that would include segments from the testimonios (as well as other new testimonios), undocumented artwork, and letters from prominent Minnesota leaders. It was to be published and sold only in Minnesota as a tool for educating the wider community while raising funds for scholarships. I was excited about our plan for statewide circulation of these stories, as was the founder of NAVIGATE. However, it couldn't be successful if I, someone outside of the DREAMer community, was the main force behind the project. The students, slammed with school, work, and familial obligations, didn't have the capacity to complete the book at the time, though we haven't given up on it as a future project.

Fortunately, I found some timely wisdom on collaborating with community participants in Paula Mathieu's *Tactics of Hope*, a book I read while serving as an undergraduate teaching assistant in a service learning course. Mathieu showed me it is best for an academic to purposefully plan for their own work timeline to be separate from their collaborators' efforts. In the book, Mathieu talks about the problems that come with pushing an academic calendar onto community organizations, and how that often leads not only to an incomplete project for the student but also to unwarranted stress on the organization. My challenge, then, was to design a project to be fully collaborative without transferring pressure to the participants. For me, the answer was to work on in a one-on-one capacity with only four people. I started conceptualizing my project as a sophomore, set up the logistics throughout my junior year (including a time-consuming Institutional Review Board approval), took the following summer, spanning four months, to do the collaborative work, and finished writing and defended my thesis the fall semester of senior year. On paper this looks like a long time, but it felt short, and I would have been better off allowing myself more time. The community-produced book still hasn't been completed, meaning that the stories I collected have yet to see widespread circulation. The experience of working collaboratively, however, helped me to understand that this does not equate to failure.

Through this project I learned the importance of redefining political power, even on a small scale. That became more clear when I realized how often such shifts in power are at odds with the academy's view. Not only do oral history projects challenge the often-strict timelines of semesters; they call into question the definition of academic authority. That was most evident in the time leading up to my thesis defense. For my particular type of thesis (for a bachelor of philosophy degree), I was to invite an outside examiner to sit on my defense board. The university would cover that professor's travel expenses and facilitate a lecture during their visit. I had been working closely with Dr. Gemignani from Duquesne University, and he was to sit on my board and have his related expenses covered. Seeing an opportunity, I wrote a letter asking if instead of bringing in a faculty member, we could facilitate a lecture by one of the narrators in my collection. I was sure that this would be a beautiful way to exemplify the power shift that we hope to create with oral history, but the university did not agree. In a brief, formal email, I was reminded that the funds were for committee members, not "guest speakers," and was told that my suggestion would not be fiscally responsible. Though there is nothing untrue or extreme about this answer, it captured what frustrated me—that, even in approving my project, the university was unable to view my narrators as voices of authority qualified to lecture on campus.

Of course I had much support from within the academy as well, most notably from my advisor, Shalini Puri, who wrote in her own work that "the object of scholarship cannot merely be to be right."[6] Instead, it is

---

6. Shalini Puri, "Finding the Field: Notes on Caribbean Cultural Criticism, Area Studies, and the Forms of Engagement," *Small Axe* 17, no. 2 (2013): 58–73, https://read.dukeupress.edu/small-axe/article-abstract/17/2%20(41)/58/98925/Finding-the-Field-Notes-on-Caribbean-Cultural.

important to consider why academic scholarship is being produced and who it is serving. Rather than using the perspectives of the narrators to support my preconceived argument, I recognized the need to let their goals reshape the collection. In many ways, the narrators' focus on other DREAMers fit the traditional goals of testimonio: the work gives authority to those who bear witness. People in power can learn from it, but the goal is not to entertain them or pander to their interest.

At the end of our last conversation, I asked Gus what he thought the collection meant as a whole. He said, "We're all saying it can be done. There have been struggles and difficulties, but at the end of the day they didn't stop us." His answer was related to the narrators' experiences as undocumented students in the United States, but I think it also fits the experience of this project. Oral history projects bombard us with new ethical questions and logistical challenges. It is important that we continue to say that those difficulties did not and will not stop us. From the perspective of the researcher, it is easy to downplay the importance of such work. I often find myself claiming to have done nothing. All I did was listen. Irma reminded me the importance of engaging in dialogue:

> I would encourage DREAMers to try to heal themselves first, and one way of doing that would be to tell your story to people. For a long time you're hidden, in many ways it's like you're living but you're not, because people don't really know you. For me, more than being in and wanting to be in the movement, it got to the point where I needed to take care of my mental state. Starting to come out really helped heal all the baggage that comes with being undocumented, so I would tell DREAMers to start there. . . .
>
> I was so ashamed and embarrassed, but now it's one of the first things I say when I meet someone. In many ways it's like I'm reclaiming it, I'm proud about it. And I would say to people like my brother, who are still coming out of that negative place, that I know you're really scared, but if you ever want to not be afraid, we need to tell our stories. If we don't, nothing will be possible for us.

TALES OF TAR SANDS RESISTANCE: VOICES FROM THE TEXAS FRONT LINES

STEPHANIE G. THOMAS

As a relative newcomer to oral history, Stephanie Thomas was curious to use the process as a means to explore the connections between storytelling, social justice, and civic engagement. Her project focuses on the southern section of the Keystone XL pipeline, which has already been constructed and is widely contested, especially in East Texas, where many of the interviews for this project took place. In this field study, Stephanie reflects on her unique "insider/outsider" status as both a former member of the oil and gas industry and a committed activist. She also articulates her initial discomfort about "talking to strangers" and how, ultimately, Tales of Tar Sands Resistance served as a powerful tool for building empathy and community, helping to expand her own definition of "resistance."

Excerpt from "Tales of Tar Sands Resistance"

As far as I know, I was the first person in the United States to be tasered while locked down.[1] Pepper spraying people who are locked down is actually fairly common, but tasering is not. For one thing, it was not physically possible for me to detach myself while they were

---

1. A "lockdown" is a form of protest where activists literally lock themselves to equipment to prevent or stall construction or destruction.

209

tasering me. I didn't have the physical control to do it. It's purely a torture item. One police officer said to me, "I'm going to inflict enough pain and cause enough fear that you will choose to do what I want once I stop doing it." The other disturbing thing was that once I was released, the police officer wanted to tell me how well I had "taken" the taser. I wonder if it was a machismo thing. He offered to show me tapes they had of other people being tasered who didn't take it so well so I can see how well I handled it instead—it really underlined the barbarism of the whole thing.

I'd never locked down before. I went up to Wood County with some cash on hand to be ready for bail if that's how things worked out. I met with some of the other people and had a good rapport with Rain Bebe,[2] whom I'd met just that night before. We did some role-play together and got along. We both think protesting the KXL is really important and stopping its construction is worth taking risks for. So we went.

At this point, the construction had come literally right up to the tree sit where eight people sat in an encampment in the trees on an East Texas property.[3] It was a really pressing issue because Trans-Canada was getting to the point where it would soon be potentially endangering people's lives with their machinery.[4] So you have Trans-Canada and its hired police officers starting to go into the territory where the blockade was active, starting to have some real impact.

So Rain and I, with a support crew, went up there and flagged the thing down. The guy immediately stopped his engine. We had a pipe that we tried to stick into the treads and we ended up putting the pipe through the backhoe's hydraulic arm. I just stood there with my arm in it while Rain got to sit on one side of the backhoe.

---

2. A noted KXL activist.

3. A "tree sit" is a form of protest where activists sit in trees, usually on constructed platforms.

4. TransCanada is a Canada-based pipeline company that is building and operating the Keystone XL pipeline.

Once we got to that point is when the operator got really upset, once he realized that we actually could lock down. He tried to shove Rain off and he tried to shove me, which didn't work very well because I'm a really big guy. I just reached over his head and put the pipe through the backhoe and locked on.

Everything was relatively calm at first. There were some attempts to taunt us from the workers who stopped working and started watching us, and then after a couple hours, more and more senior TransCanada people kept showing up and started recording us. Then the police showed up and immediately tried to arrest and detain our support crew without even saying anything. Then the cops came and started, at first, gently harassing us, and then they progressively became more aggressive. But still, not physical. And then, they start . . . and I tell them, this is a peaceful protest. I don't believe I'm actually the one trespassing since we're now on David's property,[5] which we have permission to be on, unlike TransCanada's employees. The morning I locked down was literally the first day that TransCanada was supposed to be in court over challenges on its right to use eminent domain. At that point, there had been no legal decisions at all about whether or not TransCanada was actually in the right of the law. And TransCanada's response to this was to just clear-cut everything and have a fait accompli.

Then the senior TransCanada official showed up and called the police over, and they come back, and it's a sea change. Then all of a sudden, the police tell us that we're placed under arrest. I repeat that it's a peaceful protest. The sheriff deputy tells me that since we're not obeying their orders, it can't be a peaceful protest. Then they start with pain compliance—or physical torture, depending on whose words here—on me. They're bending my arm and joints around, bending my hand behind my back. They end up handcuffing my free arm to the backhoe so they can go and get pepper spray. At which point they

---

5. David Daniel is an East Texas landowner who protested the KXL pipeline coming through his property.

pepper spray inside the pipe where Rain and I have our arms. Then, they wait ten minutes. They're very surprised that the pepper spray hasn't made us immediately let go. They start talking about how the pepper spray had expired over a year ago, which at first I thought was a joke, but later they actually showed it to me and I could see that it in fact it had expired in the year 2000, and this happened in 2012.

An officer who had been the most aggressive of all comes over and says, "Whelp, I'm going to start tasering you until one of you lets go. I'm going to say, 'Taser, taser, taser!' and then I'm going to taser you for three seconds, and then if that doesn't work, I'll say it again and I'll do it for five seconds." He decides to start on me. He tasers me in my left leg for three seconds, which was very painful. Then he tasers me in my left arm for five seconds. That's where I was concerned. Tasers frequently kill people and I will say by about the fifth second, I definitely had a firm, intense tingling in my left pec.

Being tasered is a very intense experience, especially combined with the building pain and discomfort in my arm, and then having the police officer almost choke me unconscious while bending me back to the ground. Then they started on Rain, who has an irregular heart-beat. When she expressed that, they just ignored her, though the officer who tasered her seemed to be concerned. He actually did try twice to interrupt his own count of "taser, taser, taser" to ask first Rain and then his lieutenant if he had to go through with it. He was, of course, told that he had to, so he then tasered Rain, who was clearly in intense pain and visibly upset. During the whole process, Rain and I were able to touch each other's fingers, the two fingers on our hands, through the lockdown tube. And they couldn't interfere with that.

—Benjamin Franklin Sequoyah Craft-Rendon

Background
The Keystone XL (KXL) pipeline is a partially constructed pipeline intended to transport crude and diluted bitumen ("dilbit") from Alberta,

Canada, to the Texas Gulf Coast.[6] The KXL pipeline continues to make national headlines, and stopping the construction of the pipeline has been a goal of many major environmental organizations for several reasons: its heavy toll on the environment, the effects ranging from water contamination to cancer, the long-term health impacts on communities living near refineries, and the enormous amount of carbon contained in the tar sands that contribute significantly to global warming.

As of this writing, the KXL pipeline has not been fully constructed. Yet, to this day, many people are unaware that part of the KXL has already been built. In 2012, the KXL project was divided into two projects: the northern segment, which is currently under deliberation, and the southern segment. Because State Department approval was no longer necessary since the southern leg does not cross an international border, construction began immediately on the southern KXL pipeline. The resistance encountered by TransCanada, the company building and operating the KXL pipeline, and its contractors helped shape the debate and controversy that continues to stall the construction of the northern leg of the KXL pipeline.

The oral history project I helped develop documents, shares, and bears witness to the stories of those who fought against the building of the southern KXL pipeline. From the tree sits in East Texas to lockdowns on construction equipment and projectors in corporate offices, groups of people worked hard to stall and stop the construction of the pipeline.

I left a career in oil and gas in 2013 and was drawn into activism around the KXL pipeline due to my concerns over the impacts of tar sand extraction on human health and the environment. In fall 2013, while protesting at the downtown Houston offices of TransCanada, I met several people involved in resistance against the KXL pipeline: concerned landowners whose property rights were stripped through egregious use of eminent domain, environmental activists concerned about pipeline spills into precious waterways and worried about global climate change,

---

6. Dilbit is a mixture of bitumen, an asphalt-like material derived from the tar sands of Canada, and diluent, a lighter oil that is needed for the tar sands oil to flow.

people from communities in the shadows of the refineries where the tar sands oil will be refined. The protest in which I participated led to my arrest, and I spent a night in a holding cell in Harris County Jail.

As I talked to others who have participated in the movement to stop the construction of the KXL, I heard stories not only of people risking arrests but also of harassment and physical violence as they stood up to TransCanada. I grew curious about what compelled people to take these kinds of risks, as I was processing my own engagement in environmental and social justice, and asking myself how people can challenge corporate dominance and its associated structural violence. I began to recognize the power of storytelling in shifting consciousness and in providing space for people to become heroes within the context of their own lives. Oral history was an appropriate way to recognize the lived experiences of those involved with the resistance against the southern leg of the KXL pipeline, to evaluate the impact of this campaign on both the issue itself and on the participants, and to highlight a narrative that emphasizes the power of everyday people.

For this project, I reached out to a local coalition called Houstonians Against Tar Sands. People from several of the member groups (Houston NoKXL, Tar Sands Blockade, Occupy Houston) participated. This group consisted of local folks, including some who live or had grown up in the East End of Houston, an area impacted by refinery pollution. It also included people who had moved to Texas specifically to work on the issue of the KXL pipeline. In those discussions, I heard a great deal about the wonderful people in Nacogdoches, a small city in East Texas that served as a base for Tar Sands Blockade. On the recommendation of several of the people with whom I spoke in Houston, I reached out to Austin Heights Baptist Church, where Pastor Kyle Childress warmly welcomed me in, helping me to coordinate discussions with members of his church who had been involved in the effort to stop the pipeline, supported by organizations such as NacSTOP and the Sierra Club. I also reached out to Jerry Hightower, an East Texas resident I met at a coffee shop in Houston, who described his plunge into issues of social and environmental justice after getting involved in resisting the southern KXL pipeline.

Separately, I made the acquaintance of Walter Long in Austin, who connected me with Eleanor Fairchild, a seventy-eight-year-old landowner who fought the construction of the pipeline on her property. Via email, Walter had told me a bit about Eleanor's story: "You probably know that Eleanor's husband was an oil company executive. I thought that, perhaps, based upon your common experience with oil companies (in different generations), you might find it particularly nice to get to know each other."

As I began this project, Eleanor came to mind as a person I should speak with. I was curious, in particular, about why someone who had been connected to the oil and gas industry would consider protesting the construction of the pipeline on her property.

Being new to conducting oral history, I was surprised to discover a sense of shyness; initially, I found myself a bit hesitant to reach out to people I didn't know. In fact, that sense of anxiety felt a bit prohibitive, so I decided to initiate interviews for my project first with people whom I had met before, in order to feel more comfortable. Starting dialogues with a few people who felt safe helped to strengthen my confidence and gave me permission to be a less-than-perfect interviewer. For me, perfectionism can be a challenge to overcome in any project, and speaking with friendly faces helped ease my fears. Of course, this option may not be available to everyone who takes on an oral history project. As I spoke with more and more people, it became easier to initiate conversations and to invite others to participate in this project.

Although I would have preferred to speak to more people in the flesh, I was only able to do so with three narrators: Benjamin Franklin Sequoyah Craft-Rendon, Julie Henry, and Eric Moll. I met Benjamin at my home, and I met Julie and Eric at separate times in the outdoor courtyard at a local coffee shop. While the coffee shop provided access to beverages and a warm atmosphere, the noise level was not ideal. As Eric and I spoke, an occasional strong wind created some background noise. As I transcribed our discussion, I noticed a few moments where the sound of the wind prevented me from understanding what Eric said. This particular moment highlighted the importance of meeting in relatively quiet spaces in order to ensure the quality of the recorded interview.

I spoke with all of the other narrators over the phone, using the TapeACall app to record our discussions. TapeACall is a relatively straightforward app to use. I had used it several months ago and thought I understood how it worked. However, I did not do a test run before my first interview and there was a glitch, rendering the recording unavailable. I advise anyone using TapeACall (or any other recording device or platform, for that matter) to test it briefly before the first interview to ensure that they are comfortable using the app or device so they avoid losing any precious material.

Despite my initial feelings of shyness and the technological glitch, the interviews mostly went off without a hitch. It was encouraging to observe how readily people shared their stories with me, and I became curious about how people cast themselves in their stories and how they related to the content they shared.

Oral history projects paint the cultural context from which the narrations arise. As the interviewer, I was privy not only to the stories of the narrators, but also to their backgrounds, motivations, intentions, and reflections. People shared their deeply held beliefs. One of the narrators, Steve Chism, spoke of his commitment to live in service to the world: "The world is not ours to destroy, the world is ours to be responsible for, to keep, to nurture, to hold for the next generations. That's the truth!"

Having recently come from a corporate environment, I saw, through these narratives, the world of activists as a direct challenge to the ways in which I had been trained to operate in the world. The culture described within these interviews differs from the status quo. The participants rebuked complacency and found themselves living at their edges, where the safety net falls away. This is especially true for those who took part in direct action, as Julie Henry explained in her description of her participation in a tree sit in Cherokee County, Texas:

> It was in Cherokee County where I climbed into trees, along with two others. They're called suicide platforms. Basically, our tension

lines were tied to equipment on the easement. Another line went
across the easement; that way TransCanada couldn't do anything
with their equipment. And if they tried to bring any machinery on,
they had to do so at the risk of putting us in extreme danger. It was
such chaos on the ground; the cops were purposefully kicking the
tension lines because it would shake our boards. I just remember
shouting down at them: "Don't touch that! It's very unstable." They
just kicked it anyway and laughed about it. Our direct support got
kicked out; they literally moved them out so we could no longer see
them. That's our lifeline! That's what makes you feel totally okay
about what you're doing. They're communicating with you about
what's going on. So that was hard not seeing them anymore. I remember at one point just thinking, this is one of the craziest things
that I've ever done, but it's so weird how I feel like this is totally the
right thing to do, and I am doing exactly what I should be doing right
now. There's nothing else I could be doing than sitting up in that tree.

The lockdowns arose out of frustration with the system, and many other
narrators who chose not to place themselves in a position to be arrested
highlighted that frustration. Nacogdoches resident Vicki Baggett stated:

We know TransCanada has been talking to our county for four years.
They were ahead of us. They were a couple of years selling themselves,
and who knows who they've paid off. We don't know that. We have
no way to know that. My county commissioner won't return my calls.
They don't want you to talk to the county judge unless the county
commissioner is with you. In our city—and I can't even believe this
is legal—in order to present at the city council, you have to either be
sponsored by the mayor or by three out of four of the city commis-
sioners. So there is no open mic time. And there is no open mic at
the county commission meeting. We've spoken to the mayor; we've
spoken to individuals. The mayor says clearly it's a county issue not a
city issue, even though [if the pipeline] blows, we're in the evacuation
zone depending on the way the wind blows.

    It's been hard. We've been sort of tagged as extremists, as eco-
terrorists. Around here, even *activist* is a really bad word. We went
to see the mayor and he said, "Y'all aren't activists, are you?" And we
said, "No, no, sir. We are concerned citizens." [*Laughing.*] It's really

hard. And there are still people who don't know, don't know what tar
sands are. It's a hard sell around here.

This work provides a forum for the narratives of those engaged in resisting the pipeline, and it also provides an examination of power and
privilege in several ways. For instance, interactions with the police and
experiences in jail were common themes in many of these interviews.
Those experiences allowed participants to tease out aspects of the power
relationships they faced in those situations and to address where their
own privilege arises in how they interacted with law enforcement.

Frequently, discussions of power and privilege came up as narrators
unpacked how citizens engage with the government and with corporations. In many cases, these discussions evoke stories reminiscent of
David and Goliath, in that the people resisting the pipeline faced the
behemoth TransCanada, with its seemingly endless resources of money
and people, which included not only their own employees but also the
police officers who seemed to work on their behalf. The positioning of
the underdog versus the big guy is a widely familiar theme to which many
people can relate, creating an opportunity for a mutual sighting between
the narrators and the audience.

Many of these interviews highlight the moral necessity of speaking
out on issues like climate change, environmental justice, and landowner
rights, and they also highlight the risks of doing so, such as police brutality. Another risk echoed by several narrators is the risk of going unheard
or being seen as an enemy of the people.

Ultimately, the southern KXL pipeline was not stopped. Many people shared disappointment and discouragement, but not complete de-
spondency. Eric Moll framed it this way: "We didn't manage to stop the
pipeline. Ultimately it's pumping 570,000 barrels of tar sands, which
are being refined along the Gulf Coast. We didn't manage to stop that.
All we really have done is make it a much bigger issue, a much deeper
issue than I think it would have been otherwise." My oral history project
shows some of the many difficulties of civic engagement: dealing with
bureaucracy, conflict with law enforcement, and feelings of impotence.

At the same time, the project shows many of the benefits of civic engagement. Several narrators discussed the strength of their communities when they are focused on social justice and environmental issues. For many, resisting the southern KXL pipeline was not only a logical form of action based on wanting to avoid the negative consequences of building the pipeline and encouraging greater tar sands extraction. It was also an action that they undertook on the basis of their deeply held spiritual values. Pastor Kyle Childress, who came from a family of petroleum geologists, shared his motivation in supporting the blockade: "My motivation, again, is not because I'm some kind of liberal activist; it's my Christian faith. I thought it was unjust and against the way of God I know through Jesus Christ."

Narrator Vicki Baggett's story weaves elements of her personal life, including the death of her father a week prior to receiving a call asking for her support in resisting the KXL pipeline. Her initial reaction had been to put aside the request, given the large number of pipelines running through East Texas, the other environmental issues she had been focused on, and the passing of her father. It was not a good time for her. Yet, she reluctantly said yes, and after meeting David Daniel, the quiet Texas landowner who was standing up to TransCanada, she knew what she needed to do. Reflecting upon this journey, Vicki concluded:

> This is kind of a weird thing to say, but I heart the KXL, because this has been such a deep and meaningful experience for me. I have met the most passionate, the most compassionate people in this campaign. And I continue to meet them. And it's really bonded our community and our church in a way that is so important. And I don't know how else it would have happened. There've been some really good things to come of it. I'm sorry that it had to come this way, but . . . I don't really know how to say that, but there's been some good stuff to come from it.

Oral history can show, as Vicki's story emphasizes, the capacity for transformation. Despite Vicki's initial reluctance to becoming involved, she said yes anyhow. And through saying yes, she found deep personal meaning and a stronger community. Her story and the stories of others shared in this project are a deep source of inspiration to me. They high-light the importance of taking a stand on issues of significance and the various forms that may take, from meeting with the city council, to legal action, to local community organizing, to direct action. These stories highlight not only the actions of a small group of people in Texas, but also the potential for shifting consciousness within communities.

Determining What Is Safe to Share

An unexpected component of this project was the phenomenon of nar-rators sharing others' stories during the interviews. Steve Chism spoke about some friends who took an interest in resisting the southern KXL pipeline because of their experience with a natural gas pipeline on their property that poisoned their groundwater. I witnessed Steve weave in this story as validation of the importance of the issue of the KXL pipeline and to demonstrate how people in his community are impacted. (I feel uncomfortable including the details of that story here without having spoken to his friends first, because Steve mentioned them by name and provided a few personal statements that may or may not be public knowl-edge.) I appreciate Steve's inclusion of this story because it provides a more personal context as to why the pipeline is an important issue for him and for other people in East Texas, and I plan to follow up with Steve's friends to either include their personal accounts or to ensure that including their story feels comfortable to them.

Eric Moll shared the story of David Daniel, the landowner who chal-lenged the construction of the KXL pipeline on his property. Although I haven't spoken directly to David Daniel, I feel more comfortable shar-ing his story because it has been spoken about more widely and, as Eric informed me and others have confirmed, TransCanada has placed a gag order on David Daniel.

I am generally comfortable sharing the stories of the narrators, given that I live in Texas and have myself participated in actions against the KXL pipeline. In that regard, I am considered part of the community, which is a source of trust between the narrators and me, the interviewer. Even interviewees in East Texas who didn't know me personally seemed quite eager to share their stories with me in order to give an account of what happened in Texas and use their experiences to shape discourse around the northern KXL pipeline and the larger issue of fossil fuel extraction.

Establishing good rapport with the narrators engendered trust and created a sense of safety that allowed narrators to share, in some instances, deeply personal stories. In fact, a couple of narrators continued to share their stories with me off the record because what they wanted to share delved off topic or they deemed it to be too personal to share with a wider audience. It felt like an honor to listen to all of these stories, and I know that several of the narrators felt deeply listened to. Storytelling can be a useful process in situations where the narrator experienced something traumatic. The interviewer can help create a protective space so that the narrator feels safe enough to share memories of a time when they did not experience safety. Without safety and trust, it may be more challenging for an interviewer to uncover the heart of a story that in its telling often requires the narrator to experience discomfort as she recalls her memories of pain and suffering. Such memories are often at the root of stories of resilience and transformation.

There were moments, especially when I was focused on detailed work like transcription, where it felt necessary to remind myself of the larger context of this work. Transcription can be time consuming, and if I wasn't mindful, I noticed myself feeling a bit overwhelmed and worried that I wouldn't finish transcribing the interviews in a timely manner. What helped me get through those moments was remembering the interactions I had with the narrators and how excited most of them were to share their story about their experiences with the KXL pipeline. Those reminders inspired me to work despite my hesitance.

I encountered some other challenges in transcribing. Having come from an academic background, I am accustomed to writing in a technical way, with emphasis on correct grammar and spelling, which made capturing the nuances of dialect difficult for me. In future work, I hope to attune my ear to more fully honor the voice of the narrator in that way.

Furthermore, the process of editing the voice of the narrators requires some discernment. Editing should be nuanced in a way that balances the concern for clarity with that of capturing the intention and character of what was said, so that readers can more fully understand and relate to the content.

I found this oral history project to be beneficial to the narrators because they had an opportunity to share their stories to inform other resistance campaigns. Many expressed concern about the current debate over the KXL pipeline and observed that even some large national environmental organizations seem to forget or not know that the southern KXL pipeline is in the ground and operational. Several narrators felt satisfied knowing that, through sharing their stories and setting the facts straight, the discussion about the proposed northern pipeline could be grounded in the recent histories of interactions between TransCanada, government officials, landowners, and concerned citizens.

On a more personal level, for the narrators who experienced trauma during their experiences resisting the pipeline, sharing their stories allowed them an opportunity to process some of their emotions regarding those experiences. Through this process, I've come to see how sharing stories and deeply listening to each other can provide opportunities for healing. As a narrator, one can shift one's voice from victim to hero. Following our conversation and a few conversations with others, narrator Benjamin Franklin Sequoyah Craft-Rendon decided to pursue legal action on account of the police brutality he experienced in Wood County. Oral history can help narrators find their voice and develop confidence.

Another outcome of this project is that I know myself better. I understand my idiosyncrasies a bit better, and I've learned how to work with my shyness in speaking with people I don't know. I also developed a strategy for working with the internal resistance that comes with working on a project like this, realizing that resistance tends to be a part of most major undertakings that require vulnerability, and that it, too, will pass.

This project also helped me build a larger network. I am now connected to folks not only in Houston but also in Nacogdoches and elsewhere in East Texas. I had opportunities to meet several narrators months after our phone interviews, and our original connection had forged a common space from which we could build a deeper relationship. I also felt particularly inspired after talking with the narrators about their values and motivations. Finally, this work raised questions for me regarding the general direction of the American environmental movement and how frontline communities continue to be supported or, in some cases, not supported by the broader environmental community.

It is a hope of mine that these stories will inspire readers to take action in their own communities on issues of environmental and social justice. Narrators shared not only their experiences and motivation but also what supported them through difficult times—such as meditation and their faith in God—which demonstrates how these folks can maintain their commitment despite the difficulties of civic engagement. Readers can learn new tools from the narrators or consider how they, the readers, support themselves during difficult times.

I plan to publish these stories online by reaching out to regional and national environmental blogs. My hope is to bring some renewed attention to the issue of tar sands and the KXL pipeline.

This oral history project highlights one particular challenge of civic engagement: willingly putting oneself in circumstances that are legally precarious and could be physically painful, as shared by Eleanor Fairchild, Benjamin Franklin Sequoyah Craft-Rendon, Julie Henry, and Eric Moll. It also showed the likely possibility of defeat: the pipeline was built in Oklahoma and Texas, and it seems difficult to have government officials or corporations recognize the larger impacts of their projects. Yet, almost every narrator conveyed a sense of accomplishment and some amount of hope for future endeavors. Many were fueled by a sense of compassion for others, showing how, at least among this group, there are people out in the world who embody this desire to create a healthier and more just world.

Narrators felt heard through the process of oral history, using their stories to understand themselves and their roles in resisting the KXL pipeline, as well as empowering the larger environmental movement to take action to create meaningful change. Through this project, I have gained confidence and an enthusiasm for the process of oral history and its impact. In hearing the stories of the narrators' willingness to confront TransCanada, I was inspired to question what I find to be meaningful action. Their stories provided a more robust context through which I can understand how the national NoKXL movement grew, and I've begun to develop relationships with many of the narrators outside of this particular project, which has aided in building a more cohesive network of activists in the heart of Big Oil country.

PROJECT LRN: LISTENING TO RESIDENTS AND NEIGHBORS

GENEVRA GALLO-BAYIATES

Genevra Gallo-Bayiates is a career counselor with a background in theater. In 2009, after completing her training as a counselor, she moved to the Chicago suburb of Evanston, a community with a reputation for harmonious diversity. After a few years, Genevra came to understand that the relationships between different communities in Evanston was more complicated than the city's reputation suggested: invisible barriers seemed to exist between neighborhoods, as well as between people of different ethnic and socioeconomic backgrounds. Despite limited oral history training, Genevra set out to interview people in Evanston to record their histories in the community as well as their perspectives on the community's diversity. She called her initiative Project Listening to Residents and Neighbors (Project LRN). In this field study, Genevra describes some of the unique challenges and rewards of conducting oral history projects in one's own community, as well as learning as she went, by always "saying yes" to new opportunities, ideas, and voices as they presented themselves to the project.

Excerpt from "Project LRN"

I can say what brought my family here: in short, [the] maternal line of my great-great grandmother. Apparently, her family escaped on the Underground Railroad from the South into Windsor, Canada, which is on the other side of the river from Detroit. From Windsor they came to Evanston in the late 1890s, approximately around 1897.

And then on my father's side, the paternal line, my grandfather came here when he was three, in 1903. In that time there were busloads of African American Evanstonians who were family clans, in a sense. So the Logan clan came out of the area of Greenwood, South Carolina, as a result of lynchings that were happening down there and the burning of property, because this was just after the abolishment of slavery. Our family acquired land that we lost, and there were a number of families who rush[ed] out of that area, escaping that form of oppression and racism.

There's a lot of transplants to Evanston, but I feel, being a fifth-generation Evanstonian on both lines of my family, I feel that roots me. That gives me a groundedness in the community that— just from my personal experience and observation—not a lot of transplants have [nor] a lot of Evanstonians who have been here for multiple generations. Because it's more than numbers, it's more than a chronological "how many years," it's a rootedness in the community.

I feel that Evanston is my village. That's how I approach it. So when I reflect back on my life growing up, I look through the lens of myself as a child in the village, and the elders in the village who played their role, and [the] role that the community centers played, and hence my community, and so on and so forth. It's given me a groundedness and a rootedness in the *community* of Evanston and not just the *city* of Evanston. I . . . was exposed to a lot of community servants and activists and that exposure growing up really has given me a sense of ownership.

And with that accountability, I feel responsible for what happens and what doesn't here in Evanston. I understand how it impacts all of us, despite these silos we kind of live in, in Evanston, in these different wards. I feel a connectedness and a rootedness.

I think that, as Evanston changes and evolves and gentrifies and urbanizes and so on and so forth, there's a sense that it's being lost . . . all communities feel it equally. I think the African American community has been hit really hard with that. There's money and wealth in Evanston; there's education, there's technology. So it's very modern; it has a lot of amenities and opportunities, but it's also very polarized in a sense of, you know, the extreme poverty, and the condition of our youth. So, Evanston is a polarized place. But many people live on one side or another of those polar opposites, whereas I had exposure and experience with both extremities. So that's part of my conceptualization of what Evanston is and what it means to me.

I feel like you have a lot of people in [the 5th] Ward who don't really care to go on the other side of Ridge [Avenue]. They don't feel a part of it. They don't see themselves; they don't feel connected or respected or accepted. But despite some of those barriers, I still feel, *No, that's mine, that's mine too.* You know? I don't own it, but I share it with everyone else; and no one has more of a right to it than I do, and I don't have any greater of a right than anyone else does. I'm not going to relinquish what I feel is mine.

—Gilo Kwesi Logan

Saying Yes

The creation of Project LRN began with the very intentional decision to "say yes" more often. After I completed career counseling training in 2009, my husband and I moved to Evanston, Illinois, for a job offer my husband simply couldn't turn down. We'd left nearby Chicago four years earlier and had not intended to return. However, Evanston was one of those places we had considered a Shangri-La for arts-based city dwellers looking to settle down to raise a family.

After moving into our new apartment, we quickly noticed our neighborhood near the campus of Northwestern University was very affluent. We would wander through the neighborhoods near us to gawk at the stone mansions with decorative fencing and fairy-tale yards. We felt a bit out of place and quickly realized we could not afford to buy a house in this particular area of Evanston, despite its reputation for having the best elementary schools.

In 2011, we purchased a home and moved to a new neighborhood in Evanston in preparation for our daughter's first year of school. This area was populated by people who mowed their own lawns and drove cars that looked like ours. Not only did it feel more working class, it was also more ethnically diverse, with a school that focused on community and cooperation just as strongly as it did on academics.

Yet we began to notice striking differences between our neighborhood near Northwestern and our current neighborhood. Streets were not plowed as quickly during heavy snows, and the sidewalks were rarely cleared—despite the presence of several residents who needed to travel in wheelchairs. Flooding in basements was rampant due to poor storm drainage in the streets. The biggest difference between neighborhoods seemed to be in the way the town invested in the area. We had a nearly defunct shopping plaza filled with multiple vacant buildings and a few struggling businesses, compared with the thriving commercial strips near campus, and the city seemed disinterested in improving infrastructure for the shops in our new neighborhood.

At the end of 2013, I both enjoyed and felt frustrated with my town. I was also frustrated with my work life and was looking for opportunities that would make me feel my efforts were meaningful and had purpose. I decided to remain open to any and all opportunities that presented themselves in my new community, in the hopes that clarity would follow action.

In November 2013, my friend Heather Sweeney invited me to join the steering committee at the YWCA Evanston/Northshore. I said yes. The committee was working to foster community partnerships with local organizations, and we were specifically tasked with finding arts and performance organizations to reach out to. These partnerships would then foster and promote programming linked to the nationally touring exhibit "RACE: Are We So Different?," which would be featured at the

Illinois Holocaust Museum and Education Center in nearby Skokie, Illinois. The projects were to explore the construct of race, the presence of racism, and the concept of identity in a diverse society.

Work on the committee and at the YWCA led to an invitation in January 2014 to join a new community group (I said yes again), which we eventually decided to call the Coalition for Racial Equity in Evanston. This group initially came together to discuss the idea of diversity and inclusion training in Evanston; however, we quickly moved forward with ideas for parent education, political and social advocacy, community gatherings, and advocacy within the educational system.

To me, our discussions at the Coalition for Racial Equity often seemed to boil down to identifying a lack of empathy from those in power for the experiences of others who were less privileged. As a white, able-bodied, heterosexual woman who comes from a background privileged with higher education and a very stable socioeconomic status, I increasingly felt it was essential to be aware of and acknowledge the earned and unearned privileges I enjoyed, as well as the biases, concepts, assumptions, or beliefs that have been shaped by my experience. I've always believed empathy hinges on being able to understand how someone else may or may not experience the same privilege or challenge. The Coalition for Racial Equity hoped to take that sort of personal empathy one step further and provide a call to action to build balance in the systems we inhabit so that everyone in Evanston could experience greater freedom, power, and happiness. Through my work within Evanston's social justice networks, and as a result of the inspiration I felt hearing the stories of Evanston residents who felt invisible, diminished, or eager for change, I was provided a focus and a pathway to action.

The idea for Project LRN was born through this discussion of community challenges. I decided on an oral history project consisting of one-on-one interviews about diversity and inclusion in Evanston. I would draw from my experience as a counselor, my background in interactive

and audience-focused narrative performance, and my inherent preferences as an empathic introvert. I said yes to myself and took a huge leap
of faith.

Starting "Project LRN"

I truly believe one must listen to learn, and that one of the best ways
to build empathy and understanding across multiple spheres of identity
is through hearing personal accounts and firsthand stories of someone
else's lived experiences. One of my inspirations, Eileen Hogan Heineman, put this particularly well in describing her work as the racial justice
program director at the YWCA Evanston/Northshore:

> Learning to talk *through* the issue of racism (instead of around it) re-
> quires sharing a common vocabulary and practicing our conversation
> skills by looking at events and institutions through a racial equity lens.
> We need to hear—and believe—others' stories in order to more fully
> understand the ways race impacts life. The skill we practice is listen-
> ing, deeply and with respect, to others, so we can develop the radical
> empathy necessary for transformation.

Hearing an honest narrative can shift our perception of someone in
our community away from our sometimes automatic notion of "other"
to a person who is human and recognizable, and whose experience res-
onates with at least part of our own. With Project LRN, I sought to
increase communication across multiple spheres of potential divide by
inviting residents to share their stories with the rest of their community,
thereby building a collection of narratives that would include voices who
might otherwise remain hidden, ignored, or simply missed.

My first goal for Project LRN was to explore the ways people living
within a town that prides itself on its diversity could still maintain boundaries based on socioeconomic, cultural, and ethnic identities within the
township. Evanston has nearly seventy-five thousand residents, and based
on the last census, the majority of residents identified as white (60.5
percent). Evanston's Hispanic population has increased in the last few
years, yet residents of color are still in the numerical minority, despite

Evanston's reputation as a diverse city. At the last census, 17.9 percent of residents identified as Black alone, 10 percent as Hispanic, 8.6 percent as Asian alone, 2.8 percent as two or more races, 0.2 percent as "other race" alone, and 0.2 percent as American Indian alone.[1]

Yet, despite its many cultural attributes and mix of ethnicities (due in very large part to the presence of Northwestern University and the students, professors, and families who come to Evanston for both undergrad and graduate programs), Evanston struggles with issues of affordable housing, integration and inclusion, gaps in educational opportunity for students of color, and qualitative differences between neighborhoods depending on one's particular ward. These issues lie not far below the surface-level harmonious image that Evanston has earned. They weren't visible to some residents of the city but were visible to others, and it was clear to me that I was far from the only resident—transplant or otherwise—who had come to view the city's reputation with some skepticism. Within Evanston, equity advocates and social justice groups sought to address what some residents were calling "drive-by diversity"—the presence of difference and the appropriation of such as part of a publicly paraded identity, without a true commitment to valuing diversity by honoring and including *all* members of the community in systems of power and influence.

I started my project with a number of questions I'd asked myself since moving to my new neighborhood or that had been raised in speaking to other residents: Why are some sidewalks in town pristine while others (in different wards) are cracked and buckling? Does each neighborhood have grocery stores within walking distance that offer fresh produce? How often do the police patrol each neighborhood/ward, and when they stop residents, what is the reason provided? Why do some schools outperform others when the educational curriculum is aligned across the entire district? Why does my school have such a wonderful mix of families from other countries, cultures, ethnic backgrounds—and yet we all essentially keep to ourselves or speak with others who look like us?

---

1. Census and population data provided via City-Data.com as of May 1, 2015, www
.city-data.com/city/Evanston-Illinois.html.

My personal questions and the feedback I received from others in the community led to three main objectives for the project. First, I wanted to enable community members throughout Evanston to share their life stories and opinions on matters directly affecting their wards—particularly as they applied to diversity and the perception of diversity.

Second, I wanted to provide Evanston residents with a resource such as a website, podcast, YouTube channel, or social media page through which they could access their fellow community members' interviews.

And finally, it seemed beneficial that the Coalition for Racial Equity in Evanston and other local social justice groups, with the permission of those interviewed, have access to the opinions and perspectives of traditionally underrepresented residents on issues affecting local decision making, legislation, and policy. This could strengthen such advocacy groups' efforts to work effectively on behalf of residents who might otherwise be marginalized or ignored.

My initial goal was to interview at least three residents in each of Evanston's nine wards, for a total of twenty-seven interviews. Interviews would be audio recorded, with the possibility of eventually including video interviews as well. While my only strict criterion for narrators was that they be Evanston residents, I hoped to ensure a broad diversity of identities by seeking out voices from a range of ethnicities, socioeconomic backgrounds, educational backgrounds, sexual orientations, and physical abilities.

I intended to use a set of the same twelve questions in each interview; additional follow-up questions, which would be based on each narrator's answers to the core set of questions, would yield more variation in the interviews. The idea was to achieve a balance of consistency across all the interviews, and flexibility to respond to each person as an individual as their story unfolded. My original twelve questions were:

1. What brought you to Evanston?

2. What do you like most about living here?

3. What do you love most about your neighborhood/community?

4. What do you like least about living here?

5. What makes you feel safe in your community?

6. What makes you feel unsafe?

7. As you know, Evanston prides itself on being diverse. How do you feel about that reputation or perception?

8. How has racism or discrimination affected you within the town?

9. What are the ways you see other residents being affected?

10. What's the largest issue facing your ward or neighborhood/community?

11. What do you think would help create a more equitable and open environment here?

12. Anything else you'd like to add? What did we miss that everyone should know?

After all twelve questions were answered, I would home in on details that might allow for interesting elaboration. For example, when interviewing Noelle Krimm, a white mother raising two children on her own in a highly affluent section of Evanston, she mentioned part of her experience of diversity was tied into the socioeconomic differences in her neighborhood. One of the follow-up questions I asked focused on the sense of separation she'd mentioned between herself and other moms at Orrington Elementary School in her neighborhood. She told me, "I would say that I don't really have any good friends among the moms on the playground. I tend to notice that it's like: groups of moms on one side and me by myself pushing my kid on the swing on another side. I don't know how much of that is me not making friends very easily. They do live in a very different world than I live in, with very different problems." After my follow-up question, she went on to offer a more personal and nuanced response than she had to any of the initial questions. In general, the personalized follow-up questions in the interviews led to much richer stories.

Keeping Myself Open to Discovery

As I was beginning this project, I was very lucky to receive guidance from a friend of mine, Karen Weinberg, who is a documentary film-maker with her own production company, Ten Trees Productions. Her insight into the process of documentation and the issue of consent in the oral history process was immensely valuable. She shared the permission forms she uses for filming, discussed equipment needs and best places to purchase equipment, and updated me on her latest project, *Keep Talking: Immersion in the Alaskan Wild*, which documents the efforts of the Alutiiq people to keep their native language alive. So I wasn't approaching my project without training or support, though I was still figuring certain things out as I went.

One of the first lessons I have learned as an oral history newbie is letting go—or rather, being open to (and even inviting in) change. In so many ways, this project has revealed itself to me. The direction it wants to take, the timeline it needs to follow. And so while I may have had (and still do have) very specific ideas of how I want things to go, part of the process is about loosening the grip of expectation to capitalize on the opportunity of the moment—and trusting that's exactly what needs to happen.

One important way I "let go" was to allow for conversational tangents and to base my follow-up questions on whatever I sensed the narrator wished to highlight. This flexible approach enabled the interview to go places I could not have planned on my own and let the narrator take control of the narrative. More surprisingly, tangents and detours often ended up circling back to most of the original questions anyway, only with richer and fuller responses. For example, when I spoke with Mary Trujillo, an African American long-time resident of Evanston, the answer to my questions about feeling safe or unsafe in Evanston led to a much broader discussion of the impact of racism and discrimination throughout the United States, which then moved on to the shooting of Michael Brown in Ferguson, and finally back to diversity in Evanston. Mary observed:

I think [in Evanston] we have access to diversity, and many people have multiple cross-racial, cross-cultural relationships. I think that's—kind of at a very superficial level—that's a norm. That's an expectation. I think we do better than many communities with having situations where people can have those kinds of relationships. [*Sighs.*] And it does not have to go any deeper than that.

So that's kind of the downside: that people don't have to go any deeper. The opportunities are there for meaningful relationships, but you don't really have to. And my observation is, those areas that are uncomfortable, people don't do them, Black and white. It's too hard. Those personal relationships stop or—and I'll use the word—"fail," and "fail" may be an overstatement, when those structural considerations emerge. So I can be friends with you, and we can go and have coffee and we can talk and relate on that level. But when we have to confront the fact that the experience at Evanston High School is very different for Black students, for any number of reasons, than it is for white students, there's not a need, there's not a *requirement*, for the more privileged party to deal with that. They don't have to.

In this case, allowing Mary to follow her train of thought away from the original question ultimately led to a striking observation that fit with some of my original questions perfectly.

Flexibility also was valuable when conducting the interviews, which ended up occurring all around Evanston. Some took place at the narrator's place of residence, one at my house (amid interruptions from my kids and the narrator's kids), another at the library (lots of hushed tones), and another at the narrator's office. In each case, there were potential distractions, but the selection of each location was based upon the narrator's preference, which put the narrator immediately at ease.

Another important lesson I learned was how to maintain trust and comfort when discussing potentially uncomfortable topics. My training as a counselor was highly beneficial in this regard, since I had acquired skills in active listening, interviewing, and providing an empathic and nonjudgmental presence. But we are all human, and even with this training I still noticed that I had to be mindful to explore areas of pain or disenfranchisement, rather than shy away from them when they came up. It was important to ask questions in a way that balanced concern for the narrator's feelings with determination to address the topic at hand, so that each narrator was able to share as much of the truth of their experience as possible.

It was also important to make it clear to narrators that their stories were their own, not mine. Before each interview I would go over the consent form. I would underscore the control the narrator would have over the content at all stages of the project, and made sure to leave time to answer any questions or concerns that may come up. Going over this aspect of the work at the very beginning helped to reinforce the narrator's role as a driving force in the project and as a collaborator with equal control in the outcome of his or her story. In the feedback I received from each narrator, they expressed how positive the experience was and how much they appreciated the level of control they could maintain over their story. These were all important steps in allowing the narrator to feel comfortable.

Because I am member of the community I'm exploring in this oral history project, I've had perhaps an easier time building rapport with potential narrators than I might have if I were from outside the community. Many of the people I've interviewed are acquaintances from local events or people that I met through acquaintances. This gave me an immediate starting place that felt comfortable and manageable: beginning the project was much easier because I could start with the people around me, rather than feeling like I had to chase folks down. But my goal has always been to push from the "known" into the "unknown"—both for the benefit of the project and for our process of self-growth and personal education.

The next phase of the project will include a broader focus on the narrators and their background, and ideally I will be able to speak with residents with whom I am less directly connected. I feel this is important for a number of reasons, the most important of which is to continue to honor the mission of Project LRN to highlight narratives by residents who may be traditionally marginalized or ignored.

Eileen Hogan Heineman often says, "Eliminating racism happens one conversation at a time." If this is true, then it is essential to have as many conversations as possible so that we may continue to broaden not only our lens of experience and understanding as interviewers, but also the awareness and inquiry process in which potential narrators and oral history audiences may be engaged. "Because we are a diverse community in many ways, the dominant group needs reminders that there are perceptions and experiences within our town that will be different from their lived experience," said narrator Heather Sweeney, reflecting upon the project. "Of course there will be similarities, but the idea that there will be differences is one we cannot forget or overlook."

For the interviewer, this also requires remaining aware of the ways our identities are constituted by our own ethnicity, gender, sexual orientation, socioeconomic status, education, religious and spiritual beliefs, and so forth. Without a sense of self-awareness, I recognized it was possible, for instance, to impose my perspective upon my narrator by asking questions that cater to my experience rather than the narrator's. Or in some cases I may assume I understand an aspect of a narrator's story, rather than asking for more detail or feeling comfortable with delving deeper. This is especially important to keep in mind when I work with narrators with whom I am less personally familiar or to whom I have a less immediate connection.

Much of this process has included learning as I go. For example, the process of sharing the post-interview materials requires some tough decisions. I needed to decide how much I should edit the interviews. Some oral history practitioners keep changes to transcription to a bare minimum and indicate every change, while other practitioners take greater liberties, including moving pieces of the interview around for narrative clarity and coherency.

I think I've landed somewhere in the middle for this project. I want my narrators to redact elements from their interviews if they deem it important to do so. I also want to edit out phone calls or other interruptions that were not intended to be part of the narrative experience. Yet, when I share the interviews online and make them public, I will also note where edits have taken place so that audiences understand the nature of individual documents and the archive as a whole. I also believe it's important to provide the interview in a form as true to the original event as possible; thus, I have chosen not to move paragraphs around or change the order of interview answers, as doing so preserves a type of organic, conversational flow between interviewer and narrator that ought to be honored.

While I think it is important to transcribe the interviews verbatim to ensure accuracy, editing the written text poses multiple challenges—the foremost of which is how to effectively honor each narrator's voice while honoring the truth of his or her story. I do think something is inevitably lost in the editing process, because every time I touch the story, I change it—intentionally or unintentionally. The narrative becomes one step removed from the narrator with each edit. And so providing a way for audiences to access the material in both written and audio forms, with minimal editing, remains very important to me.

What I have taken away from this initial phase (of what I hope will be a very long and fruitful project) is the reinforcement that my role is a very humble one. I am taking responsibility for others' stories, and that is a responsibility both immense and humbling. Recording someone else's story—particularly one that contains moments of pain, frustration, disenfranchisement, or a sense of separateness—requires, at its core, a lack of ego. No hidden agendas, no preconceived notions or conceptualized directions. Just listening and responding and allowing the narrator to unfold his or her experience in the way that seems best. I think this is what ultimately builds mutual trust and ensures the interviewer is just as changed and shaped by the experience as the hoped-for audience who will one day experience the stories as well.

And above all, it is what I strive most to keep improving upon as I continue this journey as a recorder of oral histories.

More Residents and Neighbors

Listening is an increasingly lost art in our modern culture. I cannot adequately express what a gift it has been to sit down with friends and strangers to learn more about their lives. One of the guiding principles I seek to live by is: there is no other. The idea of otherness depends upon separation, misunderstanding, and the absence of empathy—all of which enable the mistreatment of others. We cannot hurt or ignore someone to whom we feel inherently connected, someone who is part of our family, our "tribe," ourselves.

I believe oral history directly confronts the notion of separateness by enabling narrators to feel honored and heard and by providing listeners/readers with an opportunity to take in a direct, honest, and unmanipulated recollection of personal experience, wherein hopefully there is recognition of a shared experience, a shared humanity. Stories are linked to catharsis, and true stories—narratives we share that others know to be "real"—help us feel more united and connected within that process of catharsis.

It is my sincere hope the Project LRN Evanston interviews will not only help to spark dialogue among individuals and groups but also have the potential to widen our understanding of ourselves collectively, as a family of townspeople with common humanity and united goals. The project has certainly broadened my understanding of what residents face, particularly residents of color, and it has encouraged me to continue being active in social justice causes and to continue working on behalf of equity for everyone. It's also been amazing to see my narrators in other situations and to feel a very strong and special connection to them. I hope that, as others begin to listen to each story, a feeling of connection will grow to encompass listeners, people for whom a sense of closeness is possible perhaps even with those they've not yet met in person.

My husband and I are working on a website for Project LRN from which the Evanston interviews can be accessed. The next step will be finding some more-formal community partners to help broaden the project's reach and perhaps secure funding. Community partners might help not only in increasing the reach of Project LRN but also in encouraging more narrators with increasingly diverse experiences to participate. It is my hope the city will embrace the project and perhaps even help promote it on the town website. It has the potential to celebrate and challenge, in a very transparent way, what we both love about Evanston and struggle to change. As articulated so beautifully by narrator Yancey Hughes:

> Evanston is such a successful community in its effort to make the world a better place through the efforts and actions of diligent people as yourself and other community actions of open discussion, museum exhibitions on race and culture. We strive very hard as parents to be the best example for our children. Our efforts go beyond the "choir," and we continue to question our definition of justice [knowing it] is not necessarily the view of the dominating culture.

I'm also hopeful there will be natural and organic ways for Project LRN to explore new areas, such as providing a vehicle for oral history discussion and story sharing in other towns, or taking on local projects aimed at increasing the number and type of voices that are heard and considered in decision-making processes such as legislative, educational, and public safety–related initiatives.

There's a good chance, if you're reading this, you've got the oral history bug as well. You're either considering or have already somewhat embarked upon a project, and you're looking for guidance, inspiration, and encouragement.

My advice: Say yes. Dive in, and trust that you will be met with the support you need. Oral historians are a generous and inquisitive group, and you'll be surprised by the amount of help that is out there for anyone wishing to pursue projects that shed light on issues of inequity, injustice, or disenfranchisement by providing a platform to those most directly impacted.

If it's our collective responsibility to make sure every voice is considered, honored, and heard, then it's very worthwhile work to encourage others to share their stories and to provide the means by which a greater audience can access them. How else are we to change this world?

Say yes.

Postscript

Project LRN now has a website for the collected interviews, and new audio recordings with Evanston residents continue to be added. The project is available to the public at www.projectlrn.org.

PART THREE

STORYTELLING AND ORAL HISTORY RESOURCES

GETTING STARTED:
A QUICK GUIDE TO SETTING UP
YOUR ORAL HISTORY PROJECT

With so many questions to consider at the outset of an oral history project, getting started can feel overwhelming. The following few pages are designed as a reference for new oral historians developing their plan of approach. Also included is a modified version of the consent form we use at Voice of Witness with all of our narrators.

Identifying and Shaping a Project

Many of the determining factors that shape an oral history project are discussed in part one. This includes applications for oral history, themes or topics, intentions, potential narrators, potential audience, and more. In planning an oral history project, participants may also benefit from a discussion of the essential oral history questions that are addressed in the final section of part one and throughout the oral history field reports that make up part two. Planning a carefully considered oral history project, one that observes proper research protocol, can yield tangible benefits by enhancing the process for all stakeholders. If your project is in collaboration with a college or university, you may be subject to review by an Institutional Review Board (IRB), a committee that reviews methods of research to ensure that they meet ethical standards.[1]

---

1. An IRB is a group formed under Federal Drug Administration and Department of Health and Human Services guidelines to review and approve research studies with

Contacting Potential Narrators

When engaging in the process of selecting narrators, there are a few considerations to keep in mind. Some of these are mentioned in part one and include employing a "chain of trust" approach by building relationships, connecting with organizations that support the communities that you'd like to share stories from, and considering insider/outsider dynamics. Here are a few other considerations:

- Seek out narrators who are enthusiastic about telling their stories.

- As an interviewer or project coordinator, model a "two-way street" approach to interviewing by being willing to share details about yourself with potential narrators.

- Be clear about the intentions of your project.

- When selecting potential narrators, remember that everyone has a story and that an "unamplified" voice does not have to be someone who has suffered or is suffering through a crisis.

Interview Preparation

Many of the field reports provide strategies for interview preparation. These range from conducting informal "pre-interviews," scouting the most comfortable environment for an interview, securing permission via a release form (template provided on page 247), crafting a set of "open-ended" interview questions (questions that can't simply be answered with a "yes" or "no"), and making sure audio or video recorders are functioning properly. In our work at Voice of Witness, we've come up with others that burgeoning oral historians may find useful:

- Learn as much about your narrators as you can ahead of time.

---

human beings as subjects. The IRB's function is to ensure the protection of human subjects' rights and welfare. Revised federal guidelines took effect in 2018, stating that oral history was "not deemed to be research." As a result, the vast majority of oral history projects are no longer subject to IRB review. The guidelines stress that oral historians should follow the ethical codes developed by the Oral History Association.

- Plan enough time for each interview.

- Send a list of potential discussion topics or interview questions to your narrator beforehand.

- Bring food or snacks to share with the narrator.

Conducting an Interview

This is where an individual interviewer's "style" really emerges. Some interviewers engage their narrators in back-and-forth dialogue; others prefer to remain more quiet, letting the narrator do most of the talking. Of course, this style is also determined by the personality of the narrator. Some are natural storytellers who need very little encouragement to warm to their themes, while others need a bit more time, guidance, and nurturing. All of the field reports discuss the interview process and what the oral historians felt was particularly successful or challenging. Here are additional interview techniques to consider:

- Maintain attentive and respectful body language.

- Ask follow-up questions. Sometimes the most powerful questions during an interview are the ones you don't prepare in advance. Narrators usually appreciate hearing details of their story reflected back to them, and this also creates an opportunity to "go deeper" into the details of a story.

- Listen to your narrators without making judgments about them.

- Don't let moments of silence fluster you. Silences during an interview can be useful and may indicate your narrator is thinking, reflecting about something, or considering sharing a particular story.

- Build in "wind down" time. After the formal interview is finished, turn off the recording device and have a brief informal chat with your narrator, about anything you like. Keeping it light is usually a good idea. Taking this time affirms the human experience you've just had together.

Transcribing

Transcribing can be a time-consuming process. As a rule of thumb, it usually takes about four to five hours to transcribe an hour of audio. In the Production Resource List on pages 248–50, we list several kinds of software and apps that can make the transcription process easier to manage, although it's worth noting that there is no standard method for transcribing interviews. Some people press play, listen to six words, press pause, write down the words, and repeat. Others will listen to the whole tape, taking as many words as they can, and then return to the beginning and go more slowly through, filling out their initial notes. With both approaches, make sure you record the timecode periodically (every few minutes) so that you have an easy reference point later between the transcript and the audio files. The foremost concern when transcribing is accuracy. This means that you'll have to listen to some sections a few times to get them right. It's important to keep the speaker's word usage, syntax, and idiosyncrasies intact. Throughout the transcription process, make sure you save an unedited version of your audio or video recording!

Editing

There are many schools of thought when it comes to editing oral history transcripts, and some of them are represented throughout the earlier field report chapters. Many researchers and academics do not edit transcripts at all, while some oral historians' approaches range from very light editing all the way to a more literary style of editing, which includes reorganizing the text in order to turn the raw transcript into a polished narrative. This last approach acknowledges the myriad choices to be made when turning an audio story into one that will be read. Of course, the many possible means through which a particular oral history is ultimately shared—podcasts, video, live performance, books, and so on—can determine individual editing preferences. While there are many variables when it comes to editing, here are a few guiding principles that will serve you through the editing process:

- Honor your narrator's voice. Keep in mind that capturing the fluidity with which your narrator speaks doesn't necessarily mean leaving his or her words unaltered.

- Preserve quirks and idiosyncrasies. If the grammar reflects an accidental mistake, and it stands out, it's often best to fix it. However, if the narrator's grammar is part of his or her geographic or cultural dialect, you might choose to keep some or all of it intact.

- English language learners can still tell stories. If the grammar or word choice hinders a reader's understanding, it should be clarified, but rearranged sentence structures and incorrect tenses can still communicate a story clearly given the context.

- Translations do not have to cover every word. Preserving certain words or phrases in the original language and providing a footnote translation can center the narrator's personality and culture.

- If needed or desired, keep track of narrative length by using the word count function on your computer.

- Strive for fluidity. The goal is to produce a story that flows well and "reads" smoothly.

- Seek narrator review and approval of the final edited version. This practice is consistent with the goal of honoring individuals and wanting to present their stories in an accurate, respectful way.

Sharing and Preserving the Stories

Oral historians have a strong desire to honor the people who have told their stories, so this phase of the process entails sharing these narratives in a broader context. Oral history is often most powerful when a voice can be perpetuated. There are, of course, many ways to amplify oral histories: books, websites, podcasts, film and video, live performance, photo essays, and more. It's worthwhile to consider potential media at the start of the project, and it may help to ask the following questions:

- Who is the intended audience?

- What kinds of technical skills and financial resources do I have at my disposal?

- How will my choice of delivery system honor and support the communities where the stories came from? In other words, where does your community go for culture and information? Through books at the local library? Gatherings at the community center? Online? Through live performance? Film?

- How can I best preserve and archive the stories in a way that allows continued access? Many oral historians develop relationships through the course of their projects that enable them to have their narratives archived with local historical societies, cultural centers, museums, universities, churches, or various nonprofits. Engaging in these relationships early in your project can help to ensure that the stories will continue to be shared and preserved.

VOICE OF WITNESS SAMPLE RELEASE FORM

I, _____ (full name) hereby give permission for Voice of Witness to record, transcribe, and consider this interview for publication.

I understand that I have complete control over how my interview can be used and can choose to remain anonymous if the interview is used in any form. (This includes, and is not limited to, text or audio excerpts of the interview in newspapers, magazines, and the internet.)

I will receive a transcript and/or recording of my interview from Voice of Witness for my personal use upon my request.

Voice of Witness will not publish anything without my consent, and that they will share the final edited draft of my narrative with me for feedback and final approval before publication. In cases where it is mutually determined that follow up contact is not possible, I understand that Voice of Witness will seek my prior approval and consent and will do everything to protect my privacy. They will not share my identity or personal information with anyone else without my consent.

I grant Voice of Witness permission to use up to 15 minutes of an audio and/or video clip for purposes of promoting the book and the organization's mission only. Voice of Witness will share the clip with me and obtain my consent and final approval before using the clip. I will give my written consent or recorded verbal consent.

If I do not speak English, I will be provided with an interpreter who will explain this consent form in my language.

_____   _____
Signature   Date

_____
Address

_____
Phone #

PRODUCTION RESOURCE LIST

Recording Devices

Recording devices can be as simple or as complex as your technology needs require. Before beginning an interview, we recommend recording a "test sample" to check for ambient noises in the room and the optimal distance between speaker and microphone. Check the batteries on all devices, and when using a smartphone, activate "airplane mode" to prevent notifications and phone calls from interrupting or pausing the recording.

The following is a list of recording device options:

- Your smartphone's pre-installed applications: applications like Voice Memo for iPhone and Voice Recorder for Samsung are free and simple to use.

- Rev: a free app for iOS and Android

- Voice Record Pro: free and paid versions available for iOS

- RecForge II: free and paid versions available for Android

- TASCAM (audio product company): http://tascam.com

- Marantz (audio product company): www.us.marantz.com

Editing Tools and Services

The following is a partial list of useful and well-known transcription, audio, and video-editing tools, for varying budgets.

Transcription

Express Scribe (free trial): https://express-scribe.en.softonic.com

InqScribe (free trial): www.inqscribe.com

Wreally (free trial): www.transcribe.wreally.com

CastingWords (paid service): www.castingwords.com

Rev (paid service): www.rev.com/transcription

Audio

GarageBand: www.apple.com/mac/garageband

Audacity (free software): www.audacityteam.org

Soundslides (free software): www.soundslides.com

Video

iMovie: www.apple.com/imovie

OpenShot (free software): www.openshot.org

Shotcut (free software): www.shotcut.org

Final Cut Pro: www.apple.com//final-cut-pro

Websites

The most common way to share oral histories is online. Many oral history projects are shared on websites and online publications using simple, easy-to-use, and free website services where participants can post video, audio, images, and text. These range from blog-style postings to photography-based layouts. The following list of customizable sites feature free and paid versions:

Wordpress: www.wordpress.com

Weebly: www.weebly.com

Wix: www.wix.com

Google Sites: www.sites.google.com

Tumblr: www.tumblr.com

Issuu: www.issuu.com

Print Publishing
Self-publishing has become increasingly easy these days and relatively in-expensive. The services below are great places to start researching rates. Your local print shop is also a good starting point.

Lulu: www.lulu.com

CreateSpace: www.createspace.com

Lightning Source: www.lightningsource.com

Video and Audio Websites

Videos can be organized directly within video-sharing websites or featured on other websites such as Wordpress and Weebly. Audio can be formatted in playlists and imported into media players, embedded directly into websites, or uploaded to a podcast hosting service.

Vimeo (video): www.vimeo.com

YouTube (video): www.youtube.com

SoundCloud (audio): www.soundcloud.com

Miro (audio): www.getmiro.com

Stitcher (podcast): www.stitcher.com

Blubrry (podcast): www.blubrry.com

STORYTELLING AND ORAL HISTORY

Oral History Collections

Alexievich, Svetlana, and Keith Gessen (translator). *Voices from Chernobyl: The Oral History of a Nuclear Disaster.* Picador, 2006.

Gibson, D. W. *Not Working: People Talk about Losing a Job and Finding Their Way in Today's Changing Economy.* Penguin Books, 2012.

Griffin, Joanne. *Redefining Black Power: Reflections on the State of Black America.* City Lights Publishers, 2012.

Hurston, Zora Neale. *Barracoon: The Story of the Last Black Cargo.* Amistad, 2018.

Isay, David. *Listening Is an Act of Love: A Celebration of American Life from the StoryCorps Project.* Penguin Books, 2007.

———. *Ties That Bind: Stories of Love and Gratitude from the First Ten Years of StoryCorps.* Penguin Books, 2014.

Jones, LeAlan, and Lloyd Newman, with David Isay. *Our America: Life and Death on the South Side of Chicago.* Washington Square Press / Pocket Books, 1997.

Levinger, Laurie. *What War? Testimonies of Maya Survivors.* Full Circle Press, 2009.

Miller, Donald E., and Lorna Touryan Miller. *Survivors: An Oral History of the Armenian Genocide.* University of California Press, 1999.

Moye, J. Todd. *Freedom Flyers: The Tuskegee Airmen of World War II.* Oxford University Press, 2012.

Portelli, Alessandro. *They Say in Harlan County: An Oral History.* Oxford University Press, 2010.

Russo, Stacy. *We Were Going to Change the World: Interviews with Women from the 1970s and 1980s Southern California Punk Rock Scene.* Santa Monica Press, 2017.

Taylor, Craig. *Londoners: The Days and Nights of London Now—as Told by Those Who Love It, Hate It, Live It, Left It, and Long for It.* Ecco/HarperCollins, 2012.

Terkel, Studs. *Coming of Age: Growing Up in the Twentieth Century.* Reprint, New Press, 2007.

————. *Division Street: America*. Reprint, New Press, 2006.

————. *Hard Times: An Oral History of the Great Depression*. Reprint, New Press, 2005.

————. *Working: People Talk about What They Do All Day and How They Feel about What They Do*. Reprint, New Press, 2003.

Wilkerson, Isabel. *The Warmth of Other Suns*. Reprint, New York: Vintage Press, 2011.

Yiwu, Liao. *The Corpse Walker: Real Life Stories, China from the Bottom Up*. Anchor Books, 2009.

Zinn, Howard, and Anthony Arnove. *Voices of a People's History of the United States*. 2nd ed. Seven Stories Press, 2009.

Oral History Techniques/Methodology

Ayers, Rick. *Studs Terkel's* Working: *A Teaching Guide*. New Press, 2001.

Mayotte, Cliff. *The Power of the Story: The Voice of Witness Teacher's Guide to Oral History*. Voice of Witness / McSweeney's, 2013.

Portelli, Alessandro. *The Death of Luigi Trastulli and Other Stories: Form and Meaning in Oral History*. State University of New York Press, 1991.

Ritchie, Donald. *Doing Oral History*. 2nd ed. Oxford University Press, 2003.

Live Performance / Oral History–Based Plays

Many oral history projects culminate in live performances and play scripts. The following is a partial list of well-known oral history–based plays:

Blank, Jessica, and Erik Jensen. *The Exonerated*. Faber & Faber, 2003.

————. *Aftermath*. Dramatists Play Service, 2010 (acting edition).

Brittain, Victoria, and Gillian Slovo. *Guantanamo: Honor Bound to Defend Freedom*. Oberon Books, 2005.

Kaufman, Moises. *The Laramie Project*. Vintage Books, 2001.

Smith, Anna Deavere. *Twilight: Los Angeles, 1992*. Anchor Books, 1994.

Oral History and Visual Art

Taking the oral history narrative as inspiration, many visual artists explore personal narrative through the creation of original visual art pieces. Using technical skills and creative approaches, artists generate high-quality pieces of art using a variety of materials that examine narrative themes such as identity, culture, society, history, and more. The following book features a rich collection of case studies and serves as a great introduction to the many approaches and disciplines that combine oral history and visual art:

Sandino, Linda, and Matthew Partington. *Oral History and the Visual Arts.* Bloomsbury Academic, 2013.

Oral History–Based Graphic Memoirs

Graphic memoirs are an excellent combination of visual art and personal narrative. There are many well-known examples of oral history–based graphic memoirs. Here are just a few:

Bechdel, Alison. *Fun Home: A Family Tragicomic.* Houghton Mifflin Company, 2006.
Bui, Thi. *The Best We Could Do.* Abrams ComicArts. 2017
Delisle, Guy. *The Burma Chronicles.* Jonathan Cape Books. 2007.
Lewis, John Robert. *March: Book One.* Top Shelf Productions, 2013.
Sacco, Joe. *Footnotes in Gaza.* Henry Holt Books, 2009.
Satrapi, Marjane. *Persepolis: The Story of a Childhood.* Pantheon Books, 2000.
Speigelman, Art. *Maus, A Survivor's Tale: My Father Bleeds History.* Pantheon Books, 1986.

Organizations and Archives

Studs Terkel Radio Archive: Audio recordings of interviews, readings, and musical programs aired during Studs Terkel's tenure at WFMT Radio from the early 1950s through 1999 are part of this collection. Over five decades, Terkel interviewed individuals from every walk of life. These interviews narrate the cultural, literary, and political history of Chicago and the United States.
https://studsterkel.wfmt.com/

Columbia University Center for Oral History: The Columbia University Center for Oral History is one of the world's leading centers for the practice and teaching of oral history. Its archive, located in the Columbia University Libraries and open to the public, holds more than eight thousand interviews, in audio, video, and text formats, on a wide variety of subjects.
https://library.columbia.edu/locations/ccoh.html

Library of Congress: WPA American Life Histories from the Federal Writers Project and Recordings:
www.loc.gov/collections/federal-writers-project/about-this-collection
Oral History for Educators (including lesson plans):
www.loc.gov/teachers/classroommaterials/lessons/#topic230

Oral History Association: The Oral History Association, established in 1966, seeks to bring together all persons interested in oral history as a way of collecting and interpreting human memories to foster knowledge and human dignity.
www.oralhistory.org

Groundswell: Oral History for Social Change: Groundswell is a dynamic network of oral historians, activists, cultural workers, community organizers, and documentary artists. They use oral history and narrative in creative, effective, and ethical ways to support movement building and transformative social change.
www.oralhistoryforsocialchange.org

Oral History Center: The Oral History Center of the Bancroft Library at UC Berkeley was established in 1954. Over the decades, they have conducted four thousand–plus interviews on almost every topic imaginable. The vast majority of these interviews have been transcribed and made available online. They also offer introductory workshops and a Summer Institute.
www.lib.berkeley.edu/libraries/bancroft-library/oral-history-center

Densho: Densho is a grassroots organization dedicated to preserving, educating, and sharing the story of World War II–era incarceration of Japanese Americans in order to deepen understandings of American history and inspire action for equity.
https://densho.org

StoryCenter: StoryCenter (formerly the Center for Digital Storytelling) is a California-based nonprofit arts organization rooted in the art of personal storytelling. It assists people of all ages in using the tools of digital media to craft, record, share, and value the stories of individuals and communities.
www.storycenter.org

StoryCorps: StoryCorps is an independent nonprofit whose mission is to provide Americans of all backgrounds and beliefs with the opportunity to record, share, and preserve the stories of our lives.
storycorps.org

The 1947 Partition Archive: An oral history archive committed to documenting, preserving, and sharing eyewitness accounts from all ethnic,

religious, and economic communities affected by the Partition of British India in 1947.
www.1947partitionarchive.org

Trauma and Self-Care Resources
Video

"When Helping Hurts: Sustaining Trauma Workers," with Charles Figley. Six noted therapists and experts offer their stories and advice on dealing with compassion fatigue and discuss ways of recognizing and addressing this condition in yourself and others. Available in streaming and DVD at www.psychotherapy.net/video/compassion-fatigue.

Documentary

Braithwaite, Amy, dir., *Kick at the Darkness*, 2014.

Explores the psycho-social impact of working in environments with intense suffering, devastation, conflict, or volatility. It delves into some of the coping mechanisms commonly used when support is not always available through humanitarian organizations. Available online at https://www.youtube.com/watch?v=6YVcPH367gw.

Books

Stamm, B. Hudnall, ed. *Secondary Traumatic Stress: Self-Care Issues for Clinicians, Researchers, and Educators*. Sidran Press, 1995.

A collection of articles that raise questions about the impact of highly stressful experiences on caregivers and the potential for positive growth in the face of them. They address the psychological cost of doing trauma work, offer suggestions for ways in which therapists can create safe environments in which to work, and address ethical issues related to self-care and vicarious traumatization.

Rothschild, Babette, with Marjorie Rand. *Help for the Helper: The Psychophysiology of Compassion Fatigue and Vicarious Trauma*. Norton, 2006.

Addresses issues of burnout, vicarious trauma, and compassion fatigue. Although its theoretical perspectives and practical exercises are intended mainly for clinicians and therapists, overall this is an accessible book.

Lipsky, Laura van Dernoot, and Connie Burk. *Trauma Stewardship: An Everyday Guide to Caring for Self While Caring for Others*. Berrett-Koehler, 2009.

An accessible discussion of the consequences of trauma exposure featuring guidelines for self-care through anecdotes and cartoons. For all audiences. Also available as an e-book and audiobook.

Steele, William, and Cathy A. Malchiodi. *Trauma-Informed Practices with Children and Adolescents.* Routledge, 2011.

A sourcebook of practical approaches to working with children and adolescents that synthesizes research from leading trauma specialists and translates it into easy-to-implement techniques. Each chapter contains short excerpts, case examples, and commentary from recognized leaders in the field. Readers will also find chapters filled with activities, methods, and approaches to assessment, self-regulation, trauma integration, and resilience building.

Mathieu, Françoise. *The Compassion Fatigue Workbook: Creative Tools for Transforming Compassion Fatigue and Vicarious Trauma.* Routledge, 2012.

In addition to being a comprehensive description of compassion fatigue and vicarious traumatization, *The Compassion Fatigue Workbook* leads the reader through experiential activities designed to target specific areas in their personal and professional lives. It provides concrete strategies to help the reader develop a personalized plan for identifying and transforming compassion fatigue and vicarious traumatization.

Online Resources

Compassion Fatigue Awareness Project: To promote awareness and understanding of compassion fatigue and its effect on caregivers, CFAP is committed to gathering, documenting, and disseminating useful information that can have a positive impact on the lives of caregivers. www.compassionfatigue.org

Emergency Kits by Capacitar: Features simple, basic practices to deal with stress and manage emotions. Practices include tai chi, fingerholds, Emotional Freedom Technique (EFT), and acupressure. Available in thirteen languages and can be downloaded at www.capacitar.org/capacitar-emergency-kit.

Substance Abuse and Mental Health Services Administration's Concept of Trauma and Guidance for a Trauma-Informed Approach: This guidebook, a free, downloadable PDF prepared by SAMHSA, provides a working definition of trauma and helps practitioners to develop and implement a trauma-informed approach to care. Available at https://store.samhsa.gov /shin/content/SMA14-4884/SMA14-4884.pdf.

ACKNOWLEDGMENTS

A brief note of gratitude to former Voice of Witness managing editor Luke Gerwe, who helped wrangle the first version of this book into existence. We would like to thank Haymarket Books editor Brian Baughan for his invaluable assistance. We are also indebted to the many individuals and organizations we have learned from during the creation of this book: Jeanne Barr, Sita Bhaumik, Ipek Burnett, Linda Caballero Sotelo and the New Americans Museum, Louise Chegwidden, Shanti Elliot, Nicholas Forge, Michael Green, Sonia Hansra, Sarah Cate Jones, Susan Katz, Shabnam Koirala-Azad and the University of San Francisco School of Education, Mary Kearney-Brown, Robin Levi, Juliana Delgado Lopera, Steven Mayers, Bonnie McKelvie, Jennifer Merilees, Ruth Morgan and Community Works, Shelby Myers, Inge Oosterhoff, the Oral History Association, Molly Parent and 826 Valencia, Audrey Petty, Donzahniya Pitre, Caroline Prioleau, Chace Pulley, Phillip Reid, Kait Steele and 826 National, Teachers 4 Social Justice, Lisa Thyer, Von Torres, and Chris Wendelin. Special thanks to the Voice of Witness Education Advisory Board for their ongoing support: Bill Ayers, Rick Ayers, Diana Cohn, Praveena Fernes, Anne Germanacos, Katie Kuszmar, Nishat Kurwa, Gerald Richards, and Barbara Yasue.

CONTRIBUTORS

André Dao is a writer of fiction and nonfiction. He is the cofounder of Behind the Wire, an oral history project documenting people's experience of immigration detention, and the deputy editor of the *New Philosopher*.

Jon Funabiki is a professor of journalism at San Francisco State University. He also serves as executive director of the Renaissance Journalism Center, which incubates new models of journalism and storytelling that strengthen communities, and is former executive director of the Dilena Takeyama Center for the Study of Japan and Japanese Culture, which promotes new leadership and perspectives in the field of US-Japan relations.

Genevra Gallo-Bayiates is an instructor, counselor, and advocate. Her audience-participatory work in the Neo-Futurists, an experimental theater troupe, capitalized on direct conversation and interaction with viewers to explore issues surrounding privilege, vulnerability, power, and inequity. As a counselor, Genevra has traditionally worked with at-risk populations as a career and academic advisor, teaching young adults how to build active networks and advocating for institutional equity in policy making and programming. Her social justice and advocacy work in Evanston, Illinois, builds upon her lifelong commitment to fostering compassion and connection within communities to promote positive change.

Pendarvis Harshaw is a journalist from Oakland, California. He's a graduate of Howard University's School of Communications and UC Berkeley's Graduate School of Journalism. He is the director of the documentary film *TDK: The Dream Kontinues* and the author of *OG Told Me*, a coming-of-age memoir about Harshaw's upbringing in Oakland. He currently works as a freelance writer for a number of outlets and contributes weekly columns to KQED Arts.

Ashley Jacobs is a certified medical assistant and mother of four living in Tampa, Florida. Ashley first came to Voice of Witness as a narrator in *Inside This Place, Not of It: Narratives from Women's Prisons*. Ashley's experience telling her story inspired her to become politically active. In 2014, Ashley began conducting an oral history project with women who had been impacted by domestic violence, both as survivors and perpetrators.

Eric Marshall is a graduate of the University of New Orleans, where he studied oral history. His current projects include an oral history of New Orleans's first Black mayor, Dutch Morial, and an investigation into making digital oral history more accessible and discoverable.

Sienna Merope is a human rights advocate, lawyer, and writer. She worked as a refugee law advocate in Australia for several years and co-founded Behind the Wire in 2014. She is currently a Bertha Foundation fellow with the Institute for Justice and Democracy in Haiti, where she works to hold the United Nations accountable for bringing the world's worst cholera epidemic to Haiti in 2010.

Lauren Taylor, oral historian and psychiatric social worker, is an adjunct professor at the Columbia University School of Social Work. Lauren has been on staff since 1994 at the Service Program for Older People, a mental health clinic for older adults, and has a private practice. As an oral historian, she has conducted dozens of life history interviews, both in the United States and abroad, and is studying the subjective experience of aging through the medium of narrative in a cross-cultural context. Lauren has lectured and published on the therapeutic use of narrative.

Shelby Pasell is a graduate of the University of Pittsburgh, where she received a BA in philosophy in nonfiction writing, Spanish, and global studies. She currently lives and writes in Saint Paul, Minnesota.

Stephanie G. Thomas resides in Houston, Texas—the Petro Metro— and is an advocate for social justice and the environment. She is an earth scientist, and she currently serves as a hospital chaplain and as a mentor for the Upaya Zen Center Chaplaincy Program, where she completed a certificate in Buddhist chaplaincy in 2015.

INDEX

ABOUT THE EDITORS

Cliff Mayotte is a longtime educator and artist. He currently serves as education program director for Voice of Witness, where, among other projects, he compiled and edited *The Power of the Story: The Voice of Witness Teacher's Guide to Oral History*. Before joining Voice of Witness, Cliff worked as an arts educator and curriculum designer for many Bay Area schools and arts organizations. He is a recipient of the Beverly Kees Educator Award and a James Madison Freedom of Information Award from the Society of Professional Journalists. From 1997 to 2000, Cliff served as the education director for the Tony Award–winning Berkeley Repertory Theatre.

Claire Kiefer joined Voice of Witness as its education program associate in 2012, after six years of teaching children of incarcerated parents at a San Francisco public high school. She has developed curricula for subjects ranging from the prison-industrial complex, to collaborative poetry writing, to art responding to gang violence. Claire spent over ten years teaching in prisons and jails around the country and now works as a forensic social worker at the Georgia Capital Defender. She holds a master of fine arts in creative writing and a master of social work.

Natalie Catasús is a poet and scholar of comparative literature. During her time with Voice of Witness, she worked as a translator, assistant editor, and later, managing communications and supporting grant-writing efforts. She holds master's degrees in creative writing and visual and critical studies, and has developed multimedia oral history projects on topics such as Cuban exile in the United States and indigenous activism and gentrification in Vancouver, British Columbia.

Erin Vong is the education associate at Voice of Witness, with a special focus on oral history for English language learners and leading nationwide programs such as the Sharing History Initiative. She spent three years teaching abroad in Spain and piloting an oral history project with her students in Spanish, Galician, and English, and continues to volunteer with multilingual high school students.

VOICE OF WITNESS

Voice of Witness (VOW) is an award-winning nonprofit that advances human rights by amplifying the voices of people impacted by injustice. Cofounded by Dave Eggers, Mimi Lok, and Dr. Lola Vollen, we explore issues of criminal justice, migration, and displacement, and force space for marginalized voices to be heard. Our book series depicts these issues through the edited oral histories of people most closely affected by them. Our education program connects educators, students, and members of justice movements with oral history tools for storytelling and social change.

THE VOICE OF WITNESS SERIES

The Voice of Witness nonprofit book series amplifies the seldom-heard voices of people affected by contemporary injustice. We also work with impacted communities to create curricular and training support for educators. Using oral history as a foundation, the series depicts human rights issues in the United States and around the world. *Say It Forward: A Guide to Social Justice Storytelling* is the seventeenth book in the series. Other titles include:

SURVIVING JUSTICE
America's Wrongfully Convicted and Exonerated
Compiled and edited by Lola Vollen and Dave Eggers
Foreword by Scott Turow
"Real, raw, terrifying tales of 'justice.'" —*Star Tribune*

VOICES FROM THE STORM
The People of New Orleans on Hurricane Katrina and Its Aftermath
Compiled and edited by Chris Ying and Lola Vollen
"*Voices from the Storm* uses oral history to let those who survived the hurricane tell their (sometimes surprising) stories." —*Independent UK*

UNDERGROUND AMERICA
Narratives of Undocumented Lives
Compiled and edited by Peter Orner
Foreword by Luis Alberto Urrea
"No less than revelatory." —*Publishers Weekly*

OUT OF EXILE
Narratives from the Abducted and Displaced People of Sudan
Compiled and edited by Craig Walzer
Additional interviews and an introduction by Dave Eggers
and Valentino Achak Deng
"Riveting." —*School Library Journal*

HOPE DEFERRED
Narratives of Zimbabwean Lives
Compiled and edited by Peter Orner and Annie Holmes
Foreword by Brian Chikwava

"*Hope Deferred* might be the most important publication to have come out of Zimbabwe in the last thirty years." —*Harper's Magazine*

NOWHERE TO BE HOME
Narratives from Survivors of Burma's Military Regime
Compiled and edited by Maggie Lemere and Zoë West
Foreword by Mary Robinson
"Extraordinary." —Asia Society

PATRIOT ACTS
Narratives of Post-9/11 Injustice
Compiled and edited by Alia Malek
Foreword by Karen Korematsu
"Important and timely." —Reza Aslan

INSIDE THIS PLACE, NOT OF IT
Narratives from Women's Prisons
Compiled and edited by Ayelet Waldman and Robin Levi
Foreword by Michelle Alexander
"Essential reading." —Piper Kerman

THROWING STONES AT THE MOON
Narratives from Colombians Displaced by Violence
Compiled and edited by Sibylla Brodzinsky and Max Schoening
Foreword by Íngrid Betancourt
"Both sad and inspiring." —*Publishers Weekly*

REFUGEE HOTEL
Photographed by Gabriele Stabile and edited by Juliet Linderman
"There is no other book like *Refugee Hotel* on your shelf." —*SF Weekly*

HIGH RISE STORIES
Voices from Chicago Public Housing
Compiled and edited by Audrey Petty
Foreword by Alex Kotlowitz
"Joyful, novelistic, and deeply moving." —George Saunders

INVISIBLE HANDS
Voices from the Global Economy
Compiled and edited by Corinne Goria

Foreword by Kalpona Akter
"Powerful and revealing testimony." —*Kirkus*

PALESTINE SPEAKS
Narratives of Life under Occupation
Compiled and edited by Cate Malek and Mateo Hoke
"Heartrending stories." —*New York Review of Books*

THE VOICE OF WITNESS READER
Ten Years of Amplifying Unheard Voices
Edited and with an introduction by Dave Eggers

THE POWER OF THE STORY
The Voice of Witness Teacher's Guide to Oral History
Compiled and edited by Cliff Mayotte
Foreword by William Ayers and Richard Ayers
"A rich source of provocations to engage with human dramas throughout the
world." —*Rethinking Schools Magazine*

LAVIL
Life, Love, and Death in Port-au-Prince
Edited by Peter Orner and Evan Lyon
Foreword by Edwidge Danticat
"*Lavil* is a powerful collection of testimonies, which include tales of violence,
poverty, and instability but also joy, hustle, and the indomitable will to sur-
vive." —*Vice*

CHASING THE HARVEST
Migrant Workers in California Agriculture
Edited by Gabriel Thompson
"The voices are defiant and nuanced, aware of the human complexities that
spill across bureaucratic categories and arbitrary borders." —*The Baffler*

SIX BY TEN
Stories from Solitary
Edited by Mateo Hoke and Taylor Pendergrass
"Deeply moving and profoundly unsettling." —Heather Ann Thompson